Pioneer Studio Pottery
The Milner-White Collection

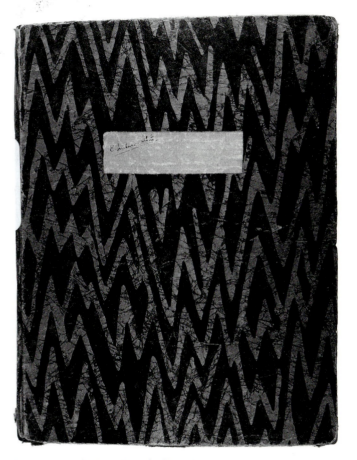

Front cover of Milner-White's album I

Milner-White's book-plate

Edited by Richard Green

Sarah Riddick

Pioneer Studio Pottery
The Milner-White Collection

Lund Humphries . London
in association with
York City Art Gallery

City of York Leisure Services

Copyright © 1990 York City Council

First published in 1990 by
Lund Humphries Publishers Ltd
16 Pembridge Road, London W11
in association with
York City Art Gallery

British Library Cataloguing in Publication Data

Pioneer studio pottery : the Milner-White collection.

1. Ceramics – Catalogues, indexes
I. Riddick, Sarah   II. York City Art Gallery
738.074

ISBN 0 85331 581 7 paperback
ISBN 0 85331 590 6 hardback

Designed by Alan Bartram
Made and printed in Great Britain by
BAS Printers Ltd, Over Wallop, Stockbridge, Hampshire

FRONT COVER
123. William Staite Murray, Jar : 'Persian Garden', 1931
BACK COVER
40. Shoji Hamada, Tea-Set, exh. 1931

74993

Contents

Foreword

Cartoon from Milner-White's album II, (?) 1936

"WELL, WHICH IS IT, SAM—A LOVELY OLD VASE OR A HIDEOUS MODERN ONE?"

The Very Reverend Eric Milner-White CBE DSO (1884-1963) was Dean of York from 1941 until his death. Known as 'Milner' to friends and colleagues, he is remembered by many in his adopted city with affection and respect. He came to York with a distinguished career as a war-time chaplain and as Chaplain, Fellow and Dean of King's College, Cambridge, behind him. Once here he quickly became involved in many different activities, quite apart from the work of the Minster, and there was hardly an aspect of cultural life in the city which was not touched by his influence. As a member of the Art Gallery Committee he provided moral support and informed advice at a crucial time – when the then Curator Hans Hess, with the backing of the Council, was transforming a war-damaged Victorian building housing a collection of little distinction into an efficient modern art gallery with a collection of international repute. Equally, if not more importantly, Milner-White provided support of a material kind in a succession of generous gifts from his collection made over the last fifteen years of his life, thereby becoming one of the Gallery's three main benefactors (the other two being John Burton and F. D. Lycett Green). These gifts divide into two groups of works both of the greatest distinction – over thirty late-nineteenth and early-twentieth century British paintings and over one hundred and seventy examples of modern stoneware pottery. The latter form the subject of this catalogue.

Milner-White was probably the most important of the early, or pioneer, collectors of what is today known as studio pottery and he assembled a group of pots of the highest quality, which it would be impossible to gather together now. He brought to his collecting an intuitive but highly discriminating aesthetic sense, supported by intellectual principles based on the philosophy of William Staite Murray and to a lesser extent Bernard Leach, two of the three potters (the third being Shoji Hamada) whose work forms the nucleus of the collection. His role as a collector was a very positive one in that he patronized and encouraged the potters concerned at a time when they were breaking new ground and, in some cases, struggling to survive: he was to be described by Murray as 'the acknowledged Spiritual Father of the Studio Potters'.

An interesting parallel may be drawn between Eric Milner-White and that other great clerical collector and patron Walter Hussey, Dean of Chichester (1909-1985), whose twentieth-century paintings and drawings are now at the Pallant House Gallery in Chichester. Astonishing though it may be, however, the pictures and pots at York City Art Gallery represent only a part of Milner-White's enormous range of interests. To those of us who did not know him, it would seem that these activities were highly compartmentalized (even the pictures and the pots for example do not for the most part make obvious bedfellows). However the factor common to them all was a pursuit of excellence and perfection.

The Dean's remarkable collection of pots came to the Gallery together with his meticulous notes and carefully preserved exhibition catalogues, press cuttings, invoices, receipts and letters. This supporting documentation makes the subject of the Dean and his pots a fascinating and rewarding one to study. It is therefore all the more surprising that the subject has hitherto received little attention, although mention should be made of two unpublished theses, one by Ruth J. [Joy] Bulmer submitted at Southampton College of Art in 1976 and the other by Melissa Anwyl Garnett submitted at the University of Manchester in 1981. Both, in their different ways, have proved useful in the preparation of this publication.

This long-awaited catalogue was commissioned by York City Council in recognition of the outstanding importance of the collection in its care and the clear need for a fully docu-

mented but attractively presented guide. It is the result of dedicated work, including important original research, on the part of the Art Assistant, Sarah Riddick (formerly Sarah Northcroft), over a period of five years. Our grateful thanks are due to her for the commitment and perseverance she has brought to the task. We have been fortunate in being able to collaborate with Lund Humphries in bringing the project to fruition.

The catalogue is, we believe, the most detailed study of a particular collection of twentieth-century pottery yet attempted. We hope that it will enhance the appreciation of the collection of those who already know it, while, at the same time, bringing the Dean's pots to the notice of a wider audience. It will, we hope, prove to be an interesting addition to the annals of York history. Lastly we hope that it will in a small way repay the enormous debt of gratitude that the Gallery and its visitors owe the late Dean, Eric Milner-White.

RICHARD GREEN

Curator

Acknowledgements

My greatest debt must be to the late Dean himself, Eric Milner-White. It has been an enormous pleasure and privilege to work on his magnificent collection; his meticulously preserved documentation has provided a rare and invaluable source of information while his written comments and insights have brought this material alive.

To my senior colleague, Richard Green, grateful thanks are due for his work on my manuscript in the final stages of this project. He has brought to the task his eye for inconsistencies, flaws in logic and inelegant turns of phrase and has added significantly to the clarity of the prose, while also suggesting useful additions. Any remaining errors are my own.

My gratitude is due to the late Harry Davis, to Anita Hoy, David Leach, Helen Pincombe, Margaret Rey and Philip Wadsworth, and to Marianne Haile, Ulla Hjorth and John Vyse, who have cheerfully answered plaguing telephone calls and letters, and who in some cases have allowed me to make exhausting demands on their time. Their revealing and helpful responses have been one of the delights of the research.

Thereafter, I would particularly like to thank Oliver Watson of the Victoria and Albert Museum for many kindnesses and ideas, but primarily for so generously sharing his scholarship. Numerous other colleagues and individuals have kindly helped in many ways and my thanks go to the following: Anne Baker, Mary Boys-Adams, Hilary Bracegirdle, Judith Bradfield, Mette Bradley, Myra Brown, Joy Bulford, L. A. Burman, Cathy Crippwell, Guillemette Delaporte, Richard Dennis, the staff of Ealing Central Library, Marjorie Eves, Dagmar Fagerholt, Murray Fieldhouse, Anne French, Craig Hartley, Gill Hedley, Andrew Isherwood, Bill Ismay, Anna Jackson, Freddy Jensen, Rose Kerr, Dorris U. Kuyken-Schneider, Emmeline Leary, Helena Moore, Kathy Niblett, James Noel White, Julia Poole, Tim Proud, Barley Roscoe, Allan Scharff, Masako Shimizu, Tessa Sidey, David Smyth, Angela Turnbull, Moira Vincentelli, Helen White, and the late George Wingfield Digby.

Thanks also go to Pam Bell, Catherine Herbert, Linda Howe, Janet Moorby, Angela O'Doherty and Margaret Severn, for converting tortuous manuscripts into immaculate typescript.

All the photographs of pots and potters' marks have been expertly taken by Charlie Nickols except for Nos 22 and 70 which are by Jerry Hardman-Jones. Credits for photographs of the potters are as follows: Seth Cardew for Michael Cardew and Ladi Kwali, Warren Mackenzie for Shoji Hamada, Evan Blandford for Bernard Leach and John Webber for William Staite Murray; acknowledgement is due to the *Yorkshire Evening Press* and ABC Television for the photograph of Eric Milner-White.

Finally I would like to thank David Alexander and my husband, Graham, without whose support this catalogue would not have been completed.

SARAH RIDDICK

The Milner-White collection of pioneer studio pottery is the finest of its kind. Formed between 1925 and 1962, it comprised at one time or another around three hundred pots representing the work of about forty potters.[1] One hundred and seventy-three of these were presented to York City Art Gallery, forty-seven to Southampton City Art Gallery, two to the Fitzwilliam Museum, Cambridge, and the remaining seventy or thereabouts were given away to friends and family.

This remarkable collection started accidentally. In Milner-White's own words:

It was by pure chance c.1925. I walked into a Bond St. Gallery [the Fine Art Society] & saw a show of stoneware pots by Reg. Wells. Transfixed. Sat there 2 hours – forgot lunch! At the end, I bought (£20) [No.151 in this Catalogue] A stranger, seeing my interest, said that in another gallery in Bond St was an exhibition of pots by an artist-craftsman of whom he thought even more highly. I went there … picking up … [William Staite] Murray.[2]

This day saw the birth of an interest which was to be sustained until the end of Milner-White's life. The collection now at York is particularly rich in the work of three potters: William Staite Murray, Bernard Leach and Shoji Hamada, the men whom the Dean recognized as 'the 3 Master Potters of the Century'. He formed a special relationship with Murray, regarding him as the most original of the studio potters. Murray's pots were far from cheap but the Dean assembled an impressive number, resulting in the finest group of the artist's work anywhere in the world. He also recognized the importance of Bernard Leach and collected some of the best examples of his work. The 'Leaping Salmon' vase – arguably Leach's most famous pot – was apparently Milner-White's personal favourite in the collection. After Murray and Leach, Milner-White bought more pots by the Japanese Shoji Hamada than by any other potter: fifty-four are listed in his MS catalogue. As well as admiring the undoubted quality of Hamada's work, the Dean was particularly fascinated by the idea of the West influencing the East, which manifested itself in Hamada's work through his connection with Bernard Leach and the English slipware tradition at St Ives. His determination to own a representative collection resulted in the best group of this potter's work outside Japan. Next in priority, the Dean assembled a particularly fine group of the works of Michael Cardew and two of his African pupils,

Halima Audu and Ladi Kwali. All these pots are stoneware, made at Abuja in Nigeria. Milner-White had admired Cardew's work for some time, but was not prepared to collect earthenware which he considered inferior pottery. It was only when he heard that Cardew was making stoneware that he started to acquire his work.[3] Cardew had been a gifted pupil of Leach, and the Dean bought work by two other Leach pupils, Norah Braden and Katharine Pleydell-Bouverie, whose notable achievement was in the field of ash glazes. From Murray's pupils, the Dean purchased examples by Sam Haile – one of the truly outstanding potters of his generation, whose life was cut short by an accident in 1948. He also bought work by Frank Barber and James Dring, and a single example each of the work of Constance Dunn (then Wade), Reginald Marlow, Margaret Rey and Philip Wadsworth. He purchased many pots by Charles and Nell Vyse – the brilliant exponents of early Chinese glaze effects – but gave most of these away, as presents.

Surprisingly Milner-White also assembled a small but interesting group of pots by French and Scandinavian ceramic artists, such as Séraphin Soudbinine and Axel Salto, the former's work being particularly rare in this country. This group, with the rest of the collection, makes an interesting contrast between European and British studio pottery in the first part of the twentieth century, as the Dean intended it should.

Eric Milner-White was born on 23 April 1884 (St George's Day), the eldest of four boys. His father was a barrister, a businessman and a knight. His mother died when he was six, but in spite of this sadness, Milner's upbringing was happy. He was encouraged to develop many different interests, and, for example, travel in the school holidays sparked a deep, life-long love of architecture and natural history. Patrick Wilkinson, the author of a perceptive memoir of the Dean which has been heavily drawn on for this introduction, commented on his formidable memory which enabled him to revisit a church fifty years later and comment on changes: '"Where has that rather curious credence table gone?" It was described, the verger unlocked the vestry, and there it was.'[4]

Milner-White was educated at Harrow and then King's College, Cambridge, where he went as a History Scholar in 1903. At King's, besides enjoying sport, and reading himself to a double first in history and the Lightfoot Scholarship in

1956

Leach Exhibition at Liberty's, Regent Street.

———————

(241) 1.   Two handled globular pot with four flattened
sides ; blue-grey glaze with chocolate-brown iron
spots ; narrow neck & collar of the same brown   18.
height 11½" Sign + B.L on base

(242) 2   Globular Pot with low neck, creamy-buff glaze
with brown everywhere ; 'mountains & hills' design with
sun, birds, leaves & *leaves*, chinese ? antelope and
peasant. iff high. Sign + B.L.   25

(243) 3   Tall Jar , inspired by my Hamada (68) +
a good match to it : iron red brown glaze   18
over cream ; low neck . Unsigned.

244 ⎫   Five small bowls   keeping Tood   Buy U/w   1
(245) ⎪   red brown outside   bowl 1   1
246 ⎬   cream inside, each   bowl 2   wedding   1
247 ⎪   with a typical bird   Flower   presents !   1
248 ⎭   animal or plant design ? Fir Tree Green army   1

249 to ⎫   Three napkin rings , Leach school   7/6
256   ⎭   (only for domestic use)

1906, he decided to go into the Church. Accordingly in 1907 he went to Cuddesdon Theological College, and thence in 1908 as Deacon to St Paul's Newington, a slum parish near the Elephant and Castle in south London. From 1909 to 1912 he was at St Mary Magdalene, Woolwich, but then lost his voice, and went abroad alone for a year to avoid talking. On his return in 1912 he became Chaplain to King's College, Cambridge, and in 1913 also Lecturer in History at Corpus Christi College and Examining Chaplain to the Bishop of London, Winnington-Ingram. In the First World War he volunteered as a chaplain to the forces, and his bravery resulted in his being awarded the DSO. After the war in 1918 he became Dean of King's College, Cambridge, and initiated the now famous Service of Nine Lessons and Carols on Christmas Eve, which has been held ever since and broadcast since 1928. His duties as Dean included teaching divinity once or twice a week at the Choir School. Although shy, he loved children. Every August from 1921 to 1939 he ran a camp at Batcombe in Somerset which those who attended as children remember with pleasure. There, whilst having enormous fun, they absorbed information about everything from architecture to the natural world. On these camps Milner-White maintained an elaborate hierarchy, in which he was 'The Archbishop' and was referred to as 'The Arch'.

Milner-White was not affluent until he inherited about £40,000 on his father's death in 1922. He also inherited his father's business acumen, a talent he enhanced by diligently learning about investment at King's from Maynard Keynes, the college Bursar and one of this century's most influential economists. More money came to him on his stepmother's death in 1951. While Milner-White developed a talent for commerce, he gave away huge sums of money to institutions and to individuals in times of need.

In 1941 Milner-White was appointed Dean of York Minster. It was to prove a memorable appointment. The new Dean became involved with many projects in the city. He was a member of the Board of the Festival Society and served on the Merchant Adventurers' Court of Assistants, he was also a founder-member of the York Civic Trust and sat on the Art Gallery Committee. He has been described as 'the first citizen of York after the Lord Mayor'.[5]

While more than ably fulfilling the duties of a Dean he gained a reputation for being a formidable character. Serenely convinced he was right, he had an uncanny gift for manipulating committees to achieve his ends. Usually, the Minster profited greatly from his machinations.

Perhaps Milner-White's biggest task at York was to replace the Minster windows which had been removed for fear of damage from air raids during the Second World War. The Minster windows contained nearly one third of all the medieval glass in England, but during the course of time it had

been so badly patched that in some cases the pictures were unintelligible. Stained glass had long been a passion of the Dean's and he persuaded the Chapter to allow him to try his hand at restoration. He used the existing staff of glaziers, which was to become the York Glaziers' Trust. 'His aim was to recapture the feeling of the original craftsmen, whose desire was simultaneously to beautify and to teach. Every morning he and his experts spent time at this gigantic jig-saw puzzle.'[6] When the work was finished the difference was striking and Milner-White was awarded the CBE, made an honorary member of the Worshipful Company of Glaziers and received the Freedom of the City of London. Although the completion of this vast undertaking was a tremendous achievement, Milner-White had not always followed strict conservation principles and his work has been severely criticized in academic circles.

The Dean loved nature and natural history. At York he became a keen cultivator of flowers and flowering shrubs and of roses in particular. It seems that 'The Duke of Edinburgh was once trapped in the Deanery by a consignment of rose-trees which happened to be unloaded on the drive while he was being entertained there.'[7] After the roses, species of 'Erica' were a great interest. Not only was he Eric, but his housekeeper was Erica. He grew a hundred varieties in his garden.

As Wilkinson has recalled, 'He was also a lover of books, including rare editions. The Library of York Minster was greatly enlarged and enriched by his care and generosity.'[8] He himself paid 'for a wing to be added to house the muniments and the Hailstone Collection of some 10,000 volumes on local history.'[9]

He was interested in all arts and crafts – from wrought iron to Persian rugs. He loved music and ballet. Eight hundred programmes stood bound on his shelves. 'He knew Margot Fonteyn and met every member of the Vic-Wells Company. They all signed a dancing-shoe and sent it to him on an occasion when he had put up two girls from the *corps de ballet* at the Deanery.'[10]

As Milner-White's income increased, he was able to buy pictures. Although he did not leave for these the meticulous documentation which has survived for the pots, his buying pattern can be discerned. Most of his pictures seem to have been bought in the later 1940s and early 1950s from London dealers and several were bought specially for immediate presentation to the Fitzwilliam Museum in Cambridge. His taste in pictures was for the small and intimate, predominantly from the late-nineteenth and early-twentieth centuries. Eleven paintings and three works on paper (as well as two Staite Murray pots and four Persian rugs) were given or bequeathed to the Fitzwilliam Museum. These works include a fine Gwen John, two Whistlers and two Pissarros.

Say Nothing about Pictures — Hess's lot…

WIVES OF CLERGY.

Said most that will be said in Paper —.

As I hinted there, English people are not naturally aware of old constituted high art in pottery. The Eastern peoples are. As painting is the supreme art in the West, a exquisite study is devoted to its history, and a critical appreciation; the same is the case with ceramic pottery in the East. Furthermore old understanding we had, was destroyed, annihilated in the 18th c. when pottery under the business genius of Wedgwood & his imitators became industrialised & commercialised. Since then, to put it v. humbly, our ceramic art have been limited to, let us say, a highly printed dinner set — Spode, however, Crown Derby etc etc. I am not denying that there can be v. pretty in colour or design, but the pieces are made in hundreds from a moulded mass produced.

It was by pure chance c. 1925. I walked into the following a gallery Bond St. & saw a show of stoneware pots by Reg. Wells. — [important!] Transfixed. Sat there 2 hours. After and. I bought (£20) a stoneware, seeing my interest, said that at another gallery in Bond St. was an exhibition of pots by an artist-craftsman of whom he thot even more highly. I went there — picking up — Barney —

Nearly all the people interested in this end of Bernard, Barney, back down to '20s would be counted on the fingers of one hand — Ennor Bennett, the A-C of the Times, Bernard Rackham, head of the department of ceramics of the V & A. & that group of poor & unknown clergymen who was myself!

Example of Milner-White's loose notes

Thirty-seven pictures came to York. These comprise half a dozen select Camden Town Group paintings by Sickert, Gilman and Gore, an outstanding Gwen John, interesting works by Greaves, Maitland, Wilson Steer and Wolmark, as well as one work from an earlier generation by Francis Danby. These purchases were discerning and unusual choices for a Dean, but it was his taste for studio pottery which was really exceptional and which led to the establishment of a unique and unrivalled collection.

In 1925, when the Dean first stumbled across 'studio' pottery, it was still a new and almost unknown phenomenon. The prevailing taste in ceramics was for fine porcelain made by factories such as Chelsea, Derby, Spode and Worcester, a taste which had developed in the eighteenth century with the importation of Ming porcelain from the East, and which still holds sway to a great extent today. The appeal of this beautiful and sophisticated type of ceramic lies in the translucency and delicate quality of its body, together with fine decoration, achieved through controlled reproduction of a master design.

A tradition of hand-made pottery had survived in England despite the increasing predominance of factory ware. By the twentieth century, however, comparatively few people bought hand-made pottery. This ceramic was often made from earthenware, which is porous when unglazed and which chips and breaks easily. Pottery made from stoneware on the other hand had other disadvantages; whilst being watertight and stronger than earthenware, its body is usually heavy and rough which scratches highly polished furniture or silver. Earthenware and stoneware pottery, though capable of vitality, is simply not as practical as true porcelain or 'china' (the popular name for ceramic which though not true porcelain is compositionally close to it). Furthermore, this type of pottery tended to be made in small country potteries, which did not have London exhibitions or other central selling outlets and whose work was not fashionable.

The major impetus for a revival of interest in hand-made pottery came from the East. This time it was the discovery of ancient Chinese ceramics mainly from the Sung dynasty (960-1279). These wares became known through the building of the Chinese railways at the turn of the century. During construction numerous ancient tombs were uncovered which contained great quantities of ceramics from this earlier period. These pots, made from stoneware rather than from porcelain, were of a completely different character from the later Ming wares. Though often technically imperfect their forms were spontaneous products of personal creativity and moreover they were covered with extraordinarily rich and exciting glaze effects. Soon examples started to find their way to Great Britain, but it was not until 1910 when the Burlington Fine Arts Club held an exhibition of early Chinese pottery

and porcelain that this ware became widely known. The exhibition was to have an electrifying effect on many people and enormous interest in the East and ancient Oriental ceramics was stimulated. The Oriental Ceramic Society dates from this time and the great collections of ancient Chinese ceramics made by men like Percival David and George Eumorfopoulos were begun then. The collection of the former can be seen at the Percival David Foundation of Chinese Art in London, whilst the best of the Eumorfopoulos collection is split between the Victoria and Albert Museum and the British Museum. Many artists and amateurs started to become interested in making pottery. Very little technical information was available but, spurred on by the example of Sung pottery, many people experimented in an attempt to discover the secrets of these beautiful glazes. Some of the earliest experimenters included William Bower Dalton, William Staite Murray, Charles and Nell Vyse and Reginald Wells.

Charles and Nell Vyse were particularly successful in reproducing the glaze effects to be seen on early Chinese ceramics, their success being due in no small part to the fact that Nell was an experienced chemist. Their most celebrated discovery was that a particularly admired blue glaze used by the Chinese was derived from iron and not from copper as had been previously thought.

The success of many of these early pioneers in producing wares with similar qualities to those in Sung pottery is attested by the fact that George Eumorfopoulos bought their work precisely because he felt it exhibited the very qualities he admired in early Chinese pottery. Staite Murray, the Vyses and Wells all had examples in the Eumorfopoulos collection. Eumorfopoulos further encouraged a contemporary interest in early Chinese wares by generously allowing any genuine enthusiast to handle pieces of his collection. Leach, Murray and the Vyses certainly visited him and found this experience of enormous value in their attempt to understand Chinese ceramics.

Shortly before Milner-White began to collect, a young British artist called Bernard Leach had returned from eleven years in Japan. There he had totally immersed himself in the Oriental approach to potting. Enthralled, he came back to England in 1920 determined to revitalize the old country-pottery tradition and to incorporate into it the lessons he had absorbed in the East. With him came Shoji Hamada and together the two men set up a pottery at St Ives in Cornwall. This pottery was to attract many pupils over the years.

Other pioneers of the studio pottery movement had become interested in ceramics through different avenues. Often women (among them Frances Richards who is represented in the collection), they were reacting against the dullness of factory-made products by turning to handicrafts, such as hand-painted pottery. Many ladies simply painted pottery

Copy from Invoice No 1.

The Rev. E. Milner White

Cambridge

5, Old Bond Street,
London, W., *8th Nov* 192*7*

WM. B. PATERSON.
Works of Art.

Telephone—Regent 949

*To a parchment glaze Pot, brush
decoration in Sepia & blue
grey (Cadence)*   *141* £*105 - - -*

Patterson's Gallery invoice for William Staite Murray's *Cadence*

which had already been made for them, but a few were real innovators and took their interest in ceramics further. They exhibited their work through outlets such as those provided by the Arts and Crafts Exhibition Society and the English-woman Exhibition.

The early studio potters struggled to succeed. There was very little technical information published and they had to learn by trial and error. By modern standards, many of the pots were badly made: often more clay was used than was strictly necessary; some were thrown badly; many warped; many were fired unevenly, or too highly; some cracked; others were thrown too thin causing a hole which then needed to be plugged. Shoji Hamada was one of the few pioneer potters to work in Great Britain with any technical training but the Leach Pottery still had enormous problems: finding the right clay; finding fuel for the kiln; building the kiln and controlling the firings. It all took an immense amount of determination and effort to succeed. Most of the potters lived very simply and only just managed to keep going.

There were few serious collectors of pots in the early decades of this century. One was Ernest Marsh who wrote many articles on studio pots for *Apollo*. His collection has gone in the main to the National Museums and Galleries on Mer-

seyside (as they are now known) and to the Museum and Heritage Centre, in Kingston. Henry Bergen, an American, was another early collector; his collection is now at Stoke-on-Trent Museum. Bernard Rackham, head of the Department of Ceramics at the Victoria and Albert Museum, was writing articles in the *Studio* and collecting for the Circulation Department of his museum. Sydney K. Greenslade, an architect and keen collector of Martinware, had been appointed by the Davies Sisters of Gregynog to acquire crafts for University College in Aberystwyth, which he did from 1919 until 1936. George Eumorfopoulos was perhaps the most respected of them all, albeit largely because of his magnificent collection of early Oriental ceramics. Then there was Charles Marriott, the Art Critic for *The Times* from 1924 until 1940, who kept the studio potters' work in the public eye.

Milner-White described the narrow circle of interest in studio pottery thus:

The people interested in the work of Wells, Murray, Leach during [the] '20s cd be counted on [the] finger[s] of one hand – Eumorphopoulos Marriott [the] A-C of the Times, Bernard Rackham, head of the department of Ceramics at the V&A. & that young & poor & unknown clergyman which was myself![11]

He and indeed they were leading taste by appreciating modern pottery (as the Dean called it; studio pottery is a term which, though first used in the mid-1920s to describe

Three Shields Gallery invoice for pots by Frances Richards

the new type of ceramic, has become the accepted term only much more recently). Milner-White was completely sure of the worth of this new pottery and was determined to own the best collection:

I knew I had come across something not only good, but v. good. I found an aesthetic delight, a thrill, over a fine pot which no other branch of art had ever been able to give me ... and worked hours, days, weeks, correcting Certificate Papers in History from schools all over England, to get the money to buy. I bought only the best. How I beat my foes![12]

Patrons like Milner-White were of enormous importance to these pioneers. William Staite Murray was being absolutely serious when he wrote to Milner-White:

I am no less grateful to you for buying my work, than you are to me in giving you pleasure by the beauty I create, for without buyers my work as a Potter would cease.[13]

Milner-White was a loyal patron once he had become convinced of the worth of a potter. In his eyes Murray was the most original of the pioneers and he was determined to own outstanding examples of his work. Over thirty-four years he purchased ninety-eight examples of Murray's work alone, costing him nearly £1,700.

He also gave valuable moral support to the potters, by writing to them and praising their work. From the replies that survive it is obvious this provided enormous encouragement. Charles Vyse wrote:

I am very grateful to you for your letter & appreciation. So very few have understood our attempt to break away in a new direction, & it is heartening to feel that you are in sympathy with it.[14]

Earlier William Dalton had written:

Your very appreciative letter touched me very much I don't feel I deserve to have such things said of my work. One struggles on & tries to realize beauty & then you get some pots in a row and ask yourself the question – have you done it.[15]

Milner-White did not only buy for himself: he gave away a large number of pots and encouraged others to take an interest in modern pottery. In a letter to the Dean of 1933 Arden Constant, a young cleric, wrote:

Dearest Arch,
    I went to see Vyse's exhibition in London on my way home, as you advised. It was a very pleasant shock. How slow I have been in appreciating his work! His glazes – remarkable! The variety of his pieces too is amazing. I had an interesting and enlightening (for me) talk with Vyse. He has great confidence but it is the confidence, I believe, of one who knows the range of his capabilities. I wanted you by my side to direct my thoughts and attention.[16]

Milner-White was a passionate and discriminating collector. He had a clear aesthetic philosophy, which was set out in the pamphlet accompanying the exhibition of his collection at York Art Gallery in 1952 (Appendix G). He purchased pots made only in stoneware, which he considered to be the aristocrat of ceramics. He looked for form, decoration and texture in a pot. When in the early 1950s George Wingfield Digby (Keeper of the Department of Textiles at the Victoria and Albert Museum) was carrying out research for his pioneering book, The Work of the Modern Potter in England, he came up to York three times to study the Dean's collection, and was enormously impressed by what he saw:

... it made a vivid impression on me – a powerful & beautiful one: you will understand this with your love for modern pottery, but the impression it made as a collection was most powerful ...

K. PLEYDELL-BOUVERIE
AND D. K. N. BRADEN

STONEWARE

AT

THE LITTLE GALLERY
3 ELLIS STREET, SLOANE STREET, S.W.1.
OCTOBER 28th—NOVEMBER 9th, 10-6. SATURDAYS, 10-1.

Announcement card for an exhibition of Stoneware by Katharine Pleydell-Bouverie and Norah Braden, 1935

The Staite Murrays one cannot easily forget, I have never seen a first-rate piece of his before. But I would like to see them again I don't feel I have quite estimated him yet. Leach & Hamada I know better, but yours are by far the finest lot of Hamada's I've seen (Leach has a few good pieces), & also the most important Bernard Leaches.[17]

After his second visit he wrote to say how helpful he found the accompanying documentation in writing his book and after the third commented particularly on the Staite Murrays:

Without your collection I don't think it would be possible to form any conception of what Murray achieved. I have searched a good deal but found no other fairly adequate representation. To my mind Murray must be judged essentially by his best pieces, his real creations.[18]

Muriel Rose also came to York, when writing her influential *Artist-Potters in England*. However, because this appeared so soon after Wingfield Digby's book, it is not surprising that it does not draw on the Dean's collection to the same extent.

Today, no serious student of the pioneer studio pottery movement can ignore the Milner-White collection. Its overall quality is consistently high, and it is a tribute to the Dean's judgement that the pots which he himself regarded most highly are generally those which are also most admired today.

At the same time, however, the Milner-White collection is not representative of early studio pottery. The Dean was interested in acquiring what he considered to be the best pieces and not in acquiring pots by every potter. From many potters he bought only one or two pieces, sometimes because

he did not think their later work fulfilled earlier promise. It is certainly true that the Dean was a man of his time in that he appreciated Oriental ceramics, and a large proportion of the collection displays qualities derived from this aesthetic. Milner-White bought many pieces by Charles and Nell Vyse who so successfully rediscovered and emulated Chinese techniques. He gave away most of his Vyse pieces, however, perhaps because he thought they would make good presents in view of the popularity of early Chinese ceramics – or perhaps his taste changed.

Milner-White was interested in the exchange of cultural ideas between countries, which was probably why he purchased a small but important group of French and Danish studio pottery. He was particularly keen to own Japanese pots which showed evidence of being influenced by the British tradition. He also bought pots by the earlier artist-potters, the Martin Brothers – but only for comparison's sake. The Martinware was bought as a group during the Second World War when there were few pot shows.

Milner-White's collecting was contained within clear and defined parameters. He could have bought work by Lucie Rie (born 1902) and Hans Coper (1920-1981) – two of the most highly regarded potters working in the later years of his life – but he did not. This is not perhaps surprising, however, as their work is so completely different from the pots in his collection.

Milner-White made most of his purchases from London exhibitions of potters' work. He retained much of the ephemeral documentation relating to these purchases, which is normally thrown away and is consequently extremely rare and valuable. Many of the exhibition private view cards and exhibition catalogues were preserved in two large albums, together with newspaper reviews of the time. Invoices and receipts were kept separately. He further kept an MS 'General Catalogue' in which he recorded most of his acquisitions and in which he made many useful observations, as also in his 'Fitzwilliam Book' (a notebook in which he started to categorize the Murray pots he intended to leave to the Fitzwilliam Museum, Cambridge, if no other museum would take his collection as a whole). The Milner-White documentation also consists of entries made in an indexed notebook, notes made on loose sheets and, as might be expected, numerous letters from the potters themselves, providing a wealth of invaluable information. All this material came to York City Art Gallery.

Milner-White was very attached to his collection of pots. He displayed them first in his rooms in King's, Cambridge, and then, when he became Dean of York in 1941, in the Deanery here. Friends noted that he would often absent-mindedly caress a pot in conversation with a guest. Towards the end of his life, as he increasingly succumbed to the cancer that would kill him, he thought seriously about the future

BEAUX ARTS GALLERY
1 BRUTON PLACE, BRUTON STREET, W.

* * *

STONEWARE POTTERY BY

W. STAITE MURRAY

AND PAINTINGS BY

BEN NICHOLSON
CHRISTOPHER WOOD

* * *

April 20th to May 10th, 10.30 to 5.30
Saturdays, 10.30 to 4

* * *

CATALOGUE, PRICE ONE SHILLING

Front cover to exhibition catalogue, Beaux Arts Gallery, 1927

of his modern pottery. In 1939 he had given forty-seven pieces to Southampton Art Gallery: the Art Gallery had opened in that year, Southampton was his home town, and he donated the collection in memory of his father. He had hoped to present the lion's share of the rest of his modern pottery to the Fitzwilliam Museum in Cambridge, the city where he had spent many happy years as Dean of King's, and where his love of studio pottery had begun. The Syndics, however, were reluctant to take on such a large number of pots, and only agreed to take the best twenty-five if no other museum would take the collection as a whole. In the event, York Art Gallery accepted the collection and only Murray's Cow and Trellis were presented to the Fitzwilliam from the original group of Staite Murray pots Milner-White had selected for it; the former is, however, regarded by many as the potter's finest work.

Between 1947 and 1967 York Art Gallery was run by Hans

Hess, a German refugee of strong opinions, who was determined to raise the standards of the collections. During that time Milner-White had served on the Art Gallery Committee as well as being involved in numerous other artistic activities in York. In November 1951 he presented two pieces of Leach pottery to the Gallery and in February 1952 the whole collection was lent for a temporary exhibition. From about 1957 the Dean's health began to decline steadily. The Fitzwilliam Museum had refused the collection of pots and he began to think of donating them to York. In 1958 he gave eighty pieces to the York Art Gallery on the understanding that he could retain some of the pieces for his pleasure during his lifetime.[19] In January 1959 he gave another one hundred and six pieces, in May five more and in December another one. The situation is rather confused because the Dean liked to rotate pots between the Gallery and the Deanery during the last years of his life. On 1 May 1963 Milner-White, at his own request, received Hans Hess at the Deanery. The purpose was to discuss the 'final distribution of his paintings'. The ones destined for York he wanted removing immediately. During the course of that meeting he asked Hess 'to take possession of all remaining pieces of modern pottery' at the Deanery. They 'had always been included in the gift of pottery made by the Dean to the Art Gallery some years ago, but at that time he had reserved the right to retain some pieces in his house for his own pleasure during his lifetime.' On 2 May 1963, Hess returned to the Deanery with the express purpose of removing the paintings destined for York. On this visit the Dean 'made it clear that he wanted them [the pictures] to come to us [the Art Gallery] as a gift and not a bequest, that is the reason he made the presentation in his lifetime. Miss Green [the Dean's secretary] suggested, and I [Hess] agreed, that the pottery should not be collected for the time being'.[20] Whatever the legal interpretation, it is reasonable to assume that the Dean also did not wish the presentation of any of his modern pottery to be recorded as a bequest.

Eric Milner-White died on 15 June 1963. He was seventy-nine. An outstanding dean, his influence and generosity touched many spheres and people. A discerning collector and benefactor of the arts, he was ahead of his time, leading taste rather than following the prevailing fashion. His vision led to the creation of the finest collection of pioneer studio pottery assembled by a private individual in the first half of the twentieth century. No other collection is comparable.

Notes

1. It is impossible to be precise about the exact number of pots in the Milner-White collection. Two hundred and ninety-five are listed in the MS catalogue. However, although Milner-White noted most of his purchases therein, there are pots at York and pots for which there is other documentary evidence which have not been recorded.
2. Milner-White MS notes, undated.
3. An invoice among the documentation records a Cardew dish as having been bought from the Artificers' Guild for 7s 6d in 1933. It does not indicate whether this was made from stoneware or earthenware, but it was not entered into the Dean's MS catalogue and its present whereabouts are unknown.
4. Wilkinson, 1963, p.6.
5. Ibid., p.41.
6. Ibid., pp.38-9.
7. Ibid., p.32.
8. Ibid., p.33-4.
9. Ibid., p.34.
10. Ibid., p.35.
11. Milner-White MS notes, undated.
12. Ditto.
13. Letter from Staite Murray, 19 December 1928.
14. Letter from Charles Vyse, 6 March 1935.
15. Letter from William Dalton, 20 December 1928.
16. Letter from Arden Constant, 20 December 1933.
17. Letter from George Wingfield Digby, 7 August 1950.
18. Letter from George Wingfield Digby, 19 December 1950.
19. 'Give over a proportion, say $\frac{2}{3}$ or $\frac{3}{4}$ the w[hole]; keeping $\frac{1}{3}$ here – change & interchange at intervals, to the benefit of both yr Gallery & my house'.
20. Typescript record of meeting between Hess and the Dean, 1 May 1963.

Place of exhibition is London unless otherwise indicated. An asterisk denotes that no numbered catalogue or checklist was published (or at least has not been located).

1925   William Paterson's Gallery, Staite Murray exhibition, November.*

1926   William Paterson's Gallery, *50 Pieces of Stoneware and Porcelain Pottery*, November.

1927   William Paterson's Gallery, Bernard Leach stoneware pottery exhibition, March.

1927   Beaux Arts Gallery, *Stoneware Pottery by W. Staite Murray and Paintings by Ben Nicholson* [and] *Christopher Wood*, 20 April - 10 May.

1927   P. & D. Colnaghi & Co., *An Exhibition of the Work of present-day Potters*, 26 October - 4 November.

1927   William Paterson's Gallery, *Stoneware Pottery and Drypoints by W. Staite Murray*, 9 November - 9 December.

1928   William Paterson's Gallery, *Stoneware Pottery and Watercolours by Staite Murray*, 1 - 28 November.

1928   P. & D. Colnaghi & Co., *An Exhibition of the Work of present-day Potters*, 28 November - 12 December.

1928   Beaux Arts Gallery, *Stoneware Pottery by Bernard Leach*, 4 - 20 December.

1929   William Paterson's Gallery, *Pottery by Shoji Hamada*, 23 May - 15 June.

1929   William Paterson's Gallery, *Stoneware Pottery by Staite Murray*, 20 November - 19 December.

1929   P. & D. Colnaghi & Co., *Exhibition of the Work of present-day Potters*, 27 November - 19 December.

1930   Alex Reid & Lefevre Ltd, *Pottery, Paintings and Furniture by Staite Murray*, November.

1931   Beaux Arts Gallery, *Stoneware Pottery and Porcelain by Kenkichi Tomimoto (of Tokyo) and Bernard Leach*, 5 - 22 May.

1931   Royal Institute Galleries, second exhibition of the National Society: Painters, Sculptors, Engravers, Potters, June.*

1931   Paterson's Gallery, *Pottery by Shoji Hamada*, 31 October - 28 November.

1931   Alex Reid & Lefevre Ltd, *New Pottery and Paintings by Staite Murray*, November.

1933   Beaux Arts Gallery, *Stoneware Pottery and Drawings by Bernard Leach*, 15 November - 2 December.

1935   Alex Reid & Lefevre Ltd, *Pots, Paintings and Drawings by Staite Murray*, November.

1936   Little Gallery, *Stoneware and Slipware by Bernard Leach*, 20 April - 3 May.*

1937   Little Gallery, *Recent Work by five Japanese Craftsmen*, 1 June - 19 June.*

1938   Brygos Gallery, *Contemporary French Pottery by Members of the Group of 'Artisans Français Contemporains'*, 20 April - 20 May.

1939   British Pavilion, Stockholm, nine pots lent 'at the request of the British Government'.

1942   Walker's Galleries, *Martin Ware from the Collection of the late Frank Knight*, 30 November - 19 December.

1946   Berkley [sic] Galleries, *Leach Pottery*, June.

1952   Dartington Hall; Edinburgh College of Art; New Burlington Galleries; and Birmingham Art Gallery, *Pottery and Textiles 1920 - 1952 made in Great Britain by Artist-Craftsmen* (Arts Council of Great Britain), June - November.

1952   Beaux Arts Gallery, *Bernard Leach and Shoji Hamada: Exhibition of Pottery*, 16 September - 10 October.*

1956   Liberty, Bernard Leach exhibition.*

1958   Primavera, *Thrown and coiled Stoneware by Katharine Pleydell-Bouverie and Helen Pincombe*, 4 - 17 November ('season 57/58').*

1958   Leicester Galleries, *Stoneware Pottery by William Staite Murray*, November.

1959   Berkeley Galleries, *Stoneware Pottery by Michael Cardew and Pupils from Abuja, Northern Nigeria* (second exhibition), 16 September - 10 October.*

1960   Museum Boymans-van Beuningen, Rotterdam, *Engelse Pottenbakkers*, 6 November - 18 December.

1961   Arts Council Gallery; City Art Gallery, Bradford; and Laing Art Gallery, Newcastle upon Tyne, *Bernard Leach: Fifty Years a Potter*; 6 January - 8 April.

1962   Berkeley Galleries, *Stoneware Pottery by Michael Cardew & Pupils from Abuja, Northern Nigeria* (third exhibition), 14 June - 7 July.*

1969   Farnham School of Art, modern crafts exhibition.*

1976   Graves Art Gallery, Sheffield, *Pottery by Bernard Leach with three Pots by Shoji Hamada*, 14 February - 7 March.

1976-7 Boymans-van Beuningen Museum, Rotterdam; (?) ..., Brussels; City Art Gallery & Museum, Bristol; National Museum of Wales, Cardiff; City Art Gallery, Leeds; Camden Arts Centre; and Gladstone Pottery Museum, Stoke-on-Trent, *Mud and Water Man: Michael Cardew: Work from England and Africa* (Crafts Advisory Committee), 20 May 1976 - 11 September 1977.

1977   Victoria and Albert Museum, *The Art of Bernard Leach: A loan retrospective Exhibition*, March - May.

1979-80 Hayward Gallery, *Thirties: British Art and Design before the War* (Arts Council of Great Britain), 25 October - 13 January.

1980   Christopher Wood Gallery, *British 20th Century Studio Ceramics*, 25 November - 6 December.

1980   Hankyu Umeda, Osaka; Mitsukoshi Museum, Nihonbashi, Tokyo; Ohara Museum of Art, Kurashiki; Meitetsu, Nagoya; and Kurosaki Sogo, Kitakyushu, *The Art of Bernard Leach: His masterpieces loaned by British Museums and Collectors: Meeting of East and West*, 4 April - 1 July.

1980-1   Holburne of Menstrie Museum, University of Bath, *Katharine Pleydell-Bouverie: A retrospective Exhibition of her Pottery from the 1920s to the Present Day*, 22 November - 22 February.

1982   Crafts Council Gallery, *The Maker's Eye*, 13 January - 28 March.

1983   York City Art Gallery; Arts Centre, University College of Wales, Aberystwyth; and Crafts Council Gallery, *Michael Cardew and Pupils*, 6 March - 28 August.

1984-5   Cleveland Gallery, Middlesbrough; and Victoria and Albert Museum, *William Staite Murray*, December - April.

1985   Tate Gallery, *St Ives 1939-64: Twenty-five Years of Painting, Sculpture and Pottery*, 13 February - 14 April.

1987   Wakefield Art Gallery, *Modern Clay*, 13 July - 3 October.

1988   Manchester City Art Gallery, *Out of Clay*, 23 July - 11 September.

1989   Whitworth Art Gallery, University of Manchester, *Off the Wheel: A New Look at Modern British Pottery*, 10 March - 1 May.*

1989   Hyogo Prefectural Museum of Modern Art, Kobe; Museum of Modern Art, Kamakura; and Setagaya Art Museum, Tokyo, *St Ives*, 8 April - 27 August.

The published works listed below are referred to in the abbreviated form 'Cooper, 1947', for example, with the exception of the final item which is abbreviated as 'Handlist, 1971'. Place of publication for books is London unless otherwise indicated.

Anon., 'Ceramic Art: Modern Exponents in France', *The Times, Trade and Engineering Supplement* ('French Porcelain Section'), 30 July 1927, p.VI.

Anon., 'Mr. W. Staite Murray's Stoneware Pottery, and Drypoints at Mr William Paterson's Gallery', *Apollo*, vi, no.36, December 1927, pp.283-4.

Anon., 'The Dean's Taste: A York Exhibition', *Yorkshire Gazette*, 22 February 1952.

Bennett, Ian, *British 20th Century Studio Ceramics* (exhibition catalogue), Christopher Wood Gallery, 1980.

Cooper, Ronald G., *The Modern Potter*, John Tiranti Ltd, 1947.

Digby: see Wingfield Digby.

Ede, H.S., 'Ben Nicholson, Winifred Nicholson and William Staite Murray', *Artwork*, iv, winter 1928, pp. 262-8.

Forsyth, Gordon, *20th Century Ceramics*, Studio, London & New York, n.d. [1936].

Haslam, Malcolm, 'William Staite Murray's Ceramics in Context', *Antique Dealer & Collectors Guide*, March 1984, pp.64-6.

Haslam, Malcolm, *William Staite Murray*, Crafts Council/Cleveland County Museum Service, 1984.

Haslam, Malcolm, 'Freedom beyond Sculpture: Early Collectors of English Studio Pottery', *Country Life*, 5 June 1986, pp.1605-7.

(Hess, Hans), 'Pottery' under 'Editorial', *Preview*, xiii, no.49, January 1960, pp.461-5.

Hogben, Carol (ed.), *The Art of Bernard Leach*, Faber and Faber, London & Boston 1978.

Holme, C. Geoffrey, & Wainwright, Shirley B. (eds), *Decorative Art 1926*, ('The Studio' Year Book), The Studio, 1926.

Holme, C. Geoffrey, & Wainwright, S.B. (eds), *Decorative Art 1930* ('The Studio' Year Book), The Studio, 1930.

Hyne, Reggie, 'William Staite Murray – Potter and Artist', *Ceramic Review*, no.92, March-April 1985, pp.10-15.

I(ngamells), J.A.S., 'The Dean's Gift of Modern Stoneware Pottery', *Preview*, xii, no.46, April 1959, pp.437-43.

Ingamells, J.A.S., 'Stoneware at York', *Museums Journal*, lix, no.6, September 1959, pp.122-5.

Leach, Bernard, *A Potter's Book*, Faber and Faber, 1940, reprinted 1976.

Leach, Bernard, *A Potter's Portfolio: A Selection of fine Pots*, Lund Humphries, 1951.

Leach, Bernard, *A Potter's Work*, Adams and Dart/Jupiter Books, 1967.

Leach, Bernard, *Hamada: Potter*, Kodansha International, Tokyo 1975; Thames and Hudson, 1976.

Leach, Bernard (introduction), *Michael Cardew: A Collection of Essays*, Crafts Advisory Committee, 1976.

Leach, Bernard, *The Potter's Challenge*, Souvenir Press, 1976.

Leach, Bernard, *Beyond East and West: Memoirs, Portraits & Essays*, Faber and Faber, London & Boston 1978, reprinted in paperback 1985.

Leach, Janet, 'Pots at the Tate!', *Ceramic Review*, no.92, March-April 1985, pp.25-6.

Marriott, Charles, *British Handicrafts*, British Council/Longmans Green, 1943.

Marsh, Ernest, 'W. Staite Murray: Studio Potter of Bray, Berkshire', *Apollo*, xxxix, no.231, April 1944, pp.107-9.

Morley-Fletcher, Hugo, *Techniques of the World's Great Masters of Pottery and Ceramics*, Phaidon-Christie's, Oxford 1984.

Pleydell-Bouverie, Katharine, 'Early days at St Ives', in a collection of articles headed 'Bernard Leach Potter', *Ceramic Review*, no.50, March-April 1978, pp.25-9.

Rose, Muriel, *Artist-Potters in England*, Faber and Faber, 1955, revised edition 1970.

Shikiba, Ryūzaburō, *Bernard Leach*, Kensetsu-sha, Tokyo 1934.

Sidey, Tessa, *Michael Cardew and Pupils* (exhibition catalogue), York City Art Gallery, York 1983.

(Watson, Oliver), ceramic entries in *St Ives* (exhibition catalogue), Hyogo Prefectural Museum of Modern Art, Kobe, etc., 1989.

Webber, John, 'William Staite Murray', *Crafts*, May-June 1975, pp.25-33.

Wilkinson, Patrick, *Eric Milner-White 1884-1963: Fellow, Chaplain and Dean, Dean of York: A Memoir prepared by Direction of the Council of King's College, Cambridge*, privately published, King's College, Cambridge 1963.

Wingfield Digby, George, *The Work of the Modern Potter in England*, John Murray, 1952.

York Art Gallery, *Modern Stoneware Pottery: Select Handlist of the Milner-White Gift*, York Art Gallery, York 1971 (abbreviated as *Handlist, 1971*).

178. Archway Road
Highgate. N6.

Dear W Milner-White

Thank you for your most
kind letter - it is a great unexpected
pleasure to hear from you about my
work - I do appreciate greatly your
opinion + your consideration in
telling me + also in telling me of
JW Murray's notice of the bowl -

I shall be very pleased indeed to do
that piece + will let you know when
I have arrived at something interesting
- I will not wait - for the perfect
thing but it shall be of my best -

Yours sincerely
Frances E Richards.

Letter from Frances Richards to Milner-White

Milner-White kept meticulous records of most of his pots and preserved a variety of documents relating to them. All of this material
came to the Gallery. It is referred to in the Catalogue under the following headings.

General Catalogue
A notebook with patterned cloth cover, measuring $7 \times 5\frac{1}{2}$ in
(17.8×14 cm), in which Milner-White recorded most of his
acquisitions of modern pottery. It is inscribed on the first page:
'Pots General Catalogue (Entered on purchase)'. The entries are
arranged under successive years but with continuous numbering
from 1 to 258. Prices are often given and place of acquisition is
sometimes noted. Further information and subjective comments are
added. The whereabouts of pots which have left his possession are
also noted.

Fitzwilliam Book
A notebook bound in leather with a design stained and gold-
embossed on the front cover, measuring 7×5 in (17.9×12.6 cm),
in which Milner-White began to catalogue and categorize his collection of William Staite Murray pots for intended presentation to the
Fitzwilliam Museum, Cambridge (only thirty-six were recorded).
It is inscribed on the first page: 'Fitzwilliam Book vol I. Staite Murray and Pupils.' Milner-White then describes the purpose of the
book:

'This is a list of ceramic pieces, which, in accordance with the terms
of my will, presenting my collection of modern stoneware to the
Fitzwilliam Museum, Cambridge, I consider to be of the highest
standard of art or interest; or typical of the particular potter's
development and work.
　　They divide into three classes.

I　Pieces of superlative merit.

II　Pieces of high Museum rank, essential to the representation of
the artist.

III　Pieces of full Museum standard; which, however, the Fitz-
william may present if it does not wish to keep them, to other
Museums, with preference to the Art Gallery of my native town,
Southampton. The collection however will be impaired, if the
Fitzwilliam does not keep at least half of Class III. It would make
no mistake in keeping all'.

At the end of the entries he writes:

'Of the 36 catalogued above, SEVEN have been given to Southampton
Art Gallery, leaving a collection of 29 pieces covering the whole of
Murray's potting career, (though somewhat weak in earlier pieces
of more derivative type) for the Fitzwilliam Museum. If kept
together it will be a collection of this remarkable potter, undoubtedly the best in the world between the two wars, which cannot be
surpassed or even remotely equalled.'

Indexed notebook
A ring-leaved notebook indexed alphabetically with floppy leather-
cover, measuring $6\frac{1}{8} \times 4$ in (15.7×10.3 cm), in which Milner-
White catalogued (presumably) seven pots by Shoji Hamada (num-
bered from 1 to 7 but 3 is missing) and twenty-five pots by William
Staite Murray.

Loose notes
Sixteen sides of rough notes, often written on the back of scrap
paper, providing invaluable insights into Milner-White's views on
his collection and on pots in general.

Letters
Thirty-three letters relating to ceramics mostly from potters represented in the collection, but also a few from potters not represented
and from non-potting correspondents.

Invoices and receipts
Seventy-one invoices and receipts cover 229 pots. Not all pots
recorded were entered in the General Catalogue (see above), while
some pots which were entered there and/or came to the Gallery
do not have corresponding invoices or receipts.

Albums I and II
Two albums covered with hand-printed (?) Japanese paper,
measuring $12\frac{1}{2} \times 9\frac{3}{4}$ in (33.2×24.8 cm) each, into which Milner-
White pasted private view cards, exhibition catalogues, reviews,
other articles and a few letters relating to the collection; their con-
tents are listed in full as Appendix E. They were given by Milner-
White to the Gallery in December 1958. Though not titled by
Milner-White, they are referred to here as Album I and Album II.

Murray's Album
An album with cloth cover, quarter-bound in leather, measuring
$12\frac{1}{4} \times 10\frac{1}{2}$ in (31.1×26.7 cm) containing newspaper cuttings relating to William Staite Murray. It was given by Murray to Milner-
White, and given by him to the Gallery in December 1958. Though
not specifically titled by either Murray or Milner-White, it is
referred to here as Murray's Album.

List of colour plates

PLATE I
Bernard Leach, Vase, c.1946 (No.72)

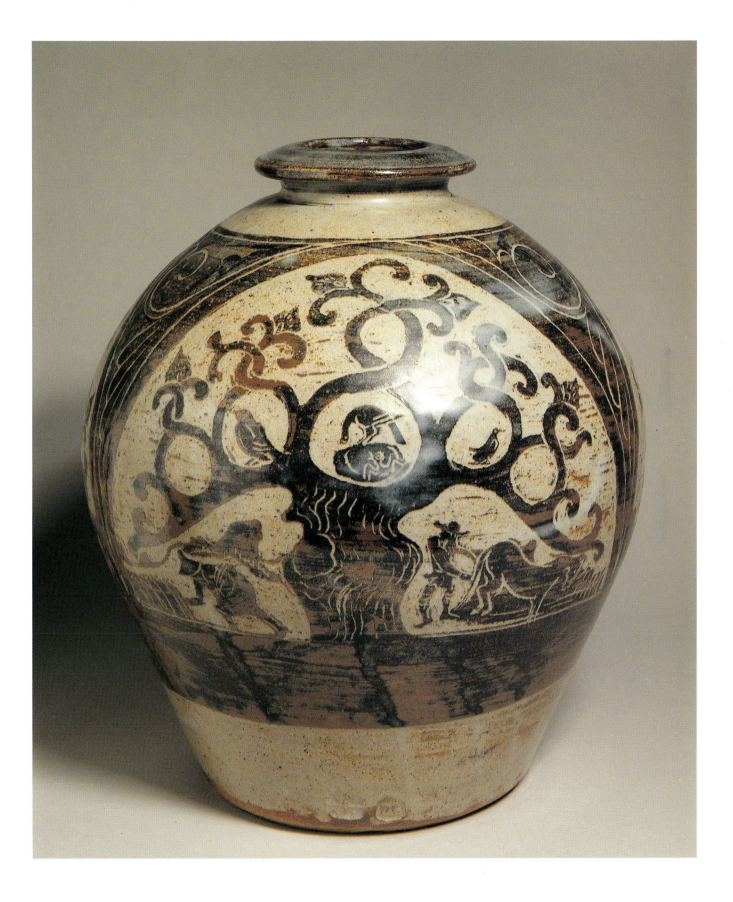

PLATE II
Reginald Wells, Two-handled Jar, exh. 1925 (No.151)

PLATE III
William Staite Murray, Pot, 1923 (No.97)

PLATE IV
Bernard Leach, Panel of Tiles: 'Well Head and Mountains', exh. 1929 (No.63)

PLATE V
Bernard Leach, Panel of small Tiles, exh. 1929 (No.64)

PLATE VI
Bernard Leach, Fruit Bowl, exh. 1952 (No.79)

PLATE VII
Bernard Leach, Vase: 'Leaping Salmon', 1931 (No.66)

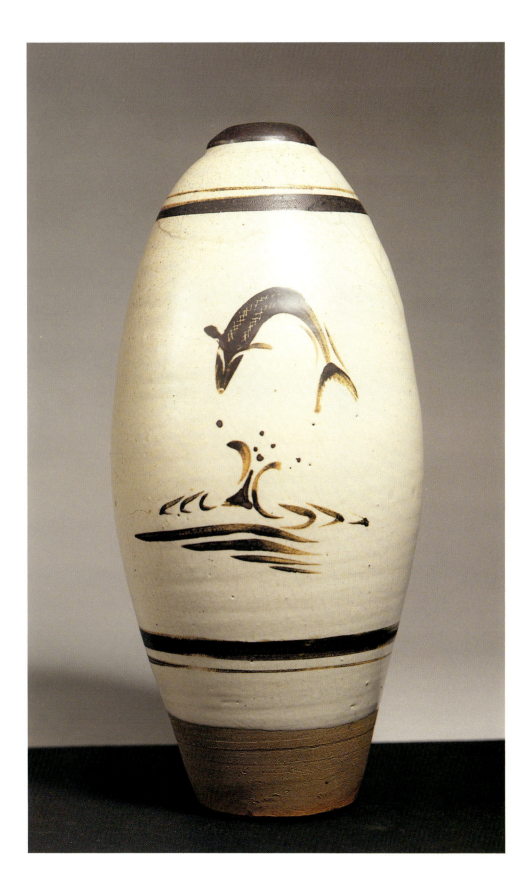

PLATE VIII
Bernard Leach, Bowl, ?1924-5 (No.55)

PLATE IX
Charles and Nell Vyse, Vase: 'Olympia', 1935 (No.145)

PLATE X
Shoji Hamada, Bottle, 1923–6 (No.24)

PLATE XI (OPPOSITE)
Shoji Hamada, Tall Jar, 1926–8 (No.26)

PLATE XII
Shoji Hamada, Bottle, c.1927 (No.27)

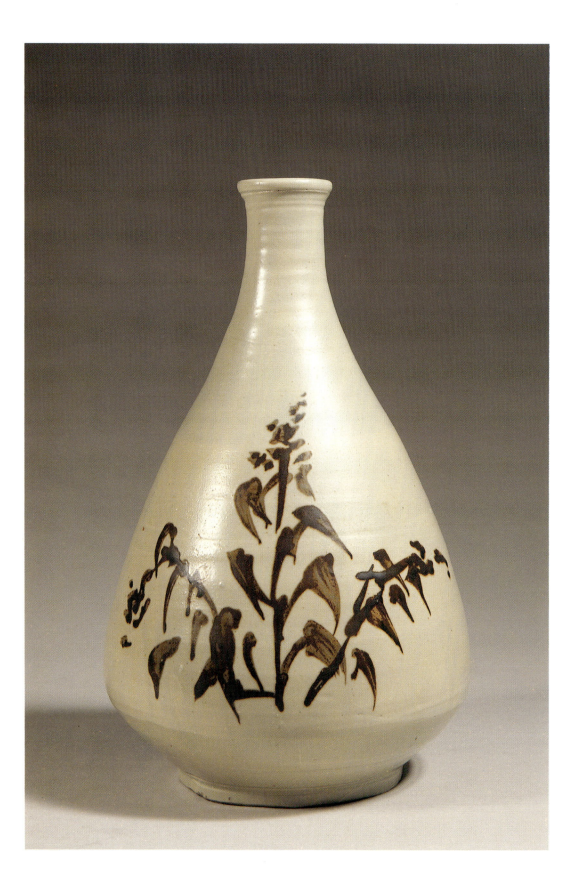

PLATE XIII
Shoji Hamada, Large Dish, exh. 1931 (No.38)

PLATE XIV
Shoji Hamada, Dish, c.1937 (No.42)

PLATE XV
Shoji Hamada, Square Dish, exh. 1952 (No.43)

PLATE XVI
William Staite Murray, Bowl: 'Vortex', exh. 1929 (No. 116)

PLATE XVII
William Staite Murray, Vase: 'Cadence', exh. 1927 (No.110)

PLATE XXI
Sam Haile, Bowl: 'Roman Baths', exh. 1936 (No.20)

PLATE XXII
William Staite Murray, Tall Jar :
'The Bather', 1930 (No.118)

PLATE XXIV
Katharine Pleydell-Bouverie, Pot, exh. 1958 (No.133)

PLATE XXV
Norah Braden, Flared Bowl, exh. 1935 (No. 3)

PLATE XXVII
Séraphin Soudbinine, Dish, 1937 or earlier (No. 139)

PLATE XXVIII
Axel Salto, Bowl, c.1946 (No.138)

PLATE XXIX
Ladi Kwali, Water Pot, exh. 1962 (No.54)

PLATE XXX
Michael Cardew, Plate, exh. 1959 (No. 11)

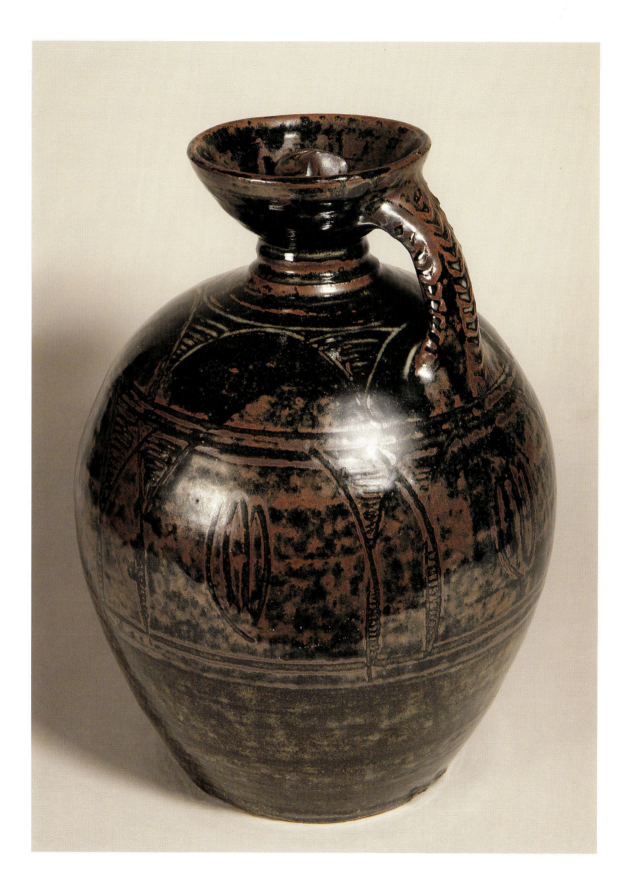

PLATE XXXII
Bode Willumsen, Jug, 1927 (No.152)

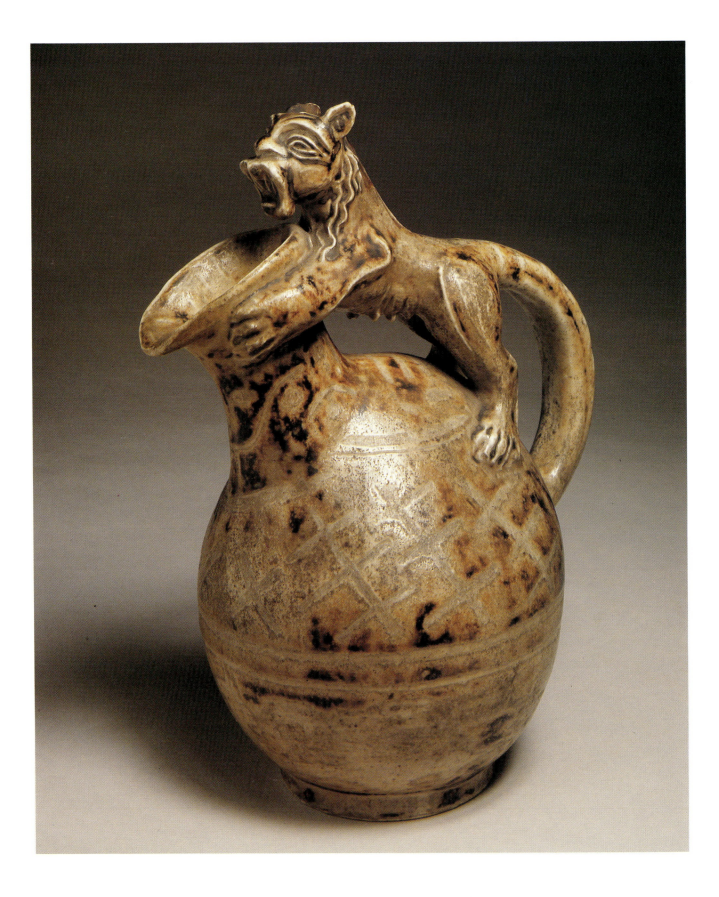

The Catalogue

Explanatory notes

All pots are stoneware, unless otherwise indicated. Measurements are correct to the nearest $\frac{1}{8}$ in and 1 mm.

All catalogued items were acquired by Eric Milner-White and subsequently passed to the Gallery, although in just one case (No. 147), indirectly.

An exhibition of Milner-White's pots was held at the Fitzwilliam Museum, Cambridge, in April 1940 and a further exhibition entitled *The Dean's Taste*, consisting of both pots and paintings, was held at York City Art Gallery in February 1952. In the absence of secure documentation, it is assumed that most of the pots owned by Milner-White in 1940 and 1952 respectively were lent to these exhibitions, but in order to avoid repetition, reference has not been made to them in the catalogue entries.

The terms 'No.' and 'Nos' with a capital N refer to items in this Catalogue.

The following abbreviations have been used:

exh.	First exhibited
H	Height
D	Diameter
PROV	Provenance
EXH	Exhibition(s)
LIT	Literature
MW DOC	Milner-White Documentation

Halima Audu

Nigerian   mid-1930s-1961

Born in Idon Kasa, a village not far from Kwali in Nigeria, the daughter of Audu, Halima married a policeman working in Abuja. Around 1959 she followed Ladi Kwali as the second of the Gwari women to work at the Pottery Training Centre,

Abuja, run by Michael Cardew. Halima Audu produced traditional hand-built water pots as well as smaller functional ware thrown on the wheel. She died from yellow fever when only in her late twenties.

I

I

1. Bowl known as 'Floating Bowl'
c.1960

Probably Cardew's body 44; the interior possibly covered in red slip with the design scratched through, the whole possibly covered in a chun glaze; wood-fired.

H $1\frac{3}{4}$ in (4.6 cm); D $8\frac{1}{4}$ in (20.9 cm)

Marks: 'H·I' and Abuja in Arabic (impressed)

Made under the instruction of Michael Cardew at the pottery centre in Abuja, Northern Nigeria, this bowl exemplifies the use of the potter's wheel and glazes, which he encouraged. The 'I' in the stamped signature is thought to stand for the name of the village where Halima was born, Idon Kasa.

PROV: Berkeley Galleries, 1962 (3gns); received on Milner-White's death, 1963 (1049/18).

EXH: Berkeley Galleries, 1962 (230); York, 1983 (46); Manchester, 1988 (41).

LIT: *Handlist*, 1971 (5).

MW DOC: General Catalogue: '19/6/62 3rd show at the Berkley [sic] Galleries of Cardew and his African pupils ... Floating Bowl by Ladi Kwali 3.3.0'; notes on loose private view leaflet: '230 Plate – Signed H.L = Halima Chun glaze dec. Ladi Kwali 3gs'.

2. Water Pot c.1960

Probably Cardew's body 49; hand-built; impressed and incised decoration inlaid with corn starch or white slip; the whole covered with transparent glaze (Cardew's AA), producing a deep green breaking to iron red where applied thinly and the iron from the body takes possession; wood-fired.

H 13 in (33 cm); D 14 in (36 cm)

Marks: 'H·I' and Abuja in Arabic (impressed)

This is a traditional hand-built Nigerian water pot, but made in stoneware, glazed and fired under the instruction of Cardew at the pottery centre in Abuja. The same glaze has been used on this pot as on Ladi Kwali's No.54. Applied thinly (as here) the effect is

2

red ; used thickly (as on the Ladi Kwali) the effect is green. This pot was previously dated c.1952 but a date nearer 1960 would seem more likely. There is a letter from Cardew in the Gallery files[1] suggesting a replacement for this pot which was broken around 1964. It was restored by Judith Larney of London in 1985.

PROV : Berkeley Galleries, 1962 (18gns) ; received on Milner-White's death, 1963 (1049/19).

EXH : Berkeley Galleries, 1962 (63).

MW DOC : General Catalogue : '19/6/62 3rd Show at the Berkley [sic] Galleries of Cardew and his African pupils. Hand built pot by Halima 18.18.0 … Halima, also a woman, younger [than Ladi Kwali], the only one at present approaching L.K.'s

standard' ; loose private view leaflet : '63 Hand Built pot by Halima 18gs. (from Idon Kasa) Flying Lizards'.

1. Letter dated 7 October 1964.

Dorothy Kathleen Norah Braden
British born 1901

Norah Braden was regarded by Bernard Leach as being perhaps his most naturally gifted pupil. She was born in Margate. From 1919 to 1921 she studied at the Central School of Arts and Crafts and afterwards at the Royal College of Art. From 1925 to 1928 she worked at the Leach Pottery, St Ives. There she began to be interested in wood-ash glazes and in 1928 went to Coleshill to join Katharine Pleydell-Bouverie, who had already embarked on an ambitious programme of ash-glaze experimentation. During the eight years Braden was to spend sporadically at Coleshill she and Pleydell-Bouverie worked closely together in a fruitful collaboration. Not surprisingly their work from those years is often very similar and it is not always easy to distinguish between the two hands. In 1936 Braden left Coleshill for the south coast and taught at Brighton School of Art. She also taught part-time at Chichester and Camberwell until she retired in 1967. Braden had rigorous standards and destroyed a great deal of her work. She made few pots after 1936 and even fewer following the war. After her retirement in 1967 she ceased potting, except when occasionally visiting Pleydell-Bouverie. Her work is rare.

3. Flared Bowl exh. 1935 (colour XXV)

Box-ash glaze in olive green and bronze, splashed iron red within (incised body code: '144': brushed glaze code: 'VII, MOI 62').[1]

H 2⅞ in (7.3 cm); D 6¼ in (15.8 cm)

Mark: If any, obliterated by glaze dribble

Presumably made at Coleshill in 1935 or before, this bowl had previously been recorded as by Pleydell-Bouverie. Both potters worked closely together for eight years and it is not always easy to differentiate between their work. However, this pot is slightly different in finish from other Pleydell-Bouverie pots in the collection. Furthermore it is not recorded in the Dean's MS catalogue, but a label on the base '106 × 1½gns' ties the pot up with a Braden receipt in the documentation and a Braden entry in the Dean's catalogue. A similar bowl by Pleydell-Bouverie is in the Southampton collection of Milner-White pottery. It seems likely that the present bowl was confused with the Pleydell-Bouverie at Southampton. Three pots by Pleydell-Bouverie bearing the glaze code 'VII MOI, are illustrated in Crafts Council, *Katharine Pleydell-Bouverie: A Potter's Life 1895-1985*, Crafts Council, 1986, pp.37, 38 and 40 in colour.

PROV: Little Gallery, 1935 (1½gns); presented, January 1959 (935/19).

EXH: Little Gallery, *Pleydell-Bouverie and D. K. N. Braden: Stoneware*, 28 October-9 November 1935 (106); Bath, 1980-1 (41).

MW DOC: General Catalogue: '1935. 171 BRADEN. Bowl, grey blue glaze with red flush. 1½'; receipted invoice: Little Gallery, 29 October (?) 1935, 'Stoneware bowl 106 × N. Braden £1.11.6'; album II: private view card.

1. In Pleydell-Bouverie's MS Glaze Recipe Notebook, under stoneware glazes for wood-fired kiln at Coleshill 1928-46, 'VII' = '2 Box ash (garden burnt) 2 Potash felspar 1 China clay slip, 1 Ball clay slip. Chamber 1: Hard (1300°c good). Beautiful grey olive, taking magnetic iron splash & pigments, 19, 21, 62 & 63 well. Chamber 2: 1350°c – 1400°c. Dark, beautiful greyish bronze – takes pigments & manganese oxide splashes very dramatically'; 'MOI = manganese'; '62' is presumably one of the pigments mentioned above.

4. Dish c.1938

Ivory-white crackle glaze with brushed iron crescents (incised body code: '144-13').

H 2⅜ in (6 cm); D 11½ in (29.2 cm)

Mark: Octagonal mark obscured by glaze (impressed)

This dish was one of Milner-White's rare purchases during the Second World War. A vase *Tornado* decorated with the same glaze and crescents is in the collection of the National Museums and Galleries on Merseyside (WAG 3620).

PROV: Unknown; purchased, 1944 (3gns); presented, January 1959 (935/78).

EXH: Rotterdam, 1960 (67); Hayward Gallery, 1979-80 (2.54); Bath, 1980-1 (164).

LIT: *Handlist*, 1971 (9).

MW DOC: General Catalogue: '1944 … 219 BRADEN Large plate, Japanese shape 3.3.0 Biscuit without; glaze ivory-white with iron splashes within. c.1938 3.3.0'.

Michael Ambrose Cardew
British 1901 - 1983

Michael Cardew with Ladi Kwali wearing her MBE medal, Abuja, 1963

Michael Cardew is widely regarded as one of the greatest British studio potters of the twentieth century. Born in Wimbledon of a professional family, he shocked his parents by leaving Oxford determined to become a potter. He learnt to throw at Fishley Holland's Braunton pottery and then persuaded Bernard Leach to take him on at St Ives. He stayed there until 1926 when he left to set up his own pottery at Winchcombe in Gloucestershire. At Winchcombe he concentrated on making slip-decorated earthenware. In 1939 he set up a new pottery at Wenford Bridge, St Trudy in Cornwall. In need of a more secure income to educate his family (he had married Mariel Russell in 1933 and now had three sons), he took over from Harry Davis as pottery instructor at Achimota College on the Gold Coast in 1942. By 1945 he had moved to the Vumé Dugamé on the Volta River. Then after a short spell back in England nursing his health he returned to Africa, this time as pottery officer in the Nigerian Government's Department of Commerce and Industry. His brief was to 'upgrade' traditional African pottery to the level of the European peasant potter as a means of establishing local industry. By 1951 he had set up the Teaching Centre for the North of Africa at Abuja. There he drew all materials from the local enviroment and concentrated on making stoneware. In 1958, 1959 and 1962 highly successful exhibitions of the work of Cardew and his African pupils were held at the Berkeley Galleries in London. As a civil servant Cardew had to retire from his post in 1965, but he continued working at his pottery in Wenford Bridge, Cornwall, until his death. He died in Truro.

For notes on bodies and glazes used at Abuja see: Michael Cardew, 'Potting in Northern Nigeria', *Pottery Quarterly*, iii, no.11, autumn 1956, p.92; idem, *A Pioneer Pottery*, Longman, 1969, pp.32 & 84; Leach (*Cardew*), 1976, p.68; Garth Clark, *Michael Cardew*, Faber & Faber, London and Boston 1978, p.74; Danlami Aliyu, 'Nigerian Pottery Tradition and New Technique', *Pottery Quarterly*, xiii, no.52, 1980, pp.175-8.

Milner-White and Cardew

All the Cardew pots in the collection are stoneware from Abuja. Milner-White had been impressed by Cardew's work for many years but was not at all interested in buying slip-decorated earthenware. It was only when he heard Cardew was making stoneware that he bought. The Dean missed the private view of the first exhibition at the Berkeley Galleries because his invitation arrived too late. Muriel Rose wisely arrived before the view and bought the best pieces for the British Council. The exhibition was very well received. If the Dean managed to get to it at all it seems probable that everything would have been sold or at least the pieces likely to interest him. He was obviously bitterly disappointed and wrote to Cardew, who promised to keep some of the best pieces in his next exhibition for the Dean (see Appendix H). From the 1959 exhibition the Dean bought seven pieces by Cardew and one by Ladi Kwali. He made the following entry in the MS catalogue:

Cardew, a first-rank pupil of Leach, was a long time (1) before he took to stoneware, & (2) before devoting his later creative life to teaching pot-making to (West) Africans. This was his second show of their work. At the first, one of Ladi Kwali's large pots was shown, & immediately bought by the V&A. Her pot opposite [No.53] and another like it were 'ordered' beforehand by myself & Sir Kenneth Clarke [sic].

At the third Berkeley Galleries show, Milner-White bought five pieces: two by Cardew, two by Halima Audu, and one by Ladi Kwali. These are the last pots recorded as being bought by Milner-White.

A cup and saucer by Cardew from Abuja (exhibited 1962) was given anonymously in 1978 (1353 a & b).

5. Oil Jar with Screw Stopper: 'Heart of Darkness' exh. 1959 (colour XXXI)

Probably body 49; red slip with linear decoration of stylized fish incised through it and inlaid with corn starch or white slip; the whole covered with transparent glaze (AA); wood-fired.

H 14¾ in (37.5 cm); D 11 in (28 cm)

Marks: MC monograms and Abuja in Arabic (impressed)

Unusually Cardew has given this magnificent pot a name, probably to emphasize its special quality. It is almost certain that No.5 is the pot which Cardew described as 'the best M.C. pot I can find', when he wrote to Milner-White promising to reserve it from the 1959 exhibition (see below and Appendix H).

PROV: Berkeley Galleries, 1959 (£25 15s.od.); received, December 1959 (952/1).[1]

EXH: Berkeley Galleries, 1959 (194, ill.); York, 1983 (22).

LIT: Hess, 1960, p.464, ill. p465; *Handlist*, 1971 (1); Bennett, 1980, p.19.

MW DOC: General Catalogue: '18/5/59 Michael Cardew and his African School – All Stoneware ... Oil Jar by M.C. 25-15-0 ... Bought at the Berkeley Galleries 18.5.59'; loose private view leaflet; letter from Cardew, 6 September 1959; see Appendix H.

1. Milner-White was authorized by York City Council on 16 December 1959 to spend up to £60 insurance money on stoneware pottery to replace damaged or stolen items. In fact he transferred Nos 5 and 6, already in his possession, together with No.78.

6. Oil Jar with Screw Stopper exh. 1959

Probably body 49; red slip, with linear decoration of stylized fish incised through it and inlaid with corn starch or white slip; the whole covered with transparent glaze (AA); wood-fired.

H 13¾ in (35 cm); D 10¼ in (25.9 cm)

Marks: MC monogram and Abuja in Arabic (impressed)

PROV: Berkeley Galleries, 1959 (15gns); received on Milner-White's death, 1963 (1049/5).

EXH: Berkeley Galleries, 1959 (192); Rotterdam, 1976 (82); York, 1983 (23).

LIT: *Handlist*, 1971 (11).

MW DOC: General Catalogue: '18/5/59 Michael Cardew and his African School – All Stoneware ... Oil Jar by M.C. 15-15-0 ... Bought at the Berkeley Galleries 18.5.59'; loose private view leaflet.

7. Screw-lidded Soy Pot exh. 1959

Probably body 49; red slip and tenmoku glaze (TK) with *sgraffito* decoration of stylized fish; wood-fired.

H 3⅝ in (9.1 cm); D 4⅛ in (10.5 cm)

Marks: MC monogram and Abuja in Arabic (impressed)

In 1945 Cardew visited the Denby factory in Derbyshire. It was here that he first saw screw-threads being tapped out by hand, although the corresponding stoppers were slip-cast. Cardew was unusual, perhaps unique, in his generation of studio potters in making screw-topped pots.

6

7 & 8

PROV: Berkeley Galleries, 1959 (2gns); received, December 1959 (952/2).[1]

EXH: Berkeley Galleries, 1959; York, 1983 (21).

LIT: Hess, 1960, p.465: *Handlist*, 1971 (7).

MW DOC: General Catalogue: '18/5/59 Michael Cardew and his African School – All Stoneware ... S'oy Pot by M.C. 2-2-0 ... Bought at the Berkeley Galleries 18.5.59; loose private view leaflet.

1. See No.5, n.1.

8. Screw–lidded Soy Pot exh. 1959

Probably body 49; red slip and tenmoku glaze (TK) with *sgraffito* decoration of stylized fish; wood-fired.

H 4 in (10.2 cm); D 4⅛ in (10.5 cm)

Marks: MC monogram and Abuja in Arabic (impressed)

PROV: Berkeley Galleries, 1959 (2gns); received on Milner-White's death, 1963 (1049/4).

EXH: Berkeley Galleries, 1959 (56); Rotterdam, 1976; York, 1983 (20).

LIT: *Handlist*, 1971 (4).

MW DOC: General Catalogue: '18/5/59 Michael Cardew and his African School – All Stoneware ... S'oy Pot by M.C. 2-2-0 ... Bought at the Berkeley Galleries 18.5.59'; loose private view leaflet.

9. Three–handled Flower Jar exh. 1959

Probably body 49; red slip covered with a local Chün glaze; wood-fired.

H 9⅛ in (23.1 cm); D 6⅜ in (16.3 cm)

Marks: MC monogram and Abuja in Arabic (impressed)

PROV: Berkeley Galleries, 1959 (7gns); received on Milner-White's death, 1963 (1049/6).

EXH: Berkeley Galleries, 1959 (197); Rotterdam, 1976 (83); York, 1983 (18).

LIT: *Handlist*, 1971 (13); Leach (*Cardew*), 1976, p.57, ill.

MW DOC: General Catalogue: '18/5/59 Michael Cardew and his African School – All Stoneware ... Flower Jar by M.C. 7-7-0 ... Bought at the Berkeley Galleries 18.5.59'; loose private view leaflet.

9

9

10. Three-handled Flower Jar exh. 1959

Probably body 49; transparent glaze (AA) and touches of zircon; wood-fired.

H $7\frac{1}{4}$ in (18.4 cm); D $5\frac{3}{4}$ in (14.7 cm)

Marks: MC monogram and Abuja in Arabic (impressed)

PROV: Berkeley Galleries 1959 (3gns); received on Milner-White's death, 1963 (1049/7).

EXH: Berkeley Galleries, 1959 (319); Rotterdam, 1976 (84); York, 1983 (17).

LIT: *Handlist*, 1971 (12).

MW DOC: General Catelogue: '18/5/59 Michael Cardew and his African School – All Stoneware ... Flower Jar by M.C. 3-3-0'; loose private view leaflet.

11. Plate exh. 1959 (*colour XXX*)

Probably body 49; red slip with a mixture of Chün and zircon glaze through which the pattern has been combed; wood-fired.

H $2\frac{3}{8}$ in (6 cm); D $16\frac{1}{4}$ in (41.3 cm)

'... the snakey swirl on the Abuja plates was known as the *river* and was designed by Cardew when he felt nostalgic about home in England. It represented a Cornish river he could see from his garden in England.'[1]

PROV: Berkeley Galleries, 1959 (9gns); received on Milner-White's death, 1963 (1049/3).

EXH: Berkeley Galleries, 1959 (10); Rotterdam, 1976 (80); York, 1983 (19).

MW DOC: General Catalogue: '18/5/59 Michael Cardew and his African School – All Stoneware. Plate by M.C. 9-9-0 ... Bought at the Berkeley Galleries 18.5.59'; loose private view leaflet.

1. Margaret Mama, 'Abuja Tankard CR 118', *Ceramic Review*, no. 121, January-February 1990, p.4.

10

12

13

12. Plate exh. 1962

Probably body 44; the top covered with tenmoku glaze (TK), the combed design and radial pattern wiped out and the whole dipped in a transparent glaze (AA); wood-fired.

H 2 in (5 cm); D 10$\frac{7}{8}$ in (27.8 cm)

Marks: MC monogram and Abuja in Arabic (impressed)

The use of combing through slip can be traced back to the Fremington baking dishes Cardew knew as a boy. A similarly decorated plate is at the Crafts Study Centre, Bath (pp.74 - 122).

PROV: Berkeley Galleries, 1962 (5gns); received on Milner-White's death, 1963 (1049/8).

EXH: Berkeley Galleries, 1962 (286A); York, 1983 (30).

MW DOC: General Catalogue: '19/6/62 3rd show at the Berkley [sic] Galleries of Cardew and his African pupils ... Plate by M. Cardew 5.5.0'; notes on loose private view leaflet: 'Cardew Plate Signed 5gs no 286A AA glaze'.

13. Ash–Tray exh. 1962

Probably body 44; the top covered with tenmoku glaze (TK), a thin line near the edge and radiating lines on the rim wiped out, and the whole dipped in a transparent glaze (AA); wood-fired.

H 1$\frac{1}{4}$ in (3.1 cm); D 6 in (15.1 cm)

Marks: MC monogram and Abuja in Arabic (impressed)

PROV: Berkeley Galleries, 1962 (15s.0d.); received on Milner-White's death, 1963 (1049/9).

EXH: Berkeley Galleries, 1962 (81); York, 1983 (28).

MW MS: General Catalogue: '19/6/62 3rd Show at the Berkley [sic] Galleries of Cardew and his African pupils ... ash tray by Cardew 15.0.'; notes on loose private view invitation; 'no 81 Ash tray black slip Two [crossed out] One Cardew Ash Trays 15/-'.

William Bower Dalton
British 1868-1965

An important early experimenter in stoneware in the Chinese manner, W.B.Dalton studied at the Manchester School of Art, then at the Royal College of Art. From 1899 to 1919 he was Principal of Camberwell School of Arts and Crafts in South London (founded 1898). There he became deeply interested in studio pottery and under his influence Camberwell provided a training ground for several potters of distinction such as Roger Fry, Reginal Wells, William Staite Murray and Charles Vyse. In 1919 he left Camberwell but remained Curator of the South London Art Gallery. A member of the Art Workers' Guild, Dalton also painted watercolours. He exhibited during the 1920s and 1930s with the Red Rose Guild, the Arts and Crafts Exhibition Society and Colnaghi's. In 1909 he designed his home at Garrow, Longfield, in Kent,

where he remained until it was bombed in the early years of the Second World War. In 1941 he moved to the east coast of America, where he continued to produce pots and paintings, as well as teaching, and wrote three books on ceramic art: *Craftsmanship and Design in Pottery*, 1957, *Notes from a Potter's Diary*, 1960, and *Just Clay*, 1962. He returned to England shortly before his death in 1965.

Dalton was unusual in that he was involved with the studio pottery movement in France and particularly admired the work of Emile Decœur. His philosophy was that ceramics should strive to develop as a fine art.

In his copy of the Arts and Crafts Exhibition Society catalogue of 1926, Milner-White noted: 'Keep eyes upon Dalton, Richards, Fox-Strangeways'.

14

14

14. Pot exh. 1928

Silver and grey matt glazes.

H 4 in (10.2 cm); D 3¼ in (8.5 cm)

Mark: WBD monogram (incised)

Wrongly accessioned as by Pleydell-Bouverie but correctly identified by Oliver Watson,[1] this was one of only two pots by Dalton purchased by Milner-White, both from Colnaghi in 1928. The whereabouts of the other pot is unknown (MS catalogue: '51 Dish, silver grey flushed rose').

PROV: Colnaghi, 1928 (2gns); presented, 1958, and received on Milner-White's death, 1963 (1049/1).

EXH: Colnaghi, 1928 (14).

MW DOC: General Catalogue: '1928 ... 50 DALTON Pot, mat [sic] silver & grey'; invoice: Colnaghi, December 1928, 'Pot, mat [sic] silver and grey by W.B.Dalton £2. 2. o.', together with receipt, 17 December 1928; album I: exhibition catalogue and review, *The Times*, 30 November 1928; three letters from Dalton, 20 December 1928, 15 November 1929 and 6 December 1936.

1. Verbally, c.1984.

Harry Davis and May Beatrice Davis

British   1910-1986
British   born 1914

Harry Davis was an inventive man with a fund of technical and theoretical knowledge about making pots. His interest in pottery was first aroused at Bournemouth art school where he was a student (though not in the pottery class). He learnt to throw in a small local commercial pottery where he was taught the traditional fingerings. Throwing was later to become his forte: he developed a capacity for making very rapidly large numbers of pots of a consistently high quality and strength.

In the 1930s he was at St Ives where he met May Scott, later to become his wife. Davis managed the pottery whilst Bernard Leach was in Japan and David Leach at Stoke-on-Trent. From 1937 to 1942, accompanied by May, he pioneered the first glazed stoneware ever made in Ghana, West Africa, and trained most of the first generation of modern Ghanaian potters at Achimota College, which he established. After the outbreak of the Second World War he went to

South America, being replaced at the College by Michael Cardew.

In 1946 the Davises returned to England and set up the Crowan Pottery at Praze near Cambourne, Cornwall. They converted a water-mill and using water power efficiently, produced moderately priced stoneware and porcelain for the table. In 1962 they emigrated to New Zealand and founded the Crewenna Pottery where they worked for ten years. They then set up a pottery training centre – the Izcuchaca Pottery – in the Peruvian Andes, returning to New Zealand in 1979. By now Harry Davis's health had declined and he could not keep up the prodigious output of former years. He spent much time instead writing and talking about the technical aspects of pottery making and the philosophy of the small workshop. With Leach and Cardew he may be regarded as one of the great post-war triumvirate of potter-writers.

15. Tea-Pot 1953-4

Olive green with brushed iron-oxide decoration; bamboo handle.

H 6⅝ in (16.6 cm); D 6⅛ in (15.6 cm)

Mark: CP monogram (impressed)

This tea-pot was wrongly accessioned as by P. Cole (and had presumably been known to Milner-White as such) but was correctly identified by David Lloyd-Jones.[1] It was made at the Crowan Pottery in Cornwall. Crowan pots, and those made at Crewenna in New Zealand, were never signed: instead the pots bear the workshop's stamp, a P inside a C in each case. Pots bearing this stamp were made by Harry or May or their daughter Nina, or anyone working with them – and there were many apprentices working at Crowan. It was part of the Davises' ethos that individual potters should not seek personal recognition. They also believed in independence from supply merchants, always using local materials. Durability was an important quality and the strongest pots in the Davis output were made at Crowan. These pots were mainly decorated with brushwork and wax-resist, executed either by May or by Harry. A diesel-oil-fired kiln was used. The date of this tea-pot, 1953-4, and technical information were supplied by the potter.[2]

PROV: Unknown; lent by Milner-White, 1958 (loan 9), and received outright on his death, 1963 (1050/3).

LIT: *Handlist*, 1971 (91, incorrectly as P Cole).

1. Verbally, c.1980.
2. Letter, 10 March 1985, in Gallery files.

15

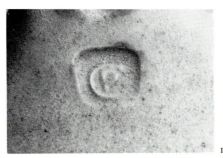

15

Emile Decœur
French   1876-1953

One of the greatest French potters of the twentieth century, Emile Decœur began his career working in the experimental decorative traditions of Art Nouveau. In 1907 he established his own studio at Fontenay-aux-Roses. Here his work became increasingly restrained in the use of ornament, and he devoted himself to glaze experiments, aiming to integrate the glaze and the body of the pot. He made both stoneware (which is fired between 1200°-1350°C) and porcelain (which is fired between 1300°-1450°C). His stoneware is very high fired – to the point at which it is difficult to differentiate between a porcelain and a stoneware body. His clay bodies tended to be thick but he nevertheless retained, through glazes, the luminous qualities associated with porcelain. His smooth, fine surfaces improved after 1927 when he began to mix kaolin (one of the ingredients of porcelain) with his glazes: his particular success may have been the result of applying many layers of the same glaze, fired separately. Decœur's degree of control is masterly.

The timing of Milner-White's purchases of Decœur pots, just before the outbreak of the Second World War, is significant. At that moment there was a concerted move to break down cultural barriers between nations, a move of which Milner-White no doubt approved.

The major difference between British and French potters at this time was that the French seemed to be drawn more towards later Chinese ceramics rather than to earlier styles. Their output was more controlled and restrained than that of their British counterparts, their aim being the beauty achieved by perfection of technique rather than the beauty derived through vitality and fitness of purpose.

16

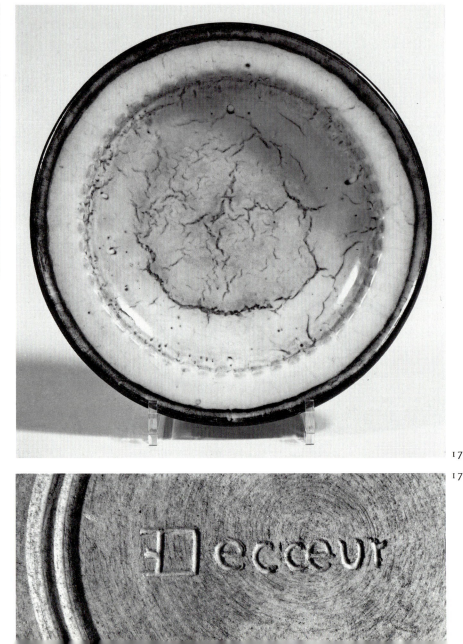

17

17

18

19

Brygos Gallery, 2 June 1938, 'Cat. No. 142 18.18.0.'; album II: exhibition catalogue and review, *The Times, Trade and Engineering Supplement*, 30 July 1927.

1. Rose, 1970, p.3.

18. Bowl exh. 1938

Thick mottled purple-brown glaze without, cream glaze within.

H 4 in (10.1 cm); D 9⅞ in (25.2 cm)

Mark: 'Decœur' (carved)

PROV: Brygos Gallery, 1938 (£16); presented, 1958, and received on Milner-White's death, 1963 (1049/10).

EXH: Brygos Gallery, 1938 (143).

LIT: *Handlist*, 1971 (93).

MW DOC: General Catalogue: '1938 ... FRENCH ... 195C E DECOEUR Large brown-purple & cream bowl (Still at Deanery) 16.0.0 ... Continental Pieces Date uncertain but at least a year before my purchase; receipted invoice: Brygos Gallery, 2 June 1938, 'Cat. No. 143 16.0.0'; album II: exhibition catalogue and review, *The Times, Trade and Engineering Supplement*, 30 July 1927.

19. Ash-Tray exh. 1938 (colour XXVI)

Fine porcelain-like body; layers of grey glaze and indigo rim.

H 1⅜ in (3.6 cm); D 4⅜ in (11 cm)

Mark: 'D' (carved)

Decœur was well known for his indigo glazes.

PROV: Brygos Gallery, 1938 (£3); presented, 1958, and received on Milner-White's death, 1963 (1049/57).

EXH: Brygos Gallery, 1938 (141).

MW DOC: General Catalogue: '1938 ... FRENCH ... 195A E. DECOEUR. Small bowl: grey glaze 3.0.0 ... Continental Pieces Date uncertain but at least a year before my purchase'; receipted invoice: Brygos Gallery, 2 June 1938, 'Cat. No. 141 3.0.0'; album II: exhibition catalogue and review, *The Times, Trade and Engineering Supplement*, 30 July 1927.

16. Jar exh. 1926 (colour XXVI)

Ribbed faintly; thick grey glaze with gold flush.

H 4½ in (11.5 cm); D 4¼ in (10.9 cm)

Mark: 'Decœur' (carved)

PROV: Unknown, possibly a gift; presented, January 1959 (935/34).

EXH: Maison Rouard, 34 Avenue de l'Opéra, Paris, La dixième exposition des artisans français contemporains, 23 November to (?)... 1926.

LIT: Gabriel Henriot, 'La dixième exposition des artisans français contemporains', *Mobilier et Decoration*, January 1927, ill. p.29.

17. Dish exh. 1938 (colour XXVI)

Linear cut-away decoration to inside rim; layers of grey glaze over blue-black within, rich bronze-black glaze without.

H 2⅜ in (6.2 cm); D 11 in (28.1 cm)

Mark: 'Decœur' (carved)

This pot exhibits the bronze-black coloured glaze praised by Muriel Rose.[1] A very similar dish was advertised in *Decorative Art 1930* ('The Studio' Year Book), 1930, p.AD.IX.

PROV: Brygos Gallery, 1938 (18gns); presented, January, 1959 and received on Milner-White's death, 1963 (935/35).

EXH: Brygos Gallery, 1938 (142); York, 1959.

MW DOC: General Catalogue: '1938 ... FRENCH ... 195B E. DECOEUR Grey Dish 18.18.0 ... Continental Pieces Date uncertain but at least a year before my purchase'; receipted invoice:

Thomas Samuel Haile

British 1909-48

Arguably the most original artist to work in clay in the first half of the twentieth century, Sam Haile was born in London in 1909. He left school at fifteen and went to work in a shipping firm. However, in 1931 he won a scholarship to study painting at the Royal College of Art. There he did not feel sympathetic to the Impressionist approach advocated by Sir John Rothenstein. A strong-minded rebel, Haile was more interested in artists who were breaking new ground, like Matisse, Picasso and Henry Moore. After the first year he changed to the pottery class under William Staite Murray where he was given more freedom. Murray's most gifted pupil, he had much in common with his tutor, notably a conviction that the maker of a pot could be as much an artist as a painter or sculptor; in fact both painted as well as potting. Haile loved the feeling of clay, and being a natural draughtsman (doodling all the time), found that once a pot was made the surface had to be covered. Both Murray and Haile had come to pottery through painting and the decoration on their pots was especially powerful and original. The sturdy, strong forms of Haile's pots show the influence of Murray; otherwise Murray's main contribution to Haile's development was in providing a sympathetic environment in which to work.

Whilst in London Haile made frequent visits to the British Museum. A knowledgeable man of wide-ranging interests, he was particularly impressed by the vitality of decoration on pre-Columbian and early Greek ceramics, as well as Eastern ceramics and those of medieval England.

After the Royal College Haile worked in both paint and clay. In 1935 he went to teach at the Leicester College of Art, but was soon back in London. He taught part-time at Kingston and Hammersmith Schools of Art in 1936, whilst work-ing at Raynes Park in a pottery workshop which he shared with Margaret Rey (q.v.). They were both to exhibit in the newly-opened Brygos Gallery in Bond Street, where in 1937 Haile shared an exhibition with James Dring. It was a great success, his pots being widely bought by museums and private collectors.

In this year Haile joined the Surrealist group at the London Gallery's Surrealist objects exhibition, so formalizing his growing attraction to the originality of the movement. In 1938 he married Marianne de Trey whom he had met at the Royal College. Together they went to the USA where, after an initial hard start, Haile studied and taught at New York State College of Ceramics, Alfred University, and later at the College of Architects, University of Michigan. He was very well received in America, where most of his work is today.

On release from military service he began potting again in England where he acted as part-time pottery consultant to the Rural Industries Bureau, now known as COSIRA. In 1946 he was making slipware at Bulmer in Suffolk and in 1947 he moved to Shinner's Bridge pottery near Dartington Hall (Leach's former workshop). Tragically in 1948 just when he was getting back in his stride after the war, a bus ran into his car in Poole, Dorset, killing him, at only thirty-eight.

Milner–White and Haile

In addition to No.20, Milner-White purchased two Haile pots from the Brygos Gallery exhibition of *Stoneware Pottery by T.S. Haile and Decorated Plates and Tiles by C.J. Dring*, 10 December 1937 to 1 January 1938: *Shepherds' Dance* (45, 7gns) and *Triumphant Procession* (52, 12gns). Both of these he presented to Southampton. The invoice and a catalogue of the exhibition are at York.

21

20. Bowl: 'Roman Baths' exh. 1936
(colour XXI)

Iron-pigment decoration of three figures over thick white glaze.

H $5\frac{7}{8}$ in (15.1 cm); D $13\frac{3}{8}$ in (34.1 cm)

Mark: SH monogram (impressed)

The decoration shows the influence of primitive art. Its apparent similarity to Picasso's work is explained by the fact that both artists were inspired by primitive art independently. This bowl was probably made in the studio Haile shared with Margaret Rey at Raynes Park and fired in her gas kiln. It would seem that *Roman Baths* was not well fired: the quantity of carbon from the firing has made the glaze rather sombre whereas Haile may well have intended it to have more vitality.[1]

PROV: Brygos Gallery, 1936 (8gns); presented, January 1959.

EXH: Brygos Gallery, *Under £10 English Pottery*, 26 November-19 December 1936 (43); Hayward Gallery, 1979 (2.63); Manchester, 1989.

LIT: Wingfield Digby, 1952, ill. p.40; *Handlist*, 1971 (3); A.W. Coysh, *British Art Pottery*, David & Charles, Newton Abbott, London & Vancouver 1976, p.92.

MW DOC: General Catalogue: '1936 ... 184 HAILE Bowl – "Roman Baths" 8 [gns]'; invoice: Brygos Gallery, 25 November 1936, receipted 15 January 1937, '1 Stoneware Bowl. (T.S. Haile.) £8.8.0'; album II: exhibition catalogue; notes: '[Disciple] of [Murray] – Haile – on his way to being a great potter'.

1. Verbal communication from Marianne Haile, 27 May 1988.

Shoji Hamada
Japanese   1892-1978

Shoji Hamada is one of the greatest potters of this century. Born in Misonokuchi in Kawasaki on the outskirts of Tokyo, he was educated at Tokyo's Industrial College where he met Kanjiro Kawai. Having decided to become a potter he followed Kawai to the Kyoto Ceramic Testing Institute, where he made extensive studies in reproducing Chinese glazes between 1917 and 1920. In 1918 he met Bernard Leach at the home of the philosopher Soetsu Yanagi. When Leach returned to England in 1920 to set up a pottery in St Ives, Hamada went with him. At the end of 1923 Hamada set off through Europe, *en route* to Japan where he arrived in 1924. From this time, in accordance with Japanese tradition, Hamada never signed another pot. In 1930 he settled at Mashiko where he built his pottery, and used clay found locally. His brushes were made from the hair of a dog forced into a piece of bamboo, while for the application of hakeme he used dried grasses. He had an enormously wide knowledge of glazes but chose to use only the narrow range available from local materials, producing an infinite variety of effects within the confines he set himself. Hamada had three kilns during his lifetime – at St Ives, Mashiko and Okinawa in the Ryukyu archipelago. All the pots at York are believed to be from Mashiko, unless stated otherwise. Hamada died in Mashiko.

Milner-White and Hamada

Hamada was recognized by the Dean as one of 'the 3 Master Potters of the century'[1] (the other two being Leach and Murray). The Dean was impressed by Hamada's emphasis on utility, strength of form and overall subtlety. He equally greatly admired the superb fluidity of his decoration. However he was also preoccupied with the idea of the West influencing the East. Enormous interest in the East had been shown in the West in the early years of the twentieth century as manifested by exhibitions and the formation of the Oriental Ceramic Society and the great Oriental ceramics collections. The Dean was greatly taken with the idea of the reverse – of Western influence being taken to the East. He always specially noted in his manuscript catalogue any pots made by

Hamada which seemed to show a hint of the West. The Dean bought his first Hamada pots in 1926 at Paterson's Gallery, after Hamada had returned to Japan. The Dean would seem to have been impatient to own more, and indeed a representative selection of his output. Judging from a letter dated 7 July 1927 from Leach to the Dean it would seem that the latter sounded out the former about the prospect of asking Hamada to send pots from Japan; he may even have asked how far £25 would go.[2] On 10 July 1927 the Dean wrote directly to Hamada enclosing a cheque for £20. From the reply of 12 September 1927, it would seem that Hamada promised to send representative pots over the years.[3] In the event, however, only two pots appear to have been sent[4] and the Dean was left to seize opportunities of buying at the rare Hamada exhibitions held in this country. Hamada though apparently pleased to supply the Dean, was heavily pressurized by collectors in his own country and perhaps found it impracticable to keep sending small parcels to England.

1. Milner-White MS notes, undated.
2. See Appendix H.
3. See Appendix H.
4. See No.27 and Appendix H.

21. Vase 1923

Tenmoku glaze with iron-oxide random decoration.

H 10¼ in (26 cm); D 4½ in (11.4 cm)

Marks: Character Sho and St Ives monogram (impressed)

This is one of the rare pots Hamada made at St Ives. Few pots of any quality were produced there at this time owing to the

experimental nature of the potting, and the difficulties experienced finding materials and making and controlling the kiln. Oliver Watson suggests that the quality of this pot may be the result of the Japanese Matsubayashi's arrival in St Ives just at the end of Hamada's stay:[1] technically Matsubayashi's experience and practical help were invaluable. This pot is delightfully simple in form and decoration. At the Municipal School of Pottery in Kyoto, Hamada

21   22

had scientifically investigated the earlier Chinese glazes, and reproduced them between 1917 and 1920. It is therefore not surprising that whilst at St Ives, his pots exhibited a gently Chinese quality. The classical Oriental shape employed here is called 'Mei-Ping' by the Chinese. The glaze, tenmoku (or temmoku), is also Chinese. Its character was described by Leach as a 'lustrous-black iron stoneware glaze some-times running to a red rust on the thinner parts.'[2] The tenmoku glaze as applied here is enlivened by spontaneous splashes of iron, an early sign of Hamada's power as a decorator. See also No.22.

PROV: Unknown; purchased, 1934 (3½?gns); presented, January 1959 (935/25).

EXH: Farnham, 1969 (5); Kobe, 1989 (c-39, ill. p.135 in colour).

LIT: *Handlist*, 1971 (20); Watson, 1989, p.135.

MW DOC: General Catalogue: '1934 ... 166. HAMADA. St Ives period. Pot, temmoku glaze Date about 1924 3½ [?gns]'.

1. Watson, 1989, p.135.
2. Leach, 1940, p.280.

22. Vase 1923

Cream ash glaze flecked with iron.

H 10¾ in (27.4 cm); D 5 in (12.7 cm)

Marks: Character Sho and St Ives monogram (impressed)

Made at St Ives, this vase exhibits a Chinese quality typical of Hamada's work of the time. A sister pot to No.21, it is also a 'Mei-Ping' shape. A similar but cruder version of this shape can be found in the Bergen Collection, City Museum and Art Gallery, Stoke-on-Trent (895P1949).

PROV: Unknown; purchased, 1934 (3?gns); presented, January 1959 (935/45).

EXH: Kobe, 1989 (c-38, ill. p.135 in colour).

LIT: *Handlist*, 1971 (16).

MW DOC: General Catalogue: '1934 ... 165 HAMADA, St Ives period, Pot, cream glaze. Date about 1924 3[?gns]'.

23. Bottle 1923

Tenmoku glaze with kaki trailing.

H 6⅝ in (16.9 cm); D 8¼ in (21 cm)

Marks: Character Sho and St Ives monogram (impressed)

Made at St Ives, this bottle exhibits a Chinese quality typical of Hamada's pots of the time. It is datable to 1923 because Colnaghi's 1927 catalogue describes the Hamada pots as 'the last group of pots made by him at the Leach Pottery previous to his return to Japan'.

PROV: Colnaghi, 1927 (25gns); presented, January 1959 (935/28).

EXH: Colnaghi, 1927 (K11), Dartington, 1952 (92); Farnham, 1969 (7); Sheffield, 1976 (16).

LIT: Ingamells (*Preview*), 1959, ill. p.443; Rose, 1970, pl.30; *Handlist*, 1971 (84).

MW DOC: General Catalogue: '1927 ... 31 HAMADA Bottle "Kaki and Tessha". Black, brush dec. in red' and '1952 The following pots were exhibited (1) Dartington Hall June-July. (2) Edinburgh Festival July-Aug. (3) Arts Council, London Sept-Oct (4) Birmingham Art Gallery Oct-Nov ... Hamada 31 "Kaki & Tessha"'; letter from G. Bell, Leach Pottery, St Ives, Cornwall, 19 December 1927: 'He [Bernard Leach] is very glad that you have got a really good example of Mr. Hamada's work, the description of which should be, "Kaki" glaze decoration or pattern over "Tenmoku glaze".'; album I: exhibition catalogue (K11 Large Bottle "Kaki" and "Tessha" ... 26.5.0.').

24. Bottle 1923-6 (colour X)

Grey-green crackle glaze with flower and band decoration.

H 7½ in (19.1 cm); D 7¼ in (18.5 cm)

Marks: Character Sho and St Ives monogram (impressed)

Made at St Ives, this bottle exhibits a Chinese quality typical of Hamada's pots of the time. Milner-White describes it as 'specially characteristic and fine in form, ornament and handling'. A note from Leach states that this pot was 'several times fired, last in April 1926, made 1923'. A similar but clearly different bottle, made in 1926 at Mashiko, is the first of two pots mentioned and illustrated in pen and ink by Hamada in a letter of 3 June 1928.[1]

PROV: Paterson's, 1926 (£10); presented, January 1959 (935/32).

EXH: William Paterson's Gallery, Bernard Leach pottery, 1926 (19).

23

24

LIT: *Handlist*, 1971 (86).

MW DOC: General Catalogue: '1926 ... 16 HAMADA Pot. Cream white flushed with sepia foliage brushwork underglaze Made at St Ives (Date 1923-26); indexed notebook: '4.POT. B. Brown G. Cream-white flushed with sepia D. Underglaze-double rim round bottle, and two foliage-bunches in grey H. 7½" × W. 7" Date. Made 1923, several times refired – last 1926. Mark. [St Ives] [character Sho] Purchased 1926 £10 at Leach Exhibn, Paterson's Gallery A pot specially characteristic and fine:– in form, ornament & handling.'; Leach MS note: 'Shoji Hamada No. 19 bottle Tz'ou chou type, stoneware bottle. Several times fired, last in April 1926 made 1923.'; receipted invoice: Wm B. Paterson, 31 May 1926, 'Bernard Leach Pottery Exhibition ... [Tzu Chou] Stoneware Bottle "Hamada" 19 [£]10'.

1. See No.27 and Appendix H.

25

25. Milk Jug probably 1926

Cream slip with iron and grey brush-decoration.

H $3\frac{3}{8}$ in (8.5 cm); D $4\frac{5}{8}$ in (11.7 cm)

Dated by Milner-White to 1926, this is an example of a pot which he believed to show Western influence on Hamada.

PROV: (?) Paterson's or Arts and Crafts Exhibition Society, 1926; W.S.Murray, by whom given to Milner-White, December 1926; presented, January 1959 (935/89).

EXH: Farnham, 1969 (10).

MW DOC: General Catalogue: '1926 ... 19 HAMADA. Jug. Cream over grey. Dec. brushwork A "milk jug". Made in Japan 1926.'; indexed notebook: 'HAMADA 7 JUG B – Salmon – brick G. Yellow-cream over gray D. Brushwork under cream glaze & so greenish; and brown overglaze. Splashes of both between brown rings round lip and base and over handle. Shape – a "milk-jug". H. $2\frac{7}{8}$" Date 1926 – made in Japan Unmarked. An interesting example of Japanese "countryware" showing the influence on Hamada of English Toftware. Given by W.S.Murray, Dec. '26'.

26. Tall Jar 1926-8 (colour XI)

Tenmoku brushwork over dark-olive glaze, wax-resist decoration revealing cream slip.

H $14\frac{1}{4}$ in (36.2 cm); D $8\frac{1}{8}$ in (20.6 cm)

The method of decoration probably used here is described by Leach. A pattern is painted 'on raw celadon glaze with wax resist' and the whole surface is then basted 'with a broad flat brush loaded with a thin wash of magnetic iron. The pigment in turn is covered with a further brushing of celadon, so that it lies between two layers of glaze.'[1] This is generally regarded as the outstanding Hamada pot at York. Leach visited Milner-White in 1951 and saw his

26

collection whilst preparing for the 1952 exhibition which opened at Dartington Hall.[2] Leach was so impressed by this pot that it inspired his own No.82. Hamada's pot was the first of two he sent Milner-White from Japan. A similar pot is in the National Museums and Galleries on Merseyside (WAG 3627): the body of this pot, made c.1935, has been paddled into a rectangular form and each face covered with wax-resist decoration. The York pot, however, retains its thrown shape and has contrasting decoration on front and back.

PROV: Sent from Japan, 1928; lent, probably 1958, and received outright on Milner-White's death, 1963 (1050/4).

EXH: Dartington, 1952 (91, pl.2), Dartington Hall only; Sheffield, 1976 (17); Tate Gallery, 1985 (C12); Wakefield, 1987.

LIT: Leach, 1951, p.27, pl.48 (frontispiece) in colour; anon., 1952, ill.; Ingamells (Museums Journal), 1959, p.123; Handlist, 1971 (85).

MW DOC: General Catalogue: '1928 ... 68 HAMADA Pot. Temmoku, brushwork (sent from Japan)' '1952 The following pots were exhibited (1) Dartington Hall ... [see No.23] ... [Hamada] 68 Tenmoku 1928' and under no.243, Leach No.82 in this Catalogue, 'Tall Jar, inspired by my Hamada (68) & a good match to it'; letter from Hamada, 3 June 1928.

1. Leach, 1976, p.232.
2. Letter in album II from Muriel Rose to Milner-White, 6 February 1951.

27. Bottle c.1927 (colour XII)

Cream matt glaze with brushed iron-oxide decoration of sugar-cane motifs.

H 12¼ in (13 cm); D 7½ in (19 cm)

Hamada used the motifs found in this decoration repeatedly. However, he would argue that the same result can never be achieved twice, and so the end product is always original. The decoration is a stem-leaf motif, originally based on a growth of sugar cane he saw in a typhoon.[1] Bottles of similar shape and decoration, dating from 1925 and c.1935 are in the Ohara Museum, Kurashiki, Japan, and the Victoria and Albert Museum (C.33-1943). This bottle is almost certainly the second of two pots described by Hamada in a letter of 3 June 1928 as having been sent 'about a week ago through Messrs. Kaitsu-sha & Co.'; both were illustrated by pen and ink drawings.[2] The only entry in Milner-White's MS catalogue to

28

which the bottle can be related is under 1929 but the apparent discrepancy in dates can be explained by the fact that the Dean possibly did not receive the pot until 1929, or at least did not pay for it until then, or that he simply misremembered the year. If No.27 is indeed the pot referred to by Hamada then, according to his letter, it was made at Okinawa in the Ryukyu archipelago, in 1927 and was representative of the output from that kiln.

PROV: Probably sent from Japan through Kaitsu-sha & Co., 1928; purchased, 1928 or 1929 (7?gns); presented, January 1959 (935/46).

LIT: Wingfield Digby, 1952, pl.16 as c.1935; Handlist, 1971 (23).

MW DOC: General Catalogue: '1929 ... 74 HAMADA. Pot, cream-white, brush decn. 7 [?gns] / Given to York'; letter from Hamada, 3 June 1928 (see above).

1. Leach (HAMADA), 1976, p.104.
2. See Appendix H.

28. Dish 1927-9

Press-moulded; slip-trailed decoration in Japanese peasant style, red-brown glaze with linear motif in black.

H 1⅜ in (4.2 cm); D 6½ in (16.4 cm)

This dish is one of a set of six purchased by Milner-White, of which four are now at York (see also Nos 29, 30 and 31) and two at Southampton. It was made in the Japanese peasant-ware style, Hamada's interest in

which had been stimulated by his contact with the English slipware tradition through Bernard Leach. Kanjiro Kawai was working in a similar vein at this time and No.28 was originally accessioned as by him (although Nos 29, 30 and 31 have always been correctly indentified as by Hamada). However, in execution this bowl is more spontaneous than Kawai's work, which is comparatively 'laboured', and it is clearly one of the set of six Hamada bowls. An earlier Hamada peasant-ware dish, of the St Ives period, is in the Bergen Collection, City Museum and Art Gallery, Stoke-on-Trent (933P1949), together with one of 1926 from Machiko (621P1949).

PROV: Paterson's, July 1929 (4gns the set); presented, January 1959 (935/36).

EXH: Paterson's 1929 (99, the set of six).

MW DOC: General Catalogue: '1929 ... 76 HAMADA. Six small plates, slipware decn. Two given to Southampton 4 [gns] / 76 Two of these plates given to Southampton; one (the best) [No.28] to York; the remaining 3 still at the Deanery all v. different, but all "Japanese peasant ware"' and (in error) '1952 The following pots were exhibited (1) Dartington Hall ... [see No.23] ... [Hamada] 76 [actually 169] and 77 Big & small plates (one each)'; invoice: Wm B. Paterson, July 1929, receipted 6 September 1929, 'No.99. A set of dishes, different patterns 4.4 –'; album I: exhibition pamphlet and reviews, Morning Post, 23 May 1929, and The Times, 24 May 1929.

29. Dish 1927-9

Press-moulded; slip-trailed decoration in Japanese peasant style, cream over grey.

H $1\frac{1}{2}$ in (4 cm); D $6\frac{1}{4}$ in (16.1 cm)

See No. 28.

PROV: Paterson's, 1929 (4gns the set); presented, 1958, and received on Milner-White's death, 1963 (1049/11a).

EXH: As for No. 28.

LIT: *Handlist*, 1971 (24).

MW DOC: As for No. 28.

30. Dish 1927-9

Press-moulded; slip-trailed decoration in Japanese peasant style, yellow over brown.

H $1\frac{3}{8}$ in (3.6 cm); D $6\frac{1}{4}$ in (15.7 cm)

See No. 28.

PROV: As for No. 29 (1049/11b).

EXH: As for No. 28.

MW DOC: As for No. 28.

31. Dish 1927-9

Press-moulded; slip-trailed decoration in Japanese peasant style, green and olive over pink.

H $1\frac{5}{8}$ in (4.1 cm); D $6\frac{3}{8}$ in (16.4 cm)

See No. 28. A small dish of 1928 with identical decoration is in the Bergen Collection, City Museum and Art Gallery, Stoke-on-Trent (626P1949).

PROV: As for No. 29 (1049/11c).

EXH: As for No. 28.

MW DOC: As for No. 28.

32. Covered Box c. 1929

Tenmoku glaze with kaki markings radiating out from centre in two circles.

29

30

32

31

33

H $2\frac{3}{8}$ in (6 cm); D $3\frac{1}{4}$ in (8.4 cm)

This box was probably made for incense. The recipe for Hamada's kaki glaze was published by Leach in *A Potter's Book*.[1]

PROV: Paterson's 1929 (5gns); presented, January 1959 (935/23).

EXH: Paterson's, 1929 (107); Dartington, 1952 (83).

LIT: Wingfield Digby, 1952, pl.16; Rose, 1970, pl.28A; *Handlist*, 1971 (17).

MW DOC: General Catalogue: '1929 ... 75. HAMADA Box, "temmoku" glaze 5 [gns]' and '1952 The following pots were exhibited (1) Dartington Hall ... [see No.23] ... [Hamada] 75 Small covered pot'; invoice: Wm B. Paterson, July 1929, receipted 6 September 1929, '107 Small covered pot, temmoku black and rust red 5.5-'; album I: as for No.28.

1. Leach, 1940, pp.137 & 170.

33. Large Dish c.1929

Sand-coloured glaze with brush-decoration in blue and green.

H $4\frac{1}{4}$ in (10.8 cm); D $15\frac{1}{2}$ in (39.4 cm)

Large plates are among the most impressive of Hamada's output. This example was one of a group of Paterson's 1929 exhibition singled out for special notice by *The Times*.

PROV: Paterson's 1929 (20gns); presented, January 1959 (935/57).

EXH: Paterson's, 1929 (27); Farnham, 1969 (1).

MW DOC: General Catalogue: '1929 ... 73 HAMADA Dish, large, brush decn. 20 [gns]'; invoice: Wm B. Paterson, July 1929, receipted 6 September 1929, '27. Large cream bowl, pattern in black, green and brown 21--'; album I: as for No.28.

34. Jar exh. 1929

Grey glaze with brushed iron-oxide decoration of sugar-cane motifs.

H 10⅜ in (26.3 cm); D 11⅛ in (28.3 cm)

The Times review of Paterson's 1929 exhibition refers to the 'combination of freedom and certainty' in this pot.

PROV: Paterson's 1929 (30gns); presented, January 1959 (935/67).

EXH: Paterson's, 1929 (1, ill.).

LIT: *Handlist*, 1971 (18).

MW DOC: General Catalogue: '1929 ... 70 HAMADA Globular jar, grey, brush decoration. 30.'; invoice: Wm B. Paterson, July 1929, receipted 6 September 1929, 'No 1, Grey pot, pattern in dark brown 31.10-'; album I: as for No.28.

35. Tea-Pot *c.* 1929

Hakeme with brushed iron-oxide decoration of sugar-cane motifs.

H 8 in (20.3 cm); D 8⅜ in (21.4 cm)

Hakeme is a type of decoration (originally Korean) which is achieved when the slip (liquid clay), into which a pot has been dipped, is partly brushed away by a small broom or a handful of dried grasses applied briskly to the surface.

PROV: Paterson's 1929 (5gns); presented, January 1959 (935/80).

EXH: Paterson's 1929 (81).

LIT: *Handlist*, 1971 (22).

MW DOC: General Catalogue: '1929 ... 72 HAMADA Tea-pot. Hakeme. 5 [gns]'; invoice: Wm B. Paterson, July 1929, receipted 6 September 1929, '81 Hakeme tea-pot pattern in rust brown 5.5-'; album I: as for No.28.

36. Ten-sided Tea-Pot *c.* 1929

Thrown and cut body; tenmoku glaze.

H 9 in (22.9 cm); D 9½ in (24.1 cm)

A similar tea-pot is illustrated in the pamphlet accompanying Paterson's 1929 exhibition and again in Leach's *A Potter's Book*.[1] A further similar example is in the Bergen Collection, City Museum and Art Gallery, Stoke-on-Trent (842P1949).

PROV: Paterson's, 1929 (12gns); presented, January 1959 (935/81).

34

35

EXH: Paterson's, 1929 (76); Sheffield, 1976 (15).

LIT: *Handlist*, 1971 (81).

MW DOC: General Catalogue: '1929 ... 71 HAMADA. Tea-pot. "temmoku" glaze. 12 [gns]'; invoice: Wm B. Paterson, July 1929, receipted 6 September 1929, '76 Temmoku black Japanese pitcher 12.12-'; album I: as for No.28.

1. Leach, 1940, p.86

37. Set of five Plates c.1929

Tenmoku glaze over cream slip, wax-resist decoration of six-petalled flower motif in centre of plate and wavy line around rim.

H 1½ in (3.7 cm); D 9½ in (24 cm) with slight variations

This set originally comprised six plates but one is now missing from the collection, presumed stolen.

PROV: Paterson's, 1929 (4gns); presented, January 1959 (935/88a,b,d,e,f).

EXH: Paterson's, 1929 (96); Dartington, 1952 (90, one only); Farnham, 1969 (2).

LIT: Ingamells (*Preview*), 1959, p.439; *Handlist*, 1971 (83 & 87, 935/88a & b).

MW DOC: General Catalogue: '1929 ... 77 HAMADA. Six plates, temmoku glaze. 4 [gns] / 77 All still at the Deanery' and '1952 The following pots were exhibited (1) Dartington Hall ... [see No.23] ... [Hamada] 76 [actually 169] & 77 Big & small plates (one each)'; invoice: Wm B. Paterson, July 1929, receipted 6 September 1929, '96 A set of dishes, temmoku black 4.4-'; album I: as for No.28.

38. Large Dish exh. 1931 (colour XIII)

Hakeme with brushed iron-oxide decoration of sugar-cane motifs.

H 3⅞ in (9.9 cm); D 14⅝ in (37.2 cm).

For a technical description of hakeme see No.35 above.

PROV: Paterson's, 1931 (12gns); presented, January 1959 (935/63).

EXH: Paterson's 1931 (60).

LIT: *Handlist*, 1971 (21).

MW DOC: General Catalogue: '1931 .. 112 HAMADA – Large Dish Design in iron-black on Hakeme 12 [gns]'; invoice: Wm B. Paterson, 27 October 1931/28 November 1931, receipted 2 March 1932, '60. Large Dish. Design in iron black on Hakeme. £12.12.0.'; album I: exhibition catalogue and reviews, *Morning Post*, 2 November 1931, *The Times*, 10 November 1931.

36

37

39. Coffee-Set (six Cups and Saucers) exh. 1931

Tessha over cream slip with brush-decoration.

Cup H 2⅜ in (9.1 cm); D 3¾ in (9.6 cm)
Saucer H 1⅛ in (3 cm); D 5¼ in (13.5 cm)
(with slight variations).

This coffee-set was selected for special mention in the *Morning Post* review of Paterson's 1931 exhibition: 'Note also the delightful ... six coffee cups and saucers (143), designed in iron black and coloured slip.' Tessha is a more metallic and broken version of tenmoku glaze. The same decoration is used on the milk jug No.25 and the tea-set No.40.

39

40

PROV: Paterson's, 1931 (4gns); presented, January 1959 (935/90 a-f).

EXH: Paterson's, 1931 (143); Farnham, 1969 (11 & 12, three cups and saucers).

LIT: Anon., 'Splendid Examples by a Japanese Craftsman', *Morning Post*, 2 November 1931; Ingamells (*Preview*), 1959, p.439.

MW DOC: General Catalogue: '1931 … 111 HAMADA Coffee-set. Design in iron-black and coloured slip 4 [gns]'; invoice: Wm B.Paterson, 27 October 1931 / 28 November 1931, receipted

2 March 1932, 'No. 143. Set of six coffee cups & saucers. £4.4.0.'; album I: as for No.38.

40. Tea–Set (six Cups and Saucers, Tea-Pot, Milk Jug and Sugar Bowl) exh. 1931

Tessha over cream slip with brush-decoration.

Cup H 1½ in (6.7 cm); D 4½ in (11.4 cm)
Saucer H 1¼ in (3.2 cm); D 6⅛ in (15.5 cm)
(with slight variations)
Tea-Pot H 7¼ in (18.4 cm); D 7¼ in (18.6 cm)

Milk Jug H 3½ in (8.8 cm); D 5 in (12.8 cm)
Sugar Bowl H 3½ in (8 cm); D 4⅜ in (11.2 cm)

A tea-set decorated with the same design, also purchased from Paterson's 1931 exhibition, is in the Bergen Collection, City Museum and Art Gallery, Stoke-on-Trent (613P1949). See also Nos 25 and 39. Spontaneously thrown and decorated in a manner typical of Hamada, the York tea-set was specially mentioned in the *Morning Post* review of Paterson's 1931 exhibition: 'Note also the delightful tea-set for six (142) ... designed in iron black and coloured slip.'

PROV: Paterson's, 1931 (8gns); presented, 1958, and received on Milner-White's death, 1963 (1049/13a-f,14,15,16).

EXH: Paterson's, 1931 (142); Farnham, 1969 (8, tea-pot and sugar bowl).

LIT: Anon., 'Splendid Examples by a Japanese Craftsman', *Morning Post*, 2 November 1931; Bennett, 1980, p.86 (cups and saucers); *Handlist*, 1971 (80, tea-pot).

MW DOC: General Catalogue: '1931 ... 110 HAMADA. Tea-Set Design in iron-black and coloured slip 8 [gns]/ 110 At the Deanery (In use on state occasions!)'; invoice: Wm B. Paterson, 27 October 1931/ 28 November 1931, receipted 2 March 1932, '142. Tea set for six. Design in iron black and coloured slip. £8.8.0.'; album I: as for No.38.

41. Set of six Plates c.1935

Black tenmoku glaze with unglazed stacking rings.

H 1½ in (4cm); D 6½ in (16.4cm)

As with so much of Hamada's output, these plates are irregular in form. However, this very irregularity is a major factor in their vitality.

PROV: Unknown; purchased, 1935 (6?gns); presented, 1958, and received on Milner-White's death, 1963 (1049/12a-f).

EXH: Dartington, 1952 (89, one only); Farnham, 1969 (3, one only).

LIT: Ingamells (*Preview*), 1959, p.439; *Handlist*, 1971 (19, one only).

MW DOC: General Catalogue: '1935 ... 169 HAMADA. Six plates, temmoku glaze 6 [?gns] and '1952 The following pots were exhibited (1) Dartington Hall ... [see No.23] ... [Hamada] 76 [actually 169] and 77 Big & small plates (one each)'.

42. Dish c.1937 (colour XIV)

Beaten, moulded and notched; kaki over cream slip, wax-resist combed decoration.

H 2¾ in (7cm); D 13½ in (34.2cm)

This pot corresponds with both Milner-White's no.204 under 1939 (£12) in his MS catalogue and the dish which he purchased from the Little Gallery in 1937 (8gns), for which there is a receipt (see MS DOC below). It seems likely that these references are to one and the same pot and that Milner-White

41

misrecorded the year of acquisition and the price.

This dish is an important example of the influence of English eighteenth-century slipware on Hamada's work. It was described by the Dean as 'Very important & delightful – showing Hamada's use of the slip decoration he learned in England in a purely Japanese dish'.

PROV: Probably Little Gallery, 1937 (8gns); lent, probably 1958; received outright on Milner-White's death, 1963 (1050/5).

EXH: Little Gallery, 1937 (31); Dartington, 1952 (87).

LIT: *Handlist*, 1971 (15).

MW DOC: General Catalogue: '1939 ... 204 HAMADA. Dish, red, bold white slip decoratn (Still at the Deanery) 12.0.0 / 204 Very important ... [as above]' and '1952 The following pots were exhibited (1) Dartington Hall ... [See No.23] ... [Hamada] 204 Dish, notched edges'; invoice: Little Gallery, 3 June 1937, receipted 1 July 1937, 'Notched dish by Shoji Hamada No 31 8.8-'; album II: announcement card.

43. Square Dish exh. 1952 (colour XV)

Beaten, moulded; impressed pattern along rim, tenmoku and nuka glazes.

H 2⅝ in (6.7cm); D 12⅛ in (30.3cm)

The influence of English slipware has been totally assimilated in this dish; the finished product is Japanese. Hamada made pots of this shape for thirty years – from 1946 to 1976.[1] The pattern was applied whilst the clay was still in the press mould. The tenmoku glaze was applied first, followed by the nuka (which is made from rice husks). A similar dish is in the Sangyobuka Kaikan, Kawasaki City, Japan.

44

PROV: Beaux Arts Gallery, 1952 (£12); presented, January 1959 (935/40).

EXH: Beaux Arts Gallery, 1952; Wakefield, 1987.

LIT: *Handlist*, 1971 (82).

MW DOC: General Catalogue: '1952 (Beaux Arts Gally. Leach & Hamada) ... 239. HAMADA. Square dish, Green-grey with raised diagonal decn. with cream wash over; the bowl, temmoku black, with resist "brush" work pattern: reverse – gouts of blue-cream glaze over black & red temmoku. V. interesting. Still at Deanery (Hall Table) 12-0-0'; album II: private view card.

1. Leach (*Hamada*), 1976, p.301.

44. Hexagonal Ash-Tray exh. 1952

Beaten, moulded; nuka and tenmoku glazes.

H 1⅜ in (3.5cm); D 4⅞ in (12.4cm)

PROV: Beaux Arts Gallery, 1952 (£1); presented, 1958, and received on Milner-White's death, 1963 (1049/17).

EXH: Beaux Arts Gallery, 1952; Farnham, 1969 (4).

MW DOC: General Catalogue: '1952 (Beaux Art Gally, Leach & Hamada) ... 238 HAMADA Ash Tray – temmoku & flecked grey 100'; album II: private view card.

Erik Hjorth

Danish   1906-1982

45

Educated in Germany at a school near Koblenz, Erik Hjorth worked all his life at the family pottery factory established by his grandfather in 1859 on the Danish island of Bornholm. He was mainly interested in glaze experiments.

45

45. Zodiac Bowl c. 1937

Raised decoration of signs of the Zodiac around exterior ; lustrous red glaze breaking to green.

H 3¼ in (8.4 cm) ; D 11½ in (29.4 cm)

Marks : 'L. Hjorth-' (incised), figure of a deer and 'Danmark.' (impressed)

This bowl was made at Bornholm.

PROV : Unknown ; presented, 1958, and received on Milner-White's death, 1963 (1049/20).

MW DOC : General Catalogue : '1937 ... 189c DANISH. HJORTH of Bornholm Bowl dec. Signs of the Zodiac Still at Deanery 1½ [gns]'.

Agnete (Anita) Hoy
British born 1914

Anita Hoy was born in Southall but her family returned to Denmark when she was four years old. She trained at the Copenhagen School of Art from 1933 to 1936 and then went on briefly to join Nathalie Krebs (q.v.) at Saxbo. By 1939 she was in England and soon met the ceramic designer Gordon Forsyth at the Burslem School of Art, then at its peak. She was introduced by him to the Bullers Studio where she was taken on as designer, reopening its porcelain studio in 1940. The range and quality of the studio's wares increased and its reputation grew. Hoy designed most of the forms, which she produced in prototype. Once they had been selected, Harold Thomas made the pots, which were given numbers and produced in small quantities on the wheel. Sometimes Hoy determined the decoration; sometimes it was left to assistants and students. Under her guidance, a successful studio department was developed, using Bullers insulator body, which operated until 1952. Thereupon Hoy joined Royal Doulton and subsequently taught at Farnham School of Art and elsewhere; she retired from teaching in 1988. She was instrumental in setting up the Craftsmen Potters Shop and has exhibited widely since the 1960s.

For further information on Hoy's association with the Bullers Studio see the exhibition catalogue, Gladstone Pottery Museum, Stoke-on-Trent, *Art among the Insulators: The Bullers Studio 1932-52*, 1977.

A bowl by Hoy was presented to the Gallery in 1990 (1452).

46. Jug 1940-6

Hard-paste porcelain (insulator body), thrown with cut spout; hare's-fur glaze with iron splashes.

H 7⅜ in (18.7 cm); D 5⅜ in (13.6 cm)

Marks: 'Made in England', AH monogram and 'By Bullers 303' (incised)

In its 'sharp-eyed animistic' form this pot follows the pattern of a type of Cypriot jug dating from around the fifth century BC, an example of which is in the British Museum (GR 1982.7-26.17).[1] Made at Bullers and glazed by Guy Harris,[2] it is not a typical Hoy form.

PROV: Unknown (possibly Heal's, through whom Bullers sold); presented, 1958, and received on Milner-White's death, 1963 (1049/58).

MW DOC: General Catalogue: '1946 ... 223 AGNETE HOY (Dane, Danish trained, naturalised in England) Jug, dark brown, lobed sides 4[?gns].'

1. Leach (*Challenge*), 1976, p.52, ill. p.53.
2. Verbal communication, c.1985.

46

46

Wilhelm Kåge
Swedish 1889-1960

Wilhelm Kåge was born in Stockholm into a cultured Swedish family. After art school he took up painting and made a name for himself as a poster artist. He joined the Gustavsberg ceramics factory in 1917 as artistic adviser but with no previous experience of ceramics. Soon afterwards he designed a range of pottery which was intended to bring beauty into the lives of working-class people. Ironically it was too expensive for this market and was bought mainly by young intellectuals. Nevertheless it was upheld as an example of good design and continued in production for years. Other ranges produced included 'Pyro' ware in 1930 and 'Praktika' in 1933. He continued successfully inventing new forms for domestic ceramics through the 1930s.

Alongside these lines, Kåge designed individual pieces of stoneware. He began experimenting in 1926 and by 1930 had launched 'Farsta' stoneware, the distinctive feature of which was that its body was fired high, but its glazes were applied in several stages and fired lower. The intrinsic qualities of stoneware were brought out through engraved or sculpted ornamentation.

Kåge enjoyed an international reputation. In this country for instance, his work was illustrated in 'The Studio' Year Book for 1926, while the Contemporary Art Society bought two pieces of his 'Farsta' ware in 1931 from the exhibition of Swedish arts and crafts. Kåge gave up ceramics for painting in 1949.

A copy of the publication *Porslin*, 1951-2, was sent to Milner-White from Gustavsberg with Kåge's compliments. However, No.47 was the only Kåge pot acquired (or at least recorded) by the Dean.

47

47. Bottle c.1935

Rust-brown body; incised diamond pattern; brownish-yellow glaze.

H 6¼ in (15.9 cm); D 4 in (10.2 cm)

Marks: 'GUSTAVSBERG', 'KAGE', unidentified monogram and 'FARSTA' (incised)

This bottle is one of the individual 'Farsta' stoneware pots designed by Kåge for the Gustavsberg factory.

PROV: Unknown; purchased, 1935 (1½gns); presented, 1958, and received on Milner-White's death, 1963 (1049/22).

MW DOC: General Catalogue: '1935 ... SWEDE. KÄGE (Wilhelm) (Gustafsberg-) [sic] Pot. Brown glaze, handled. 1½[gns]'.

Kanjiro Kawai
Japanese 1890-1966

Kanjiro Kawai, Shoji Hamada and Kenkichi Tomimoto were considered the three greatest Japanese potters of their day. All three were honoured by being made 'Living National Treasures'. Today Kawai's house and workshop in Kyoto have become a potter's shrine maintained by the National Museum. A prolific and original artist, Kawai made a major contribution in the field of glazes, developing in particular a multicolour glaze effect which combined slip-trailed decoration and coloured glazes, contrasted with a coloured base.

Kawai began his career with a thorough technical grounding at the ceramic division of the Tokyo Technical College which he attended from 1910 to 1914 and then at the Kyoto Municipal Institute of Ceramics where he worked from 1914 to 1917. At the latter he studied Chinese ceramics which were then little known in Japan. This influence was to form the basis for his style. In 1920 he set up as a potter in Kyoto, where he continued to work all his life. His output can be divided into three periods: 1915-28, characterized by technically superb pots clearly derived from Chinese ceramics; 1929-35, when this influence was integrated into work inspired by everyday Japanese crafts; 1949-66, his last period, which saw an eccentric creative flowering. During this final phase he made frequent use of casting moulds to create shapes, one of the most idiosyncratic being that of a hand holding a lotus flower, often large scale. In accordance with Japanese tradition Kawai did not sign his work.

Hamada was a great friend of and positive influence on Kawai. He showed him the slipware bowl brought back from England whilst staying at St Ives with Leach. This sparked experiments which eventually led to the powerful trailing-glaze effect, for which Kawai is well known. It was Hamada who introduced him to the philosopher Soetsu Yanagi, who with the two potters founded the 'Mingei' (folk craft) movement. In 1929 he arranged for Kawai to have his first exhibition in Europe at the Beaux Arts Gallery, London, thereby presenting his work to an international audience. Although Kawai never came to England himself, he was to have two further exhibitions in London – in October 1932 at Yamanaka and Co. and in June 1937(?) at the Little Gallery (the latter as part of a group show).

Milner-White and Kawai

Milner-White purchased five pieces of Kawai's work all from the end of the early period/beginning of the middle period. His interest seems to have sprung from his fascination with the interaction between East and the West, especially influences from the West on the East. He wrote of his pots intended for York:

The Vast Proportion of these being of the 3 Master Potters of this Century, Staite Murray, Leach & Hamada with a few contemporary Continental pieces for comparison's sake, & IMPORTANT a few of Japanese native potters [e.g. Kawai], showing how English potting tradition & methods have, through Hamada, influenced, for the first time in history, influenced the Pottery of the Far East.[1]

1. MS notes.

48. Dish exh. 1929

Red-brown glaze with horse's-eye pattern in black.

H 1¾ in (4.4 cm); D 6⅝ in (16.9 cm)

This dish dates from a time when Kawai was making the transition from his first period to the second. It shows the influence of British slipware and, more particularly, Japanese peasant ware. See also Hamada Nos 28, 29, 30 and 31.

PROV: Beaux Arts Gallery, 1929 (8gns); presented, January 1959 (935/37).

EXH: Beaux Arts Gallery, *Stoneware Pottery by Kanjiro Kawai*, 9-27 July 1929 (77).

LIT: *Handlist*, 1971 (8).

MW DOC: General Catalogue: '1929 ... 78 KANJIRO KAWAI. Plate, slipware, horse's eye pattern / 78 Valuable as showing the influence of English slipware decn established via Hamada in Far Eastern pottery'; invoice: Beaux Arts Gallery, 11 July 1929/26 July 1929, receipted 14 August 1929, '77. Dish "horse's eye"; pattern in iron on white (by Kawai) 8.8. .'; album I: exhibition catalogue.

48

49

50

49. Rectangular lidded Box exh. 1932

(?)Slab-built; tessha glaze with symmetrical cream-slip decoration.

H 3 in (7.6 cm); D 4 in (10.2 cm)

This box is a product of Kawai's middle period, when his borrowings from Chinese ceramics were becoming well integrated. The central decorative motif on the lid also appears on the lid of a casket dating from 1930 in the Kawakatsu collection of Kawai's work at the National Museum of Modern Art, Kyoto (98). Another casket with similar decoration also of 1930 is in Kawai's house, Kyoto.

PROV: Yamanaka and Co., 1932 (£2 10s. od.); presented, January 1959 (935/27).

EXH: Yamanaka and Co., *Stoneware Pottery by Kanjiro Kawai*, October 1932 (151).

MW DOC: General Catalogue: '1932 ... 118 KANJIRO KAWAI Box. [£] 2½'; invoice: Yamanaka & Co. Ltd, 5 November 1932, receipted 7 November 1932, 'Ex. 151. Box, oblong quatrangular, brown glaze painted symetrical [sic] ornaments. 2.10.0'; album II: exhibition catalogue.

50. Bowl exh. 1932

Yellow slip-trailed interlaced design with overglazes of brown and tessha.

H 2⅜ in (6 cm); D 7⅜ in (18.8 cm)

This bowl, made in Kawai's middle period, exhibits his distinctive trailed glaze effect, which shows that he had successfully incorporated the lesson of the British slip-ware tradition into his art. It was broken in February 1981 and repaired by Judith Larney at West Dean College, West Sussex.

PROV: Yamanaka and Co., 1932 (£2); presented, January 1959 (935/30).

EXH: Yamanaka and Co., *Stoneware Pottery by Kanjiro Kawai*, October 1932 (76).

LIT: *Handlist*, 1971 (96).

MW DOC: General Catalogue: '1932 ... 117 KANJIRO KAWAI Dish dec cream slip. [£] 2'; invoice: Yamanaka & Co. Ltd, 5 November 1932, receipted 7 November 1932, 'Ex. 76. Do. [Circular dish, yellow and brown glaze.] 2.0.0'; album II: exhibition catalogue.

Nathalie Krebs
Danish   1895 - 1978

Nathalie Krebs trained as a chemical engineer and then entered the porcelain manufacturing firm of Bing and Grøndahl, where she gained a thorough grounding. In March 1929 she started a firm with Gunnar Nylund called Nylund and Krebs; its mark was a kiln with flames. In December 1930 she set up her own workshop called 'Saxbo' (a combination of Gladsaxe, where the ceramics were made, and BO, the firm in Amagertorv, Copenhagen, through whom they were marketed and sold). At Saxbo she produced porcelain and stoneware, aiming to achieve pure colours and simple forms in line with the functionalist ideas prevalent at

the time. Her interest lay in the technical side of ceramics and, not being a designer herself, she collaborated with other craftspeople. Glazes were her strength – their composition, application and firing; these she developed for stoneware dividing them into 'families' according to colour. Well-known Danish artists came to Krebs to have their work glazed and fired, Jais Nielsen (q.v.) and Axel Salto (q.v.) amongst them. Through a number of successful exhibitions Krebs's work became well-known. She was remarkable in achieving cheap mass production of high quality stoneware, which was sustained until 1968 when Krebs closed the workshop.

51

51

51. Large Dish c.1935

Flying duck applied in relief to centre.

H 4⅝in (11.2 cm); D 16½in (42.2 cm)

Marks: Nyland and Krebs symbol, 'SAXBO' and two unidentified (?)flame symbols (impressed)

PROV: Unknown; purchased, 1935 (9?gns with No.52); presented, January 1959 (935/82).

MW DOC: General Catalogue: '1935 ... 170A DANE KREBS (Nathalie) (Saxbo) Large dish [with] DANE KREBS. Ash tray. 9 [?gns].'

52. **Ash-Tray** c.1935

Cream and brown glazes.

H $\frac{3}{4}$ in (1.8 cm); D $5\frac{1}{8}$ in (13 cm)

Mark: '61' Nylund and Krebs symbol 'II'/ 'SAXBO' (impressed)

PROV: Unknown; purchased, 1935 (9?gns with No.51); presented, 1958, and received on Milner-White's death, 1963 (1049/52).

MW DOC: As for No.51.

52

52

Ladi Kwali
Nigerian c.1925-1984

Ladi Kwali became internationally famous in the late 1950s. Her first name means 'born on Monday'; Kwali is the name of her birthplace, one of the towns of the Gwari Yamma people of Northern Nigeria, thirty miles south of Abuja. Almost every woman there made traditional coiled pots from childhood. These comprised large jars with wide mouths for carrying and storing water, jugs for corn beer, casseroles and cooking pots, and small gourd-shaped water bottles. Michael Cardew was much impressed by her work when he first saw it at the home of the Emir of Abuja in 1950. When he met Ladi Kwali in 1951 he invited her to work with him at the Pottery Training Centre in Abuja, when completed. Three years later in 1954 she joined him there, as the only woman in the Centre. She began using the wheel, in addition to traditional coiling, producing beakers, dishes and bowls, often with *sgraffito* decoration scratched through a red or black slip. Cardew took the unusual step of glazing and firing her coiled pots. In 1958 Ladi Kwali's work was exhibited to great acclaim at the Berkeley Galleries in London, and again in 1959 and 1962. This helped the Pottery Training Centre, which had not proved to be the financial success envisaged by the authorities. In 1962 Ladi Kwali spent three weeks in England demonstrating coiling. In 1963 she was awarded the MBE and invited to give demonstrations in Germany. In 1972 she toured America and Canada with Cardew.

For Nigerian hand-building see: Michael Cardew, 'Pottery Techniques in Nigeria', introduction to Sylvia Leith-Ross, *Nigerian Pottery*, Ibadon University Press, Ibadon 1970, p.10; Geoffrey Ireland (photographs), 'Hand Building the Ladi Kwali Way', *Ceramic Review*, no.65, September-October 1980, pp.14-15; Peter Stoodley, obituary, *Ceramic Review*, no.92, March-April 1985, p.51.

For Nigerian decoration see: Malam Hassan, Sarkin Ruwa, Malam Shuaibu and Mukaddamin Makarantar, *A Chronicle of Abuja* (translated from Hausa), Ibadon University Press, Ibadon 1952, pp.40-2; Michael Cardew, 'Potting in Northern Nigeria', *Pottery Quarterly*, iii, no.11, 1956, pp.95-6; Michael Cardew, 'Ladi Kwali', *Craft Horizons* (American Crafts Council), April 1972, pp.34-7; Leach (*Cardew*), 1976, pp.68-9.

53. **Water Pot** exh. 1959

Probably Cardew's body 49; hand-built; impressed and incised geometric decoration; Chün glaze over red slip; wood-fired.

H 13⅛ in (33.4 cm); D 14⅝ in (37.3 cm).

Mark: 'L K' (incised)

'Ladi Kwali obtains her impressed decoration by rolling pieces of home-made string or roulettes made of wood over the surface of the clay sometimes, as here, as horizontal banding and sometimes in vertical panels. For *sgraffito* decoration she uses a blade-like palm rib for the big pots and a porcupine quill for the smaller thrown ware'.[1] The patterns used by the Kwali villagers to decorate pots are the same as those used in tattoos on girls' backs.

PROV: Berkeley Galleries, 1959 (15gns); presented, December 1959 (935/98).

EXH: Berkeley Galleries, 1959 (?161); York, 1983 (47).

LIT: Hess, 1960, p.465, ill. front cover; *Handlist*, 1971 (6).

MW DOC: General Catalogue: '18/5/59 Michael Cardew and his African School – All Stoneware … Waterpot by Ladi Kwali (his first & greatest pupil) 15-15-0 … Bought at the Berkeley Galleries 18.5.59 … This was his second show of their work. At the first, one of Ladi Kwali's large pots was shown, & immediately bought by the V&A. Her pot opposite & another like it were 'ordered', beforehand by myself & by Sir Kenneth Clarke [sic].'; loose private view leaflet.

1. Sidey, 1983, under no.47.

53

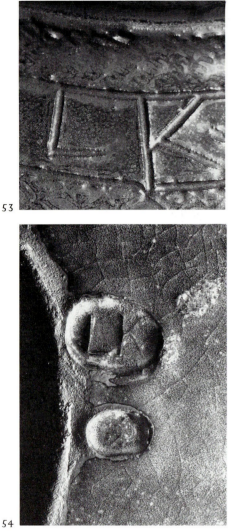

53

54

54

54. Water Pot exh. 1962 (*colour XXIX*)

Probably Cardew's body 49; hand-built; impressed and incised decoration of geometric designs and alternating birds and praying mantis in traditional Kwali style; white slip or corn starch rubbed into the decoration, the whole covered with transparent glaze (AA); wood-fired.

H 14¼ in (36.1 cm); D 14⅜ in (36.6 cm)

Marks: 'L K' and Abuja in Arabic (impressed)

Large coiled pots such as this created enormous interest when exhibited in London. For an account of the purchase of this pot see Sidey.[1] It is probably the glaze effect on this pot which was referred to by Cardew in 1976.[2]

PROV: Berkeley Galleries, 1962 (20gns); presented, 1958, and received on Milner-White's death, 1963 (1049/21).

EXH: Berkeley Galleries, 1962 (26); York, 1983 (52, pl.15); Manchester, 1988 (48).

LIT: *Handlist*, 1971 (95).

MW DOC: General Catalogue: '19/6/62 3rd Show at the Berkley [*sic*] Galleries of Cardew and his African pupils. Handbuilt Pot by Ladi Kwali 21.0.0 ... Ladi Kwali, the greatest African potter, died in 1961 [actually 1984; it was Halima Audu who died in 1961], thus the Y.A.G. has two of her finest works. Halima, also a woman, is younger. & the only one at present approaching L.K's standard.'; notes on loose private view leaflet: '26 20 gs Hand Built Pot by Ladi Kwali = Born on Monday at Kwali Decorated by [?]Bakin Allah from Gidan dara 20 gs.'

1. Sidey, 1983, n.p.[p.5].
2. Leach (*Cardew*), 1976, p.68.

Bernard Howell Leach and the Leach Pottery
British   1887 - 1979

Bernard Leach was born in Hong Kong and spent part of his early childhood in Japan. He studied painting and etching at the Slade, under Henry Tonks and Frank Brangwyn respectively, and in 1909 returned to Japan to teach etching. He was first introduced to pottery-making at a raku party, which inspired him to learn the craft from Ogate Kenzan, the sixth Kenzan of a line of master potters. Whilst in Japan he was particularly impressed by Korean pottery and Chinese ware of the Sung dynasty. In 1920 he returned to England with Shoji Hamada to set up a pottery at St Ives in Cornwall. There he sought to combine the Oriental approach assimilated in Japan with indigenous British traditions, in making by hand everyday pottery as an alternative to mass-produced factory ware. Leach would have preferred to do so in slipware but by 1928 he had realized that there was not a big enough market for this and he concentrated thereafter on stoneware. He envisaged a team of potters working together, each a fully responsible craftsman, yet producing a common line of work designed by Leach. Alongside this reasonably-priced everyday ware (which just before the Second World War was developed into the 'Standard Ware' range), finer exhibition pieces were made to be sold at higher prices. Leach continued making pots at St Ives until his sight failed in 1972. He died in Hayle, Cornwall. Leach attracted many pupils : through them and their pupils in turn the Leach tradition continues. He also lectured and wrote widely. He is usually regarded as the 'father' of the modern pottery movement.

Milner-White and Leach

Milner-White recognized Leach as one of 'the 3 Master Potters of the century'.[1] He bought more pots by Leach than by any other potter : there is documentary evidence for eighty-three pots, of which thirty-three came to York City Art Gallery. The Dean bought none of Leach's slipware, as he was interested only in stoneware, and acquired virtually nothing deriving from the British medieval tradition : nearly all the pots at York owe their inspiration to the East. Milner-White's favourite pot (in the whole collection) was apparently Leach's famous 'Leaping Salmon' vase, No.66.

As well as the exhibition pieces, Milner-White also bought some of Leach's Standard Ware. He was at pains, however, to keep the two categories apart and did not usually include any of the latter in his gifts to York or Southampton, the notable exception being No.80, which bears masterly

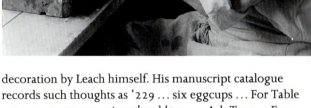

decoration by Leach himself. His manuscript catalogue records such thoughts as '229 ... six eggcups ... For Table use ... not museum pieces' and '237 ... Ash Tray ... For household use'.

Although the Dean did not establish the same relationship with Leach as he did with Staite Murray, he corresponded with him and entertained him at the Deanery. Two letters in the Milner-White correspondence show that he sought Leach's advice on collecting more Hamada pots. The Dean was also interested in the work of Leach's most important pupils Braden, Cardew and Pleydell-Bouverie.

All Bernard Leach's pots in the Milner-White collection at York were made at St Ives. Leach was not personally involved, however, in all the pots made there despite the fact that many pieces produced by his team of craftsmen bear his impressed mark. It is likely, however, that pieces bearing the painted monogram were decorated by Leach himself. In this catalogue all pots impressed 'BL' or marked in any way with the BL monogram are assumed to be by Bernard Leach ; the remaining pots are catalogued as from the Leach Pottery.

55. Bowl ?1924-5 *(colour VIII)*

Tenmoku glaze with iron-red decoration of three six-dot floral motifs within and pine-needle decoration without.

H 2½ in (6.3 cm) ; D 6¼ in (15.8 cm)

Marks : BL and St Ives monograms (impressed)

This bowl is the earliest Leach in the collection and the one made most consciously after an Oriental model. Leach's success at reproducing an Oriental style is attested by the fact that the bowl previously belonged to George Eumorfopoulos, who amassed one of the greatest collections of early Chinese ceramics, the cream of which is now divided between the Victoria and

Albert Museum and the British Museum. A bowl with similar external decoration is illustrated by Forsyth.[1] A bowl decorated with the same floral decoration, dating from 1925-6, is in the Victoria and Albert Museum.[2]

PROV : Almost certainly George Eumorfopoulos ; probably his sale, Sotheby's, 20-21 April 1944, first day (113, with four others), bought Lessore (£13 the lot); presumably Beaux Arts Gallery and thence purchased (2gns); presented, January 1959 (935/15).

LIT: *Handlist*, 1971 (26); Haslam, 1986, p.1605, pl.2 in colour.

MW DOC: General Catalogue: '1944 ... 218 LEACH – Bowl, Temmoku glaze, red & black dec. with stars of five spots within "pine-needles" without ?1924 or 5 Early work From the Eumophopoulos [*sic*] Collection dispersed at Sotheby's in. 1944 April 20 2.2.0'.

1. Forsyth, 1936, p.89.
2. Hogben, 1978, pl.30.

56. Vase exh. 1926

Cut-away T'zǔ Chou type decoration; grey slip.

H $8\frac{7}{8}$ in (22.4 cm); D $7\frac{3}{8}$ in (18.3 cm)

Marks: BL and St Ives monograms (impressed)

This vase consciously reproduces ancient Oriental form and decoration. The base cracked during production and had to be mended. A drawing of a similarly shaped and decorated pot is in the collection of Mrs Janet Leach.[1]

PROV: Paterson's, 1926, or Arts and Crafts Exhibition Society, 1926; presented, January 1959 (935/24).

EXH: Paterson's, Bernard Leach pottery, May 1926, or Royal Academy, thirteenth exhibition of the Arts and Crafts Exhibition Society, 1926; V&A, 1977 (36).

LIT: Holme, 1926, p.129, pl.IV; *Handlist*, 1971 (51).

MW DOC: General Catalogue: '1926 ... 21 LEACH. Bottle Tzu Chow type, decoration grey slip, cut away'; album I: review of Paterson's exhibition, *Morning Post*, 24 April 1926.

1. Exh. Osaka, 1980 (180, ill. p.140).

57. Bowl c. 1926

Grey-brown glaze on reddish ground.

H $2\frac{3}{8}$ in (5.9 cm); D $4\frac{1}{2}$ in (11.4 cm)

Mark: St Ives monogram (impressed)

Leach Pottery. Oriental in inspiration, this bowl was recorded by the Dean as 'Exquisite'.

56

57

PROV: National Society: Painters, Sculptors, Engravers, Potters, 1939 (£1 10s.); presented, May 1959 (935/94).

EXH: Royal Institute Galleries(?), exhibition of the National Society: Painters, Sculptors, Engravers, Potters, 1939 (1); Stockholm, 1939.

LIT: *Handlist*, 1971 (31).

MW DOC: General Catalogue: '1939 202 LEACH. Small Bowl, Brown & grey glaze on reddish biscuit 1.10.0 / 202 at Deanery. Potted c.1926 Exquisite' and '1939. Collection Lent to Stockholm at the request of the Government ... [LEACH] (202) Small Bowls, smoke grey. [Insured for £]1-10'; receipt: National Society etc., 28 February 1939, 'Thirty shillings in payment of Pottery by Bernard Leach (No.1)'.

58. Tea-Pot Stand c.1927

Tile with 'Tree of Life' design in cream and brown glazes; beaten copper frame.

H and width 6⅛ in (15.8 cm); depth 1¼ in (3.2 cm)

Marks: BL monogram (painted); thirteen St Ives monograms (impressed)

PROV: Paterson's, 1927 (£2); presented, January 1959 (935/21).

EXH: Paterson's, 1927 (56); Stockholm, 1939.

LIT: *Handlist*, 1971 (44); Morley-Fletcher, 1984, p.168, ill. in colour.

MW DOC: General Catalogue: '1927 ... 26 LEACH. Tile. dec. pattern. Tree of Life' and '1939. Collection Lent to Stockholm at the request of the Government ... [LEACH] Tile [Insured for £]4-4'; invoice: Wm B. Paterson, 17 March 1927, receipted 25 April 1927, 'Tile teapot stand decorated. Tree Animals. Birds fish &c. No 5 6 2 - -'.

59. Tea-Pot c.1927

Brown decoration of six-petalled flowers and two double 's' and dot motifs over light brown ground.

H 5 in (12.8 cm); D 8⅝ in (21.9 cm)

Mark: St Ives monogram (impressed)

Leach Pottery. This tea-pot is part of a set which also included five cups and saucers: see Appendix B3 (1049/59a-e) and 1049/60). In the compiler's opinion, it is likely to date from the same period as No.58. The decoration is an Oriental six-dot flower pattern. A similar tea-pot is in the Bergen Collection, City Museum and Art Gallery, Stoke-on-Trent (563P1949).

58

59

PROV: Possibly Leach Pottery via Colnaghi, 1927; presented, 1958, and received on Milner-White's death, 1963 (1049/61).

EXH: Possibly Colnaghi, 1927 (stand J, not listed in catalogue); Sheffield, 1976 (4).

LIT: *Handlist*, 1971 (36).

MW DOC: General Catalogue: not listed; No.59 can possibly be linked with a receipt: Leach Pottery, 19 December 1927. 'Twelve guineas' for unspecified item(s); album I: exhibition catalogue.

60. Bowl c.1928

Crackled cream-grey glaze.

H 2⅞ in (7.4 cm); D 4¾ in (12 cm)

Marks: BL and St Ives monograms (impressed)

This pot is Oriental in inspiration.

PROV: Beaux Arts Gallery, 1928 (3gns); presented, January 1958 (935/6).

EXH: Beaux Arts Gallery, 1928 (68).

LIT: *Handlist*, 1971 (45).

MW DOC: General Catalogue: '1928 ... 67 LEACH. Small bowl, crackled, grey.'; invoice: Beaux Arts Gallery, 20 December 1928, receipted 22 December 1928, 'POTTERY BY BERNARD LEACH 68 Bowl crackled grey 3.3.0'; album I: exhibition catalogue and review: *The Times*, 6 December 1928.

61. Bottle exh. 1928

Porcelain-like body; carved and incised geometric pattern covered with grey glaze.

H 4⅜ in (11.1 cm); D 4⅛ in (10.5 cm)

Marks: BL and St Ives monograms (impressed)

PROV: Beaux Arts Gallery, 1928 (7gns): presented, 1958, and received on Milner-White's death, 1963 (1049/24).

EXH: Beaux Arts Gallery, 1928 (112).

MW DOC: General Catalogue: '1928 ... 65 LEACH. Small engraved white porcelain bottle [the whole entry crossed out]'; invoice: Beaux Arts Gallery, 20 December 1928, receipted 22 December 1928, 'POTTERY BY BERNARD LEACH No.112 Small engraved white porcelain bottle 7.7.0'; album I: exhibition catalogue and review, *The Times*, 6 December 1928.

62. Moulded Tea-Jar late-1920s

Four-sided, made in two diagonal halves; wax-resist panel decoration of alternating fleur-de-lys motifs and lattice pattern under a thick opaque olive-green glaze.

H 5⅝ in (14.2 cm); D 3½ in (8.9 cm)

Leach Pottery. This tea-jar is the only unmarked piece of Leach pottery in the collection. A similar example is in the Crafts Study Centre, Bath (P.74.4).

PROV: Beaux Arts Gallery, 1931 (4gns); presented, January 1959 (935/9).

EXH: Beaux Arts Gallery, 1931 (222, 'Celadon tea Jar; wax reserve'); Stockholm, 1939; Dartington, 1952 (56); Sheffield, 1976 (2).

LIT: Leach, 1967, pl.15; *Handlist*, 1971 (32).

MW DOC: General Catalogue: '1931 ... 107 LEACH Olive tea jar, dec. fleur-de-lys 4[gns]', '1939. Collection Lent to Stockholm at the request of the Government ... [LEACH] Olive Tea-Jar [Insured for £]4-4' and '1952 The following pots were exhibited (1) Dartington Hall ... [see No.23] ... [Leach] 107 Tea Caddy'; invoice: Beaux Arts Gallery, 23 May 1931, receipted 22 June 1931, 'Tea-jar by Bernard Leach 4.4.0'; album I: exhibition catalogue.

63. Panel of Tiles: 'Well Head and Mountains' exh. 1929 (colour V)

Nine square tiles decorated with an overall picture of a well-head in a mountainous landscape in *sgraffito* with iron brush-decoration in shades of brown glaze on a mottled cream background, the whole set in a wooden frame.

Overall H and width of tiles: 27 in (68.5 cm)

With frame: H 32⅞ in (83.5 cm); depth 1 in (2.5 cm)

Individual tiles: 9 in (22.5 cm) square

Marks: BL and St Ives monograms (painted on bottom right-hand and bottom left-hand tiles respectively)

One of Leach's most famous pieces, this panel was exhibited at Colnaghi's in 1929 as 'Mountains' and Milner-White recorded it in his MS catalogue as 'The Mountains' (which is also lettered on a tablet attached to the wooden frame). However it is titled 'The Well Head' in an undated *Catalogue of Tiles, Fireplaces, Pottery* issued by the Leach Pottery in about 1930, where it features as a photograph on a loose, inserted sheet. In *A Potter's Work* it was captioned by Leach himself as 'Well Head and Mountains'.[1]

60

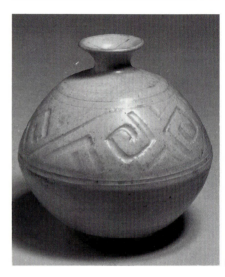

61

62

The mountains, the well-head, the horse eating seaweed, the pottery in the distance and the plants, which constitute the decoration, appear over and over again in Leach's work. In *A Potter's Work*, he wrote of this panel: 'The technique is *sgraffito* and brushwork with an iron pigment which varies in colour between black and raw rust red. I would not describe this subject matter as symbolic. The design is imaginary but derived from things seen and felt in the mountains of Japan, although the various elements had, to me, a long-term significance of a pictorial kind.'[2] In *Beyond East and West*, he wrote more generally: 'the peaks of the high Japan Alps became part of a dreamland which I often drew or even painted on pots. That picture has remained with me all through life.'[3]

The Leach Pottery produced large numbers of individual tiles, which were often used in fireplace surrounds or as teapot stands (e.g. No.58); such tiles could easily be combined to make decorative panels (e.g. No.64). The present work, however, is a very fine example of Bernard Leach's panels where a single pictorial scheme covers a group of tiles. Two further examples were in Colnaghi's 1929 exhibition – 'Tiger' (1) and 'Tree of Life' (2); the former was probably the six-tile panel now in the Ohara Museum of Art, Kurashiki,[4] while the latter was probably the nine-tile panel subsequently reproduced in *A Potter's Work*.[5] Yet another example is a four-tile panel depicting a horse eating seaweed of 1928 in the Japan Folk Craft Museum (Mingeikan), Tokyo.[6]

PROV: Colnaghi, 1929 (30gns); presented, January 1959 (935/91).

EXH: Colnaghi, 1929 (Leach 2, 'Mountains'); Arts Council Gallery, 1961 (33); V&A, 1977 (43).

LIT: Holme, 1930, ill. p.155 (2); Shikiba, 1934, pl.51; Ingamells (*Museums Journal*), 1959, p.124; Leach, 1967, pl.36 (incorrectly as 1940); Nuffield-Chelsea Curriculum Trust, *Pottery* (in the Nuffield 'Working with Science' series), Longman, 1977, fig.4.2; Hogben, 1978, p.180, pl.36 (as c.1928).

MW DOC: General Catalogue: '1929 ... 94 LEACH. Tile-Picture – "The Mountains." [£] 31½'; invoice: Colnaghi, December 1929, 'Pottery: – Bernard Leach. No. 2. Set of Stoneware Tiles, "Mountains" £31.10.0' (together with receipt, 23 December 1929); album I: exhibition catalogue, review, *The Times*, 30 November 1929, and photograph; loose catalogue: Leach Pottery, *Catalogue of Tiles, Fireplaces, Pottery*, Leach Pottery, St Ives n.d. (c.1930).

1. Leach, 1967, caption to pl.36.
2. Ditto.
3. Leach, 1985, p.73.
4. Exh. Kobe, 1989 (c-45, ill. in colour).
5. Leach, 1967, pl.35 (incorrectly dated 1940).
6. Exh. Kobe, 1989 (c-46, ill. in colour).

64. Panel of small Tiles exh. 1929
(*colour IV*)

Twenty-five square tiles decorated with pictorial images in brown and blue glazes on a creamy ground alternating with twenty-four plain mottled buff and green tiles within a border of thirty brown rectangular tiles, the whole set in a wooden frame.

Overall H and width of tiles: 33 in (84 cm)

With frame: H and width 38 15/16 in (99 cm); depth ¾ in (1.9 cm)

Individual tiles: 4 in (10 cm) square and 4 × 2 in (10 × 5 cm)

Marks: BL and St Ives monograms (painted on most of the tiles)

Like No.63, this is a deservedly well-known work by Bernard Leach. It features on a loose, inserted sheet in an undated *Catalogue of Tiles, Fireplaces, Pottery* issued by the Leach Pottery in about 1930. The sheet is headed 'Sample Set of decorated Tiles' and bears a photograph of the panel within a grid of letters and numbers, so that clients may order their own combination of tiles by giving grid references and indicating 'a preference in colour scheme'. According to the caption, this particular set of tiles was made as a summer screen for a fireplace and the tiles were 'painted by Mr. Leach personally'.

John Gould Fletcher wrote of Leach's tiles: 'in his stoneware tiles for use as wall decoration or in fireplaces, Leach has brilliantly combined old Delft mediæval heraldic ornament, and Chinese invention into a product so peculiarly his own that it resembles nothing that has been done before'.[1]

Some of the tiles were slightly damaged in 1985; they were repaired in the same year by the York Archaeological Trust.

PROV: Colnaghi, 1929 (10gns); presented, January 1959 (935/92).

EXH: Colnaghi, 1929 (Leach 4); V&A, 1977 (44).

LIT: Ingamells (*Museums Journal*), 1959, p.124; Hogben, 1978, p.180, pls 33 & 34.

MW DOC: General Catalogue: '1929 ... 95 LEACH. Tiles – framed together. 10[gns]'; invoice: Colnaghi, December 1929, 'Pottery:– Bernard Leach ... No.4. Set of Stoneware Tiles, varied.

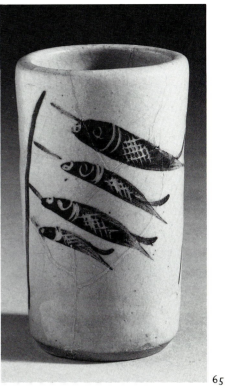

65

£10.10.0.' (together with receipt, 23 December 1929); album I: exhibition catalogue, review, *The Times*, 30 November 1929, and photograph; loose catalogue: Leach Pottery, *Catalogue of Tiles, Fireplaces, Pottery*, Leach Pottery, St Ives n.d. (c.1930).

1. John Gould Fletcher, 'The Pottery and Tiles of Bernard Leach', *Artwork*, summer 1931, p.123.

65. Pot: 'Fish Banners' exh. 1931

Cream-grey glaze, decorated in sepia with two groups of fish kites (four and five respectively) hanging from poles.

H 3⅜ in (8.5 cm); D 2 in (5.1 cm)

Mark: St Ives monogram (impressed)

Leach Pottery. The decoration is inspired by a Japanese festival in which each fish kite represents a son in the family: 'A forty-foot pole on the lawn outside flies lazy cotton carp twenty-five feet long, in bright colours, to celebrate Boys' Day, May 5th – one fish for each boy – the eldest, the biggest fish.'[1] According to Milner-White's MS General Catalogue, this pot was 'broken to pieces' while at the Birmingham showing of the 1952 *Pottery and Textiles* exhibition. Repaired soon afterwards, it was fully restored in 1985 by Judith Larney of London.

66

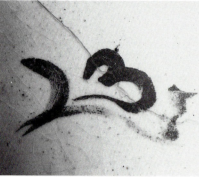

66

PROV: Beaux Arts Gallery, 1931 (1gn); presented, January 1959 (935/7).

EXH: Beaux Arts Gallery, 1931 (254); Dartington, 1952 (59).

LIT: Wingfield Digby, 1952, p.98, pl.4(d); Handlist, 1971 (47); Morley-Fletcher, 1984, p.167, ill. in colour.

MW DOC: General Catalogue: '1931 ... 106 LEACH. "Fish-banners" 1' and '1952 The following pots were exhibited (1) Dartington Hall ... [see No.23] ... [Leach] 106 Fish Banners (broken to pieces at Birmingham) (Both [Nos 65 and 71] wonderfully mended)'; invoice: Beaux Arts Gallery, 23 May 1931, receipted 22 June 1931, '254. Pot by Bernard Leach 1.1.0'; album I: exhibition catalogue.

1. Leach, 1978, p.175.

66. Vase: 'Leaping Salmon' 1931
(colour VII)

Oxidized matt-white bracken-ash glaze made with equal parts feldspar, bracken ash and pike clay applied thickly over a pale body with delicate iron brushwork decoration of a leaping salmon.

H $12\frac{7}{8}$ in (32.7 cm); D $6\frac{1}{8}$ in (15.5 cm)

Marks: BL monogram (painted verso), BL and St Ives monograms (impressed) and an unidentified monogram (incised)

Leaping Salmon is one of Leach's finest and most famous pots. Made in 1931, it is one of the rare pots covered with the famous bracken-ash glaze which was made with great effort. Leach wrote of this glaze: 'It made a creamy white, big-crackled glaze, which we have never since equalled. It was velvety white, it took pigment on its surface with gentleness, it did not look mechanized, it was hard and it was soft at the same time. We attempted that same effect in successive years, but never got it again. The reason for this was partly the season in which the dried vegetable was taken from the hills, and partly, no doubt, the amount of salt in the sea air that had dried onto the bracken.'[1] Another vase, of c.1931, decorated with the same glaze is in the Victoria and Albert Museum (c.144-1931). Later versions of the fish vases use smaller quantities of bracken ash, and being oil- rather than wood-fired, have glazes of lesser subtlety.[2] A later version of this pot is at Paisley Museum and Art Gallery (398-1962).

The decoration of the Leaping Salmon is Leach at his best. It is a superb example of control and lyricism at the same time and could not have been painted by anyone else. The form, however, was almost certainly not thrown by Leach: an unidentified mark incised on the base is presumed to be that of the thrower. Although very similar to the mark of Warren Mackenzie, he was not working in St Ives at this date. The base of the Victoria and Albert Museum's bracken-ash pot is incised with the monogram PLK, which is also unidentified.

Leaping Salmon was reputedly Milner-White's favourite pot. Sadly the top was broken in April 1959; it was repaired fairly crudely, presumably soon afterwards.

PROV: Beaux Arts Gallery, 1931 (30gns); presented, January 1959 (935/71).

EXH: Beaux Arts Gallery, 1931 (129); V&A, 1977 (65, ill. p.12; Hayward Gallery, 1979 (2.73, ill.); Tate Gallery, 1985 (C3, ill. p.94 in colour); Kobe, 1989 (C-40, ill. in colour).

LIT: Shikiba, 1934, pl.59 (in photograph of a room); E.A.Lane, Style in Pottery, Oxford University Press, Oxford, 1948, pl.34; Wingfield Digby, 1952, p.98, pl.2; Ingamells (Preview), 1959, p.439, pl.441; Ingamells (Museums Journal), 1959, p.124, fig.30; Leach, 1967, pl.21; Handlist, 1971 (39); Hogben, 1978, p.181, pl.56; Janet Leach, 'Pots at the Tate!', Ceramic Review, no.92, March-April 1985, ill. p.26 in colour.

MW DOC: General Catalogue: '1931. 105 LEACH Bottle "Leaping Salmon" white matt glaze, brown brushwork 30 [gns]'; invoice: Beaux Arts Gallery, 23 May 1931, receipted 22 June 1931, '129. White matt bottle; "Leaping Salmon" by B.Leach 31.10.0'; album I: exhibition catalogue; note: '[Illustrate] Grace by Salmon = Expression of an Inspiration'.

1. Leach (Hamada), 1976, p.48.
2. Oliver Watson in exhibition catalogue, Tate Gallery, 1985, p.230.

67. Lidded Ink Pot exh. 1933

Nine-sided cut decoration; glazed in autumn-leaf colours.

H $2\frac{7}{8}$ in (7.4 cm); D 3 in (7.7 cm)

Marks: BL and St Ives monograms (impressed)

Hamada is believed also to have made cut-sided ink pots.[1]

PROV: Beaux Arts Gallery, 1933 (2gns); presented, January 1959 (935/22).

EXH: Beaux Arts Gallery, 1933 (78, 'Cut autumn leaf Ink Pot', ?ill. front cover); Rotterdam, 1960 (10).

LIT: Leach, 1951, p.28, pl.56(3); Wingfield Digby, 1952, p.98, pl.4(a); Handlist, 1971 (40).

MW DOC: General Catalogue: '1933 ... 134 LEACH Ink Pot, "Cut Autumn Leaf" 2[gns]'; receipted invoice with letter: Beaux Arts Gallery, 19 December 1933, 'Pottery by Bernard Leach ... Cut autumn leaf Ink Pot 2.2.-'; album II: exhibition catalogue and review, The Times, 5 December 1933.

1. An example attributed to Hamada and dating from about 1928 is in the Bergen Collection at Stoke-on-Trent City Museum and Art Gallery (898P1949).

68. Bowl exh. 1933

Twelve-sided cut decoration; greenish-red glaze.

H $3\frac{5}{8}$ in (9.1 cm); D $10\frac{1}{2}$ in (26.6 cm)

Marks: BL and St Ives monograms (impressed)

67

68

69

69

MW DOC: General Catalogue: '1936 … 179. LEACH.
Small plates (4) (3 given away + 1 — Fritillary
design, to York) £1.10./179 3 given away; one
'the Fritillary York'; invoice: Little Gallery, 30
April 1936, receipted, (?) 7 June 1936,
'Stoneware by Bernard Leach. 6 small plates a 7/-
2.2.-'; album II: announcement card with MS
note 'Four Small Plates 1-10-0' and review, *The
Times*, undated.

A similar bowl is in the studio ceramics collection at Paisley Museum and Art Gallery
(59-1961).

PROV: Beaux Arts Gallery, 1933(10gns);
presented, January 1959 (935/79).

EXH: Beaux Arts Gallery, 1933 (60, 'Variegated
rust cut Bowl'); Stockholm, 1939; Dartington,
1952 (61); Rotterdam, 1960 (9); Sheffield,
1976 (5); Hayward Gallery, 1979 (2.74).

LIT: *Handlist*, 1971 (38).

MW DOC: General Catalogue: '1933 … 131 LEACH.
Bowl "Variegated rust, chestnut & green oil spot
10[gns]' and '1939. Collection Lent to Stockholm
at the request of the Government … LEACH Bowl,
12 facets [Insured for £]10½'; receipted invoice
with letter: Beaux Arts Gallery, 19 December
1933, 'Pottery by Bernard Leach Variegated rust
cut bowl 10.10.-'; album II: exhibition catalogue
and review, *The Times*, 5 December 1933.

69. Dish c.1936

Painted flower in centre under crackle
celadon glaze.

H 1½ in (3.7 cm); D 6 in (15.3 cm)

Mark: 'BL' and St Ives monogram
(impressed)

The flower on this dish is derived from the
genus Fritillaria, and the design, one often
used at the Leach Pottery, is known as the
'Fritillary': it may also be seen, for example,
on the tile panel No.64.

PROV: Little Gallery, 1936 (7s. according to
invoice or one of four priced at £1 10s. together
according to MS catalogue); presented, January
1959 (935/4).

EXH: Little Gallery, 1936.

70. Bowl c.1936

Smooth, thick, dark-green glaze.

H 3⅝ in (9.3 cm); D 6 in (15.2 cm)

Marks: 'BL' and St Ives monogram
(impressed)

The quality of Leach's output is not con-
sistent, much of his throwing being disap-
pointing. This bowl, however, is beautifully
made and glazed. As Oliver Watson writes,
'This bowl shows Leach at his purest – trying to recapture the "Sung" aesthetic. He
must have highly valued it, for it was priced
at 12gns (£12. 60p.) – a considerable sum
for a smallish piece of his in 1936!'[1]

PROV: Little Gallery, 1936(12gns); presented,
January 1959 (935/5).

70

EXH: Little Gallery, 1936; Dartington, 1952 (70); Rotterdam, 1960 (12); Kobe (c-47, ill. in colour).

LIT: Leach, 1951, p.28, pl.56(2); Wingfield Digby, 1952, p.98, pl.4(c); Handlist, 1971 (42).

MW DOC: General Catalogue: '1936 178 LEACH. Bowl, dark green. 12[gns]' and '1952 the following pots were exhibited (1) Dartington Hall ... [see No.23] ... [Leach] 178 Dk Green Bowl'; invoice: Little Gallery, 30 April 1936, 'Stoneware by Bernard Leach. Bowl Ruli 12.12.'; album II: announcement card with MS note 'Bowl, dark green. 12' and review, The Times, undated.

1. Watson, 1989, p.139.

71. Bottle c.1940-6

Off-white glaze, brushed iron-oxide decoration of twelve leaping fish.

H 15⅞ in (40.4 cm); D 6¼ in (16 cm)

Marks: 'BE' and St Ives monogram (impressed)

Bottles of this shape and with this decoration were often repeated, and are probably Leach's most famous and easily recognizable production. An early, perhaps the earliest, example is in the Victoria and Albert Museum (C.144-1931); another example is in the Ohara Museum of Art, Kurashiki, Japan. Leach wrote of a 'fish' bottle made in 1970: 'I have made quite a few of these, perhaps fifty. The pattern is made with iron pigment on a white slip. Bands are the first means of decorating a pot, but they create sections which then demand further pattern; otherwise the space looks a bit empty. Free calligraphic use of a brush does not come easily to a European, for we are accustomed from childhood to the heavier pressure of a pencil or the scratch of a pen. For that reason I have found it best to limit my efforts to a few rhythmic strokes. The fish are made by one brush stroke which is then combed.'[1] According to Milner-White's MS General Catalogue, the lip of this bottle was broken by Leach himself while it

was at Dartington for the 1952 Pottery and Textiles exhibition. It was repaired soon afterwards.

PROV: Probably Berkeley Galleries, 1946(20gns); lent, 1958, and received outright on Milner-White's death, 1963 (1050/6).

EXH: Probably Berkeley Galleries, 1946; Dartington, 1952 (60); Sheffield, 1976 (8).

LIT: Leach, 1951, p.28, pl.56(1); Wingfield Digby, 1952, p.98, pl.4(b); Handlist, 1971 (48).

MW DOC: General Catalogue: '1946 ... 221 LEACH Tall pot, white matt glaze, brown brushwork of fishes 20[?gns]./221 still at Deanery' and '1952 The following pots were exhibited (1) Dartington Hall ... [see No.23] ... [Leach] (221) Fish decoratn (lip broken by Leach at Dartington) (Both [Nos 65 and 71] wonderfully mended)'; album: outside pages of exhibition catalogue.

1. Leach (Challenge), 1976, p.132, ill. p.133.

72. Vase c.1946 (colour I)

Incised with three 'Tree of Life' motifs.

H 12½ in (31.6 cm); D 11 in (28.1 cm)

Marks: 'BE' and St Ives monogram (impressed)

This pot is one of Bernard Leach's most famous. The design makes a strong and distinctive decorative pattern around the generous and well-thrown form. The 'Tree of Life' decoration was a recurring theme in Leach's work and it is likely that he used stencils to reproduce it in its different guises. Oliver Watson writes of this pot: 'The "Tree of Life" was considered to be symbolic by Leach. The design is taken from Chinese temple stone-carvings of the Han period which Leach must have seen during his visit to China in 1914-16. He used it regularly from the 1920s onwards; the Plough constellation is his own addition.'[1]

PROV: Probably Berkeley Galleries, 1946(50?gns); presented, January 1959 (935/70).

EXH: Probably Berkeley Galleries, 1946; Dartington, 1952 (65); Rotterdam, 1960 (14, ill.); Arts Council, 1961 (73, pl.VI); Sheffield, 1976 (7); V&A, 1977 (96); Tate Gallery, 1985 (c5, ill. p.95 in colour); Kobe, 1989 (c-53, ill. in colour).

LIT: Leach, 1951, p.28, pl.57; Wingfield Digby, 1952, p.98, pl.3; Ingamells (Preview), 1959, ill. front cover; Ingamells (Museums Journal), 1959, p.124, fig.31; Handlist, 1971 (46); Pleydell-Bouverie, 1978, ill. p.27; Hogben, 1978, p.182, pl.82 and front cover both in colour.

MW DOC: General Catalogue: '1946 220 LEACH Large Globular Pot with Tree of Life decoration 50 [?gns]' and '1952 The following pots were exhibited (1) Dartington Hall ... [see No.23] Leach. (220) Tree of Life'; album II: outside pages of exhibition catalogue.

1. Oliver Watson in exhibition catalogue, Tate Gallery, 1985, p.230.

73. Jar c.1951

Sgraffito decoration through a brown ground in two horizontal bands, the lower one with design of mountains, trees, shrine, (?)figures, animals and an unidentified geometric motif, the upper one with design of mountains, trees and birds, the upper two-thirds with grey overglaze.

H 12in (30.5 cm); D 10in (25.4 cm)

Marks: 'BL' and St Ives monogram (impressed)

The provenance of this pot and No.74 is uncertain as there are no relevant invoices or receipts in the Milner-White documentation. However, they are listed among a group of Leach pots under 1951 in the Dean's General Catalogue and it is known that two other pots in this group (Nos 75 and 76) were purchased direct from the Leach Pottery in that year. It is likely, therefore, that both Nos 73 and 74 were also purchased direct from St Ives. The form of the jar and the motifs which decorate it recur regularly throughout Bernard Leach's career.

PROV: Probably Leach Pottery, 1951 (£18); presented, January 1959 (935/68).

EXH: V&A, 1977 (102); Shipley Art Gallery, Gateshead (alongside Northern Potters Association exhibition), 19 August – 10 October 1978.

LIT: *Handlist*, 1971 (41).

MW DOC: General Catalogue: '1951 ... 226 LEACH. (B) Large Pot, light blue grey, sgraffito decoration 18.0.0'.

73

73

74. **Large Bowl** c. 1951

Cream glaze within speckled with iron from the clay body, red rust around the rim, thick band of blue without.

H 4¾ in (12 cm); D 12¼ in (31 cm)

Marks: 'BL' and St Ives monogram (impressed)

See No.73.

PROV: Probably Leach Pottery, 1951 (£7); presented, January 1959 (935/75).

LIT: *Handlist*, 1971 (27).

MW DOC: General Catalogue: '1951 ... 228 LEACH. B. Large bowl, blue, grey & cream glaze 7.0.0'.

75. **Pot** c. 1951

Cream glaze under iron-red glaze to the upper three-fifths, the whole speckled with iron from the clay body, brushed iron-oxide decoration on top.

H 10⅜ in (26.2 cm); D 10⅛ in (25.6 cm)

Marks: 'BL' and St Ives monogram (impressed)

This pot and No.76 were the first two gifts of pottery from Milner-White to York City Art Gallery and the first examples of twentieth-century studio ceramics to enter the collection. They were purchased by the Dean especially for presentation. Although there are no relevant invoices or receipts in the Milner-White documentation, the entries in the Gallery's accessions register indicate that the two pots were bought direct from the Leach Pottery (for £15 and £2 respectively). Two similarly shaped pots also of 1951 are in the Victoria and Albert Museum (C.136-1952 and C.137-1952).

PROV: Leach Pottery, 1951 (£15); presented, November 1951 (592a).

LIT: *Handlist*, 1971 (37).

MW DOC: General Catalogue: '1951 ... 231 LEACH B. Large pot – brown & grey 15.0.0 ... These two [Milner-White's nos 231 and 232, Nos 75 and 76 in this Catalogue] were bought for York City Art Gallery and Given to it 1951'.

74

75

76. Plate c. 1951

Speckled cream ground with iron-red rim
and brushed decoration of a willow tree in
blue and brown.

H $1\frac{3}{8}$ in (3.6 cm); D 9 in (22.9 cm)

Mark: St Ives monogram (impressed)

Leach Pottery. This plate was bought by
Milner-White especially for York City Art
Gallery, together with No.75 (q.v.). Leach
owned a Japanese stoneware dish made at
Seto in the eighteenth or nineteenth century
and decorated with a willow-tree pattern in
brown and blue. He described it thus:
'Another country dish (probably painted by
a child). The bend of the willow trunk
painted with a single attenuating stroke of
the brush in iron brown, set against the
rhythmic touches of the drooping leaf in
pale-grey blues, provides at once the objective image of a popular subject and the subjective requirements of pure decoration.'[1]

PROV: Leach Pottery, 1951 (£2); presented,
November 1951 (592b).

LIT: *Handlist*, 1971 (25).

MW DOC: General Catalogue: '1951 ... 232 LEACH
B. Plate, Willow drawing 2.0.0 These two
[Milner-White's nos 231 and 232, Nos 75 and 76
in this Catalogue] were bought for York City Art
Gallery and given to it 1951'.

1. Leach (*Challenge*), 1976, p.110, ill. p.111.

76

77

77

77. Pot c.1951

Blue glaze with iron-red patches.

H 5¼ in (13.3 cm); D 5¼ in (13.4 cm)

Marks: 'BL', St Ives monogram and 'ENG-LAND' (impressed)

This pot is very close stylistically to Nos 75 and 76, two pieces in a group presumably purchased by Milner-White from the Leach Pottery, St Ives, in 1951. No.77 is not recorded in the Dean's MS catalogue but, in the absence of further information, may be assumed also to have been acquired from St Ives in 1951.

PROV: Probably Leach Pottery, 1951; presented, 1958 and received on Milner-White's death, 1963 (1049/25).

LIT: *Handlist*, 1971 (29).

78

78. Vase 1952 or before

Impressed, incised and painted design, with transparent, dark grey and iron glazes.

H 16¼ in (41.1 cm); D 6¼ in (15.9 cm)

Marks: St Ives monogram and presumably 'BE' (impressed), the latter nearly obliterated by glaze.

The date of this pot is uncertain: Rose dates it to 1952 but the catalogue of the Arts Council exhibition of 1961 assigns it to 1945. The pot's provenance is equally unclear. When reproduced by Rose in 1955 it was with Bendicks (Mayfair) Ltd. Milner-White, may have purchased it from Bendicks at about that time. On the other hand, it was one of three pots which he transferred to the Gallery in December 1959, to replace damaged and stolen items, and it might have been specially purchased then.[1]

The form of this pot recurs in Leach's work but the decoration is unusual. It derives from a type of T'zŭ Chou Sung ware, a particular example of which he illustrated and described in *The Potter's Challenge*: 'The dotted background of circles has been done with a section of bamboo – almost certainly the wrong end of a Chinese brush. The pattern, as with many which reiterate circular forms, is within a wave movement ...'.[2]

PROV: With Bendicks (Mayfair) Ltd, 1955; ...; received December 1959 (953/3).

EXH: Arts Council, 1961 (72).

LIT: Rose, 1955, pl.A (frontispiece) in colour; *Handlist*, 1971 (50).

1. See No.5, n.1.
2. Leach (*Challenge*), 1976, p.82, ill. p.83.

79. Fruit Bowl exh. 1952 (colour VI)

Painted decoration of a willow catkin branch in brown and blue glazes on a speckled cream (?)slip ground within, iron-rich brown glaze over cream (?)slip without and around rim.

H 4½ in (11.3 cm); D 12 in (30.7 cm)

Marks: BL and St Ives monograms (painted and impressed respectively)

This bowl exhibits one of the forms developed as part of the Leach Pottery's range of Standard Ware. It has been decorated by Leach himself and shows the delicate lyricism with which he could use a brush. It has

80

been hitherto dated c.1931, but the grounds for this are unknown. A similar bowl, dating from 1949, decorated with a fritillary design (again by Leach himself) is in the Victoria and Albert Museum (C.171-1950).

PROV: Beaux Arts Gallery, 1952 (£5); presented, January 1959 (935/76).

EXH: Beaux Arts Gallery, 1952; Sheffield, 1976 (3).

LIT: *Handlist*, 1971 (33).

MW DOC: General Catalogue: '1952 (Beaux Art[sic] Gally Leach & Hamada) 233 LEACH (B) Bowl – Willow Catskin brushwork design in brown & blue. Bowl, cream within: red-brown chocolate without 5.0-0'; album II: private view card.

80. Dish exh. 1952

Celadon glaze with floral six-dot decoration in green and tomato-red glazes.

H 2 in (5 cm); D 11¼ in (28.7 cm)

Marks: BL and St Ives monograms (painted and impressed respectively).

PROV: Beaux Arts Gallery, 1952 (£4); presented, May 1959 (935/93)

EXH: Beaux Arts Gallery, 1952.

LIT: *Handlist*, 1971 (35).

MW DOC: General Catalogue: '1952 (Beaux Art[sic] Gally, Leach & Hamada) ... 234 LEACH (B) Plate, cream, with dark cream rim. [illegible word] the blossom in tomato-red petals Still at Deanery/ 4.0-0' [see also No.81]; album II: private view card.

81

81. Plate exh. 1952

Pale celadon glazed ground, brown-green
around rim, mountain motif in dark green
glaze, tree and building motifs in red glaze.

H $1\frac{1}{4}$ in (3.3 cm); D $6\frac{1}{2}$ in (16.4 cm)

Mark: St Ives monogram (impressed)

Leach Pottery. The design on this plate
recurs frequently in Leach's work. See also
No.63.

PROV: Beaux Arts Gallery, 1952($3); presented,
January 1959 (935/8).

EXH: Beaux Arts Gallery, 1952.

LIT: Handlist, 1971 (34).

MW DOC: General Catalogue: '1952 (Beaux
Art[sic] Gally Leach & Hamada) ... 235 LEACH.
Small Plate, same colour, brushwork design in
dark green, & in the same glaze (These [Milner-
White's nos 234 and 235, Nos 80 and 81 in this
Catalogue] are the first two instances of the use
of this glaze in pottery) 3.0-0'; album II: private
view card.

82. Tall Jar exh. 1956

Lustrous bronze glaze breaking to red, wax-
resist wavy decoration revealing cream slip.

H $13\frac{1}{2}$ in (34.4 cm); D $8\frac{1}{8}$ in (20.6 cm)

Mark(s): Obliterated by glaze (?impressed)

According to Milner-White, this jar was
inspired by Hamada No.26, which Leach
probably saw in 1951 when he visited the
Deanery in York with Muriel Rose.

PROV: Liberty, 1956($18); presented, January
1959 (935/69).

EXH: Liberty, 1956.

82

83

84

LIT: Ingamells (*Preview*), 1959, p.439; Ingamells (*Museums Journal*), 1959, p.124; *Handlist*, 1971 (49).

MW DOC: General Catalogue: '1956 Leach Exhibition at Liberty's, Regent Street ... 243 3 Tall Jar, inspired by my Hamada (68) & a good match to it: iron red-brown glaze over cream; low neck. Unsigned.[£]18'.

83. Vase exh. 1956

Body flattened into four sides with two small handles; iron and iron-speckled blue glazes.

H 11$\frac{3}{8}$ in (29 cm); D 9$\frac{1}{4}$ in (23.6 cm)

Marks: 'BL' and St Ives monogram partly covered by glaze (impressed)

PROV: Liberty, 1956(£18); presented, January 1959 (935/72).

EXH: Liberty, 1956; Sheffield, 1976 (1); V&A 1977 (122).

LIT: *Handlist*, 1971 (30); Hogben, 1978, p.182, pl.86.

MW DOC: General Catalogue: '1956 Leach Exhibition at Liberty's, Regent Street ... 242 1. Two handled globular pot with four flattened sides; blue-grey glaze with chocolate brown iron spots: narrow neck & collar of the same brown Height 11$\frac{1}{2}$" Sign & B.L on base [£]18.'

84. Bowl exh. 1956

Cream glaze with brush decoration of a leaping toad in blue and brown within, dark bronze glaze without.

H 1$\frac{7}{8}$ in (4.8 cm); D 4$\frac{7}{8}$ in (11.8 cm)

Mark: St Ives (impressed)

Leach Pottery. The motif of the leaping toad is identical to the uppermost of the 'Young frogs' in a drawing of spring 1935 reproduced in *Beyond East and West*.[1]

PROV: Liberty, 1956(£1); presented, 1958, and received on Milner-White's death, 1963 (1049/23).

EXH: Liberty, 1956.

LIT: *Handlist*, 1971 (28).

MW DOC: General Catalogue: '1956 Leach Exhibition at Liberty's, Regent Street ... 244 [in a group of five, 244 to 248] Five small bowls red brown outside cream within, each with a typical Leach animal or plant design Leaping Toad [etc.] Bought for wedding presents! [£1]'.

1. Leach, 1978, fig.9, p.158.

85. Pot exh. 1956

Iron slip with design of mountains, trees, suns, birds, animals and figure to the upper three-quarters.

H 12 in (30.3 cm); D 10½ in (26.7 cm)

Marks: 'BL' and St Ives monogram (impressed)

The process of decorating this pot appears to have been elaborate. The upper three-quarters of the pot were 'dipped into a heavy iron bearing dark slip, and much of its area was cut away in sgraffito. Some of the pattern was incised through this slip into its buff coloured body, and some of the bare areas were painted in brush stroke dark slip.'[1] The contrast between light on dark and dark on light makes a pleasing and well-balanced effect. The motifs on this pot recur regularly throughout Leach's work.

PROV: Liberty, 1956(£25); lent, 1958, and received outright on Milner-White's death, 1963 (1050/7).

EXH: Liberty, 1956; Sheffield, 1976 (6).

LIT: Handlist, 1971 (43).

MW DOC: General Catalogue: '1956 Leach Exhibition at Liberty's, Regent Street … 242 2 Globular Pot with low neck, cream underglaze, brick brown overglaze, ? mountains & hills? design with sun, birds, bears & hares, chinese? antelope and peasant. i ft hight.[sic] Sign & B.L. [£]25'.

1. Letter from Janet Leach, 22 June 1990.

85

85

David Andrew Leach

British born 1911

David Leach was born in Tokyo, the eldest son of Bernard Leach. Having decided not to go to university, he learnt to pot from his father at St Ives, with whom he worked closely for over twenty-five years. From 1934 to 1936, he improved his knowledge of the technical aspects of making pottery on the pottery managers' course at the North Staffordshire Technical College, Stoke-on-Trent. The knowledge gained here was of crucial importance to the survival of the Leach pottery, which was organized on philosophical ideas with very little technical grounding. On his return he was to take charge of the running of the St Ives pottery when his father was away in Japan. After the war, in 1946, father and son formed a partnership which was to last ten years. Many improvements were implemented under David Leach's persuasion, such as the introduction of machinery, and the development of a new stoneware body. His modernizations enabled the Standard Ware range to succeed. In 1956 he set up his own workshop, Lowerdown Pottery near Bovey Tracey, South Devon. This was originally organized on similar lines to St Ives – a small team making domestic ware with time for individual work. His output gradually moved away from repetitive domestic ware, however, to individual pots sold in one-man or joint shows. He made slipware and, from 1961, stoneware and porcelain also. His style is similar to that of his father. Since the late 1970s he has conducted three- or four-week lecture-demonstrations on the Continent, including Scandinavia, and in the USA and Canada. An outstanding thrower, he works alone today. In 1987 he was awarded the OBE.

86

86

86. Fruit Dish c.1951

Grey body; thick cream glaze breaking to brown where the glaze is thinnest, delicate incised linear decoration around rim.

H $2\frac{3}{8}$ in (6.1 cm); D $10\frac{3}{8}$ in (26.4 cm)

Marks: DL and St Ives monograms (impressed)

PROV: Probably Leach Pottery; purchased, 1951 (£4); presented, 1958, and received on Milner-White's death, 1963 (1049/26).

MW DOC: General Catalogue: '1951 ... 230 DAVID LEACH – Fruit dish, cream & brown 4.0.0/ For Table use 230 ditto [i.e. not museum pieces], but v. pleasant'.

Emile Lenoble
French 1876-1939

One of the greatest French potters of the twentieth century, Emile Lenoble spent seven years in industry before moving to Choisy-le-Roi in 1903 to work in the studio of his father-in-law, Ernest Chaplet. There he experimented with stoneware. Throughout his working life he was to be concerned primarily with perfecting various ranges of coloured slips, called in French *engobe*, and with stylized abstract *sgraffito* decoration. His vases and bowls have a richness of style typical of the best French applied arts between the wars.

Originally interested in Japanese folk ceramics, Lenoble later became fascinated with Chinese pottery of the T'ang and Sung dynasties: the T'zŭ Chou wares of the latter dynasty were especially important for him. The colour ranges of these early Chinese pieces are restricted to white, brown and black, and Lenoble also restricted himself throughout his working life to a fairly narrow range of colours – black, green, grey, various shades of brown, blue (including a vivid turquoise first developed by his grandfather) and rose.

Having perfected his technique by 1913, Lenoble spent the First World War years in a German prison camp. After the war he returned to Choisy-le-Roi, where he continued to refine his glazes and decoration. During the 1920s his decoration became more geometric.

87

87. Pot 1937 or before

Very rough pale body; brown, yellow and black mottled glazes.

H 4⅛ in (10.4 cm); D 5⅛ in (13 cm)

Mark: EL monogram (impressed)

This pot is listed in the accessions register as by an unidentified potter. However, the mark has recently been identified as that of Emile Lenoble by Dorris U. Kuyken-Schneider, Keeper at the Department of Decorative Arts and Design, Boymans-van Beuningen Museum, Rotterdam.[1] This enables the pot to be linked with a fair degree of certainty to an entry in Milner-White's MS catalogue. For examples of the same impressed mark see two Lenoble bowls at the Victoria and Albert Museum (C.184-1931 and C.185-1931), both dating from c.1931.

PROV: Brygos Gallery, 1938 (£20); presented, 1958, and received on Milner-White's death, 1963 (1049/54).

EXH: Brygos Gallery, 1938 (111).

MW DOC: General Catalogue: '1938 … LENOBLE. Pot, resist decn. 20.0.0/Continental Pieces Date uncertain but at least a year before my purchase'; invoice: Brygos Gallery, undated, receipted 2 June 1938, '4 pieces of French ceramics … 111 20.0.0'; album II: exhibition catalogue.

1. Letter in Gallery files, 1 June 1988.

87

Martin Brothers
British

The Martin brothers were: Robert Wallace Martin (1843-1924), Charles Douglas Martin (1846-1910), Walter Frazer Martin (1857-1912) and Edwin Bruce Martin (1860-1915). Working as a team, they produced highly distinctive saltglazed stoneware, known as Martinware. Robert Wallace (known as Wallace) was the founder, leading figure and sculptor of the group. Walter was the technician and made all the larger vases, Edwin made many of the very small Martinware vases, excelling at surface design. Charles initially helped with decoration but soon took over administration of the business. The firm of R. W. Martin had been founded in 1873 in Fulham. In 1877 it moved to Southall, about a mile east of Southall Green, where the brothers developed the production and decoration of their distinctive ware. They opened a showroom at 16 Brownlow Street, Holborn, in 1879.

Cosmo Monkhouse's article in the *Magazine of Art* of 1882 referred to the corporate nature of the brothers' pottery and was probably the spur to the use of a mark acknowledging the contribution of them all;[1] hitherto R. W. Martin's name

had been used in isolation without reference to the part his brothers played. The marks 'Martin Brothers London and Southall' and 'R. W. Martin & Bros London & Southall' were both used from 1882 until 1914 when the London (i.e. Brownlow Street) showroom closed. The dates on the pots refer to when they were decorated and not when they were fired, which was in many cases much later. All the marks on the bases of the pots in the collection were incised by Edwin, who had a talent for incised work and executed most of this type of decoration.

In 1910 a serious fire destroyed much of the brothers' work at their Brownlow Street shop. Charles Martin died in the same year. In 1912 Walter died suddenly of a cerebral haemorrhage taking with him the technical knowledge of the wares. The remaining two brothers struggled on, providing less important pieces, but closed the shop in May 1914. Edwin died in 1915 bringing the activities of the firm to a close. Robert Wallace lived on until 1923. During their lifetime they were never financially successful. Today, however, they are considered amongst the first studio potters of

1. Cosmo Monkhouse, 'Some original Ceramists', *Magazine of Art*, v, 1882, pp. 443-8.

the modern English school and their work is recognized as an inspired ceramic venture, Wallace's owls and grimacing-face mugs being particularly well-known.

Milner-White, who described his Martinware collection as 'a few typical: none important', bought eight of his nine pieces (if not all nine) together, probably from Walker's Galleries. All had come from the dispersal of the collection of the late Frank Knight of Brixton Hill in 1942. Knight worked for Frank Nettlefold, who was one of the Martins' earliest and most important patrons. A large part of the Frank Knight and

Mrs H. M. Knight's collection was given and bequeathed to Southall Borough Council between 1943 and 1953.

Information on the Martins has largely been drawn from Malcolm Haslam's *The Martin Brothers: Potters*, Richard Dennis, 1978, and the Sidney Greenslade MS papers held in the local history section of Ealing Central Library (Greenslade Papers 551-641).

The Gallery has ten further pieces of Martinware, which were presented by Stuart Syme Esq. in June 1958 (926/1958a-j).

88. Bowl 1889

Pale body; elaborate incised floral pattern in an Italian Renaissance style with blue, cream, orange and brown salt-glazes; small hole through side of base for hanging.

H 2⅛ in (5.4 cm); D 8⅛ in (20.7 cm)

Mark: '12-1889 R. W. Martin & Brothers London & Southall'

From 1885 onwards there were two styles of decoration which the Martins used predominantly – floral designs in a Japanese manner and Renaissance ornament. This bowl is in the Italian Renaissance style which had become popular in the 1880s. The style was developed at the Martins' factory whilst H. F. Fawcett was there in the early 1880s. He had briefly decorated for the William de Morgan studio. He drew competently and passed his skills on to Edwin Martin and Walter Edward Willy, who had worked for the Martins since around 1873. During the 1880s Walter Martin greatly expanded the range of colours used, developing different shades of blue, green, yellow and brown, which gave the brothers' stoneware a richness to meet the taste for colourful painted wares. The 1880s were the height of success for the brothers.

PROV: Frank Knight; Walker's Galleries; purchased, 1942 (2gns); presented, January 1959 (935/20).

EXH: Walker's Galleries, 1942 (?25, 'Plaque. Dark brown and cream. Diameter 11 inches £2 2s. od.').

MW DOC: General Catalogue: '1942 Purchase of MARTIN Ware at the dispersal of the Collection of the late Frank Knight ... 210 Plate. Black with elaborate formal design in blue, brown & cream – signed 12-1889 R. W. Martin & Brothers London & Southall Decoratn bad but typical 2.2.o.'; album II: exhibition catalogue and article, *The Times*, 19 April 1958.

88

89. Vase 1896

Pale body; incised and painted dragons on an orange-brown ground, sea creatures incised around the neck, salt-glazed.

H 15 in (38 cm); D 8⅝ in (22.1 cm)

Mark: '11-1896 R. W. Martin & Bros. London & Southall' (incised)

The decoration on this pot combines Japanese and Renaissance influences, the main sources of inspiration for the Martins. The dragons are partly derived from a decorative motif found in Renaissance ornament but are also clearly Oriental in style.

PROV: Frank Knight; Walker's Galleries; purchased, 1942 (6gns); presented, 1958, and received on Milner-White's death, 1963 (1049/37).

90

EXH: Walker's Galleries, 1942 (2, 'A Large Pot.
Brown background, incised with blue and brown
dragons. Height 21 inches £6 6s. od.', or possibly
3, 'Pot, similar to above £6 6s. od.').

MW DOC: General Catalogue: '1942 Purchase of
MARTIN Ware at the dispersal of the Collection of
the late Frank Knight 205. Pot, brown, dec. with
dragons Height 21 inches. Signed 11-1896
R.W. Martin & Bros. London & Southall. Coarse &
poor shape 6.6.0'; album II: exhibition catalogue
and article, The Times, 19 April 1958.

90. Small flattened Pot 1903

Pale body; sea-urchin shape; incised lines
through a dark green glaze filled with a
cream glaze, salt-glazed.

H 1½ in (4 cm); D 4¾ in (12 cm)

Mark: '5-1903 Martin Bros. London and
Southall' (incised and red clay rubbed in)

Around 1900 the Martins decided to modify
their style to keep abreast of changes in taste
and to try to improve their flagging sales. In
that year they visited the Paris *Exposition
Universelle* in search of inspiration, and found
the stylized organic forms popularized in
Continental Art Nouveau – with which
Edwin had been experimenting quite independently since the end of the 1890s. During the next ten years, the principal feature
of their work became the use of modelled
surfaces, texturings and ribbings, often
based on natural forms. These new pieces
(considered by many to be the finest of their
career) were largely the achievements of
Walter and Edwin. Walter was a fine
thrower and mixer of an extraordinary
range of colours for salt-glaze. Edwin,
without an art school training and almost a
generation younger than Wallace, was the
most receptive of the brothers to new ideas.
His talents were ideally suited to salt-
glazing, the advantage of which is that it

89

89

allows carved and incised decoration to retain a clearer definition than when liquid glazes are used.

From 1899 the brothers had been firing only once a year. The success of the firing was therefore even more critical than in the case of the previous biannual firings. Firings were always problematic and that of September 1903, which presumably included this pot, was no exception.

PROV: Unknown; presented, 1958, and received on Milner-White's death, 1963 (1049/29).

91. Four-sided Vase 1904

Pale body; cream salt-glaze ground with incised decoration of flowers and leaves in blue and olive-green salt-glaze.

H 4⅛ in (10.5 cm); D 1¾ in (4.5 cm)

Mark: '11-1904 Martin Bros London & Southall' (incised)

The mid-1880s saw the introduction by the Martins of decoration in the form of birds, hedgerow flowers, reeds and grasses, presumably studied along the banks of the canal at Southall. This decoration was a logical development from the imitation of asymmetrical Japanese motifs, but was also in sympathy with the trend towards naturalism resulting from the teachings of John Ruskin. Direct copying from nature was complemented by the extensive use of late-eighteenth-century and early-nineteenth-century prints which were collected for the studio at Southall by Charles. To work in the naturalistic style the Martins needed a skill in pictorial as opposed to geometric design which they had learnt at Lambeth. H. F. Fawcett provided this training.

The firing of 1904, in November, was not a success – perhaps partly because the year was one of friction between the brothers – and this vase shows signs of being badly fired. Edwin produced very little work in protest against Wallace and he may have made this vase at the last moment for firing: the scale and decoration suggest his hand.

PROV: Frank Knight; (?)Walker's Galleries; purchased, 1942 (7s. 6d.); presented, January 1959 (935/12).

EXH: (?)Walker's Galleries, 1942 (not in catalogue).

MW DOC: General Catalogue: '1942 Purchase of MARTIN Ware at the dispersal of the Collection of the late Frank Knight ... 214 Small jar, Cream with blue floral decn 4-1909 Martin Bros. London & Southall 7.6'.

92. Square Jug 1906

Moulded pale body; matt black salt-glaze with wavy incisions.

H 9 in (23 cm); D 3 in (7.6 cm)

Mark: '7-1906 Martin Bros London & Southall' (incised)

This jug was made while the Martins' brother James was visiting from Australia and when relations between the brothers were better than they had been for some time. The kiln was fired on 17 August before Walter's wedding in September, after which relations deteriorated again. A similar jug is in Southall Library (320).

PROV: Frank Knight; Walker's Galleries; purchased, 1942 (£1 10s.); presented; January 1959 (935/2).

EXH: Walker's Galleries, 1942 (47).

MW DOC: General Catalogue: '1942 Purchase of MARTIN Ware at the dispersal of the Collection of the late Frank Knight ... 208 Jug. square shaped, with handle. Bronze with wavy incisions Height 9 inches. Signed 7-1906 Martin Bros. London & Southall. 1.10.0'; album II: exhibition catalogue and article, *The Times*, 19 April 1958.

93. Vase 1907

Pale body; gourd-shaped; gouged bands filled with incised lines and impressed pomegranate-seed decoration at regular intervals; pale pink-brown ground with green glaze rubbed into decoration, brown glaze around lip, salt-glazed.

H 9¼ in (23.5 cm); D 7⅞ in (20 cm)

Mark: '6-1907 Martin Bros. London and Southall' (incised)

This pot in its fruit-like form and surface decoration may be compared with the productions of Continental Art Nouveau. The decoration was finished in June 1907, but there was no firing in that year. The next firing was to be in 1908 and was described as a bad one. The surface of this pot certainly shows many burst air bubbles and other blemishes and the bottom of the pot clearly stuck to the kiln shelf. The Martins always had trouble with their firings. Even with a successful firing they expected a third of the

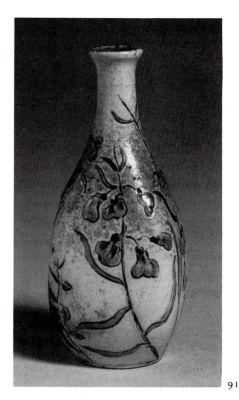

91

92

94

95

95

93

contents of a kiln to be lost, another third to be saleable and only the last third to be perfectly fired.

PROV: Frank Knight; Walker's Galleries; purchased, 1942(2gns); presented, 1958, and received on Milner-White's death, 1963 (1049/28).

EXH: Walker's Galleries, 1942 (40).

MW DOC: General Catalogue: '1942 Purchase of MARTIN Ware at the dispersal of the Collection of the late Frank Knight ... 207 Globular Pot. Brown-green, pomegranate markings. Signed 8-1907 Martin Bros. London & Southall 2.2 0'; album II: exhibition catalogue and article, The Times, 19 April 1958.

94. Bowl 1908

Pale body; four-sided; raised decoration of four fish against a roughly lined background and a toothed lip; brown, blue and green glazes.

H 3¼ in (8.2 cm); D 5¾ in (14.7 cm)

Mark: '1-1908 Martin Bros. London and Southall' (incised)

Aquatic-life forms first made an appearance in the Martins' work in the mid-1880s. They were presumably studied from the waters of the Southall Canal. Further humorous motifs of extraordinary fishes and birds soon developed. It was Edwin who had a talent for raised decoration, as seen here. This pot was presumably fired in May 1908, a firing which was not generally considered a success. The years 1908 to 1911 were to be a slack time at the pottery; firings, when they happened at all, were unsuccessful.

PROV: Frank Knight; (?)Walker's Galleries; purchased, 1942(£1); presented, January 1959 (935/10).

EXH: (?)Walker's Galleries, 1942 (not in catalogue).

MW DOC: General Catalogue: '1942 Purchase of MARTIN Ware at the dispersal of the Collection of the late Frank Knight ... 212 Bowl, foursided, brown & green, raised decn of fishes, serrated lip, blue 1-1908 Martin Bros. London & Southall 1.0.0'; album II: exhibition catalogue and article, The Times, 19 April 1958.

95. Bowl 1911

Pale body; mottled brown and green salt-glaze punctuated by unglazed cream raised ribbings on the exterior; blue and dark blue salt-glaze over smaller incised ribbings and contours on the interior.

H 2½ in (6.5 cm); D 5¾ in (14.7 cm)

Mark: '8-1911 Martin Bros London & Southall' (incised)

The ribbed decoration derived from Continental Art Nouveau is still being applied here, although its principal period of use was 1900 to 1910. On 16 November 1911 the kiln was fired, as so often, unsuccessfully: 'a horrid dryness – or a still more horrible "glazey" apperance' was noted – 'dull, dirty & uninteresting – in the other hand, unsympathetic and "varnishy"'.[1]

PROV: Frank Knight; (?)Walker's Galleries; purchased, 1942(1gn); presented, January 1959 (935/13).

EXH: (?)Walker's Galleries (not in catalogue).

MW DOC: General Catalogue: '1942 Purchase of MARTIN Ware at the dispersal of the Collection of the late Frank Knight ... 213 Bowl. Exterior, brown with cream rib Interior, blue, incised pattern decn. 8-1911 Martin Bros. London & Southall 1.1.0'; album II: exhibition catalogue and article, *The Times*, 19 April 1958.

1. Greenslade diary, 2 December 1911.

96. Vase 1911

Pale body; hand-built, hexagonally segmented; inlaid apple-blossom motifs in cream against a black salt-glazed ground.

H 10½ in (26.7 cm); D 6¼ in (16 cm)

Mark: '6-1911 Martin Bros. London and Southall' (incised)

The asymmetrical floral decoration on this jar is Japanese in manner but there is an element of originality to it which suggests direct observation. The workmanship is superb, the quality of the inlay being particularly noteworthy. This pot was presumably fired in the 16 November 1911 firing, which was not, overall, a success.

PROV: Frank Knight; Walker's Galleries; purchased, 1942(3gns); presented, January 1959 (935/73).

EXH: Walker's Galleries, 1942 (43).

MW DOC: General Catalogue: '1942 Purchase of MARTIN Ware at the dispersal of the Collection of the late Frank Knight ... 206 Black Vase dec. Apple Blossom in Cream Height 10½ inches. Signed 6-1911 Martin Bros London & Southall. 3.3-0'; album II: exhibition catalogue and article, *The Times*, 19 April 1958.

96

William Staite Murray
British 1881 - 1962

William Staite Murray, one of the most original artists of the 1920s and 1930s, was born in Deptford of Scottish parents. From an early age he showed an aptitude for painting. His father, however, refused to allow him to follow this inclination and in 1895 sent him, aged seventeen, to Holland to learn the trade of a bulb and seed merchant. Having returned to England around 1902, he married Kathleen Medhurst in 1905. From about 1909 to 1912 he attended evening classes in pottery at Camberwell School of Art. After the First World War he took up pottery professionally, in large measure stimulated by the early Chinese ceramics which had been discovered at the turn of the century. Now in his late thirties he began his life's work of raising pottery to the level at which it would be accepted on equal terms with painting and sculpture. This objective was in contrast to that of the other great potter of the time, Bernard Leach, whose aim became that of mass-producing functional pottery which in its own, different way would enhance the status of the craftsman potter. The early years of Murray's potting life were spent in experimentation, getting to know intimately the materials with which he was working. His first workshop was in the basement of a house at Yeoman's Row in London. There he made pots from earthenware. After the war, in 1919, he set up his own pottery at Rotherhithe with the intention of making stoneware in emulation of Chinese ceramics from the Sung dynasty. In 1924 he moved to Wickham Road, Brockley (near Lewisham), where he set up an oil-fired kiln; this was operational certainly by June of that year, when he announced his new 'furnace' in an advertisement in the *Daily Express*, and he subsequently patented improvements to it. In 1925 he became pottery instructor at the Royal College of Art and soon afterwards became head of the department. In 1929 he moved to Bray in Berkshire. In 1939 he left England for Rhodesia (now Zimbabwe) for a three-month visit. In fact he remained there for the rest of his life, never to make another pot. On 7 February 1962 he died of cancer in Umtali.

Milner-White and Staite Murray

Milner-White was Murray's greatest patron. He bought more and better pots by Murray than any other collector (see No.112). Right from the beginning, when he purchased his first pot by him in 1925 (No.97), the Dean recognized in Murray a highly original artist and backed him throughout his potting life, giving considerable moral support, not to mention financial support by paying the enormous prices he charged for his most outstanding creations. Milner-White had a special relationship with Murray, and made perceptive comments on his development. He kept a notebook specially devoted to entries on thirty-six of his Murray pots, which he called his 'Fitzwilliam Book', categorizing the pots for possible presentation to the Fitzwilliam Museum in Cambridge. The comments found here, often provide useful information on the pots unavailable elsewhere. Equally useful is an album of newspaper cuttings about his exhibitions (referred to in this catalogue as 'Murray's album'), which the potter gave to Milner-White.

97. Pot 1923 (colour III)

Coarse white body with iron specks; flambé glaze, blue within and green-orange at rim, heat blisters and burst bubbles in glaze (incised code: 'L.D. [?]8').

H 6⅛ in (15.4 cm); D 6½ in (16.5 cm)

Mark: 'W.S.Murray London 1923' (incised)

This is the second pot, and the first by Murray, which Milner-White purchased. It marks the beginning of a special relationship between the potter and the Dean. It was made early in Murray's career when he was working in the vein of the early experimenters such as W.B.Dalton (who was principal of Camberwell when Murray took evening classes there). These potters were influenced by early Chinese pottery, the forms and more particularly the glazes of which they were striving to recreate; a study of the copper-red glazes had been published in the *Transactions of the Oriental Ceramic Society*, 1921-2, a copy of which Murray owned. This pot, which bears Murray's incised signature and date 1923, belongs to his first group of independent stoneware produced in the early 1920s and is the only pot in the collection dating from before the introduction of the pentagon stamp in 1924. It was made in a gas-fired kiln at Rotherhithe, where Murray's brothers – partners in the Murray Engineering & Foundry Co. – gave him workshop space and power. The distinctive shape of the neck is to be found on ware made by Carter's of Poole, which Murray undoubtedly knew (he had worked with Cuthbert Frazer Hamilton, who in turn knew Roger Fry, who had worked at Carter's from 1914 to 1915). A similarly shaped pot, also dated 1923, is at the Crafts Study Centre, Bath (P.75.27).

PROV: Paterson's, 1925(10gns); presented, January 1959 (935/62).

97

98

General Catalogue 4. No. under foot 3. Date 1924. Bowl ''Hare's Fur'', light-brown and green-gold. Signed. A fine example of Murray equalling – yet in a novel colour – the work of Sung potters, (whence his inspiration came,) both in shape and glaze.'; indexed notebook: 'MURRAY. 3 BOWL. B – red-brown G. Hare's-Fur (red-brown speckled with green-gold) Lip – red-brown H 2¾″ × W. 6″ date 1924 or 5. Mark Ṁ Purchased 1926 £10.10. (Leicester Gallery) Jason'; invoice: Ernest Brown & Phillips, Leicester Galleries, 28 January 1926, receipted 29 January 1926, '''Bowl'' – Hares fur markings W.S.Murray £10.10.'

99. Jar 1924-5

Pale body with tiny flecks of iron, toasted orange; bronze glaze flushing to red and green (incised code: 'R').

H 10⅝ in (27 cm); D 5⅝ in (14.9 cm)

Mark: Murray's pentagon (impressed)

Like No.98, this pot provides an early example of the pentagon stamp, which Murray started to use in 1924. It was made in conscious emulation of the Oriental traditions which he admired so much and was oil-fired at Wickham Road.

PROV: Leicester Galleries, 1926(£21); presented, 1958, and received on Milner-White's death, 1963 (1049/31).

EXH: Leicester Galleries, 1926.

LIT: Handlist, 1971 (71).

MW DOC: General Catalogue: '1926 … 5 MURRAY Pot. Red flushed with green (Date 1924 or 5.); indexed notebook: MURRAY 4. POT B – red-brown G.Light crimson with strong passages of dark green. (mouth = blue green inter[10]r = greenish gray H. 10¾″ × W. 6″ (greatest) Date 1924 or 5. Mark Ṁ Purchased 1926 £21. (Leicester Gallery) Orion'; invoice: Ernest Brown & Phillips, Leicester Galleries, 12 June 1926, receipted 24 June 1926, 'Scarlet blue & green stoneware pot. W.S.Murray £21 ..'

100. Tea-Bowl 1925

Grey body, with tiny iron specks, toasted orange; luminous, smooth red glaze marred by a few burst bubbles (painted code: '6').

H 2½ in (5.9 cm); D 4⅛ in (10.4 cm)

Mark: Murray's pentagon (impressed)

There were severe technical problems to be overcome before any studio potter could successfully imitate the glaze effects of the Sung dynasty. Murray and others attempting to do this were working in the dark. In

EXH: Probably, Houldsworth Hall, Manchester, annual exhibition of the Red Rose Guild, 1923;[1] Paterson's, 1925; Middlesbrough, 1984.

LIT: Handlist, 1971 (78); Webber, 1975, ill. p.27 in colour; Haslam (Murray), 1984, pl.IV in colour.

MW DOC: General Catalogue: '1925 … 2. MURRAY. Pot. Red and Gold. (Date 1923) Fitzwilliam Book: '1. Class III Number in General Catalogue ..2 Number under the foot .. 1 Date 1923. POT, red and gold, white biscuit, signed ''W.S.Murray London 1923'' Lip & interior, dark green and gold. An early example of M.'s work.'; indexed notebook; 'MURRAY 1 POT. Biscuit – white   Glaze – gold-red, spotted with iron. (Interior) sage-green Height – 6″ Width (greatest) 6½″ Date 1923 Mark W.S.Murray, London. Purchased, 1925, £10-10-0.'; notes: 'c.1925 … A stranger, seeing my interest, said that in another gallery in Bond St was an exhibition of pots by an artist-craftsman of whom he thought even more highly [than of Wells]. I went there … picking up … Murray.'

1. It is almost certainly one of the pots visible in a photograph of Murray's stall at the exhibition, now at the Crafts Study Centre, Bath (reproduced Haslam (Murray), 1984, p.19).

98. Bowl c.1924-5

Pale body with tiny iron specks, toasted orange; 'hare's fur' glaze with impurity in middle (painted code: '6').

H 2¾ in (7.2 cm); D 6½ in (16.5 cm)

Mark: Murray's pentagon and '91' (impressed)

This pot, like No.99, exhibits an early example of the 'Ṁ' in a pentagon stamp, which Murray started to use in 1924. Made in emulation of early Chinese ceramics, it was oil-fired at Wickham Road.

PROV: Leicester Galleries, 1926(10gns); presented, January 1959 (935/51).

EXH: Leicester Galleries, 1926.

LIT: Handlist, 1971 (76).

MW DOC: General Catalogue: '1926 … 4. MURRAY. Bowl. Hare's Fur, brown & green-gold (Date 1924 or 5); Fitzwilliam Book: '3. Class II No. in

99

101

100

1921 Murray met Bernard Leach, the first person he knew with direct experience of Oriental methods and materials who was willing to share his knowledge with him. Through Leach, Murray met Shoji Hamada, which was of vital importance for Murray. Hamada showed him how to make foot-rings and how to hold a decorating brush in the Oriental way, and helped him with glaze recipes. In technical virtuosity Murray made enormous advances during the five years he worked at Rotherhithe, gaining sufficient competence to produce accomplished imitations of Sung wares by 1924. This pot was oil-fired at Wickham Road.

PROV: Given by Murray to Milner-White, 1926; presented, 1958, and received on Milner-White's death, 1963 (1049/30).

EXH: Probably Paterson's, 1925.

MW DOC: General Catalogue: '1925 ... 3 MURRAY. Tea-Bowl, red.'; Fitzwilliam Book: '2(a). Class III No. in General Catalogue 3 No. under foot 2 Date 1925 Tea-bowl, dark red Signed M in a Pentagon (henceforth the usual Murray signature) Simple & Pleasant, but not of the charm of – 2(b) ... General Catalogue 203'; indexed notebook: 'MURRAY. 2 BOWL (Small tea-) B – reddish-brown G. dark crimson H. 2½″ × W. 4″ Date 1925 Mark. Ṃ Given, [?] Jan? '26 by W.S.M.'

101. Jar: 'The Roundabout' exh. 1926

Pale body with small flecks of iron, toasted orange; grey ground with black and white inlaid decoration of five figures on a roundabout.

H 8⅜ in (21.3 cm); D 10⅜ in (26.5 cm)

Mark: Murray's pentagon (impressed)

Murray became increasingly interested in Oriental art and philosophy. He was one of the earliest British converts to Buddhism. Through Buddhism he believed that,

although each pot was in itself an inanimate object, nevertheless it was the manifestation of an animate consciousness and had within it the emotions and life-force which had created it. This was one reason he named his pots, although the names were also an expression of his belief that a pot was as much a work of art as a painting or sculpture and was therefore equally worthy of being individually titled.

This pot shows his intention of evolving a contemporary 'Western' form of decoration, whilst at the same time perfecting what he realised was an essentially derivative style based on ancient Chinese ceramics. The use of inlay here is an original synthesis derived from Korean incised decoration and Western motifs and style. Inlay is rare in Murray's *œuvre* perhaps because of the comparative lack of spontaneity involved in the process. It is achieved by engraving a design on the surface of a pot when the clay is at the leather-hard stage; the surface is then brushed with slip and, when the pot is dry, gently shaved until the inlaid pattern is revealed. The pot may then be dipped in a transparent glaze and fired. The *Birdcage* (No. 111) and the *Crinolines* bowl[1] are other examples of inlaid decoration. This pot was made in the oil-fired kiln at Wickham Road.

This pot was referred to as 'the Roundabout' by the Dean in his General Catalogue, Fitzwilliam Book and indexed notebook, and this is the title by which it is generally known. The name 'Bellerophon', however, also appears in the indexed notebook. Despite the somewhat inappropriate coupling of the name of the classical hero who rode Perseus's horse Pegasus with the riders of the fairground horses on the jar, this could be an alternative title.

It has been suggested that the introduction of figurative designs in Murray's work resulted from his friendship with the painter Ben Nicholson.[2] Murray met Nicholson around 1924 and was to exhibit with him several times; both were members of the Seven and Five Society.

PROV: Paterson's, 1926(35gns); presented, January 1959 (935/47).

EXH: Paterson's, 1926 ('Selected Pieces' 1); Middlesbrough, 1984-5; Manchester, 1989.

LIT: (?Charles Marriott), 'Art Exhibitions', *The Times*, 15 November 1926; *Illustrated London News*, 18 June 1927, ill.; R H Wilenski, 'Art Collectors, wise and foolish', *Sphere*, 18 June 1927, ill. p.304; Ede, 1928, ill. p.265; anon., 1952, ill.; Wingfield Digby, 1952, p.72; *Handlist*, 1971 (63); Haslam (Murray), 1984, pl.VIII in colour.

MW DOC: General Catalogue: '1926 ... 13 MURRAY Pot. Cold grey-green. Inlay dec. "the Roundabout".'; Fitzwilliam Book: '9. Class I No. in Catalogue 13 No. underfoot 12. Date 1926. POT. "the Roundabout" Cold gray-green, inlaid decoration of a Roundabout. This & the next pot [*Bird Cage*, No.111] are the two finest examples of a completely original form of decoration by elaborate "inlay", expressive of the "mood" of the pot. They show Murray wholly emancipated from Chinese precedent, and are like nothing else in the long history of ceramics. Murray never repeated the type after 1927, so these two pots stand as monuments of a striking stage in the development of his art. Their form, too, is very grand. "Roundabout" was illustrated in the Illustrated London News. June 18, 1927. Cf. also The Times 15.11.26.'; indexed notebook: 'MURRAY 12 POT. B. G. Cold grey-green D. Inlay decoration in black & white "The Roundabout." H. 8½" × W 10" Date 1926 Mark Ṃ Purchased 1926 £36-15-0 after the Nov. Exhibn (No.1.) See critique in "Times" Bellerophon'; album I: exhibition catalogue ('1.' underlined and 'the Roundabout' written beside entry by Milner-White) and reviews, The Times, 15 November 1926, and Sphere, 18 June 1927; album II; review, *Yorkshire Gazette*, 22 February 1952; Murray's album: review, *The Times*, 15 November 1926.

102

103

1. Private collection, ill. Haslam (Murray), 1984, pl.12.
2. Haslam (Murray), 1984, pp.28-9.

102. Bowl: 'Petal' *c.*1926

Pale body with iron specks toasted orange; parchment glaze streaked with paler tones, sepia decoration of seven-petalled flower and three-fold bud (painted code: ?'2/9').

H 2⅝ in (6.8 cm); D 6¾ in (17 cm)

Mark: Murray's pentagon (impressed)

This bowl provides a typical example of the brush decoration in the Oriental manner which Murray used between 1926 and 1929; see also *Cadence*, No.110. Flowers frequently occur as decoration on Murray's pots; his training as a bulb and seed merchant had given him a thorough knowledge of botany. The number of petals and the number of bud heads have significance in that seven and three are sacred numbers in Buddhist philosophy. Although not inappropriate, it is not known how the name 'Petal' became attached to this pot: it does

104

EXH: Paterson's, 1926 (64).

LIT: *Handlist*, 1971 (70).

MW DOC: General Catalogue: '1926 ... 14 MURRAY. Bowl, Porcelain-white dec. brushwork, "wings."'; indexed notebook: 'MURRAY 1 3 BOWL. B. Porcelain body-white G. White D. Brushwork "wings" of iron pigment, which has eaten into the body H. $2\frac{7}{8}$" × w. $4\frac{1}{2}$" Date 1926 (one of the two first successful pieces in this body by M.) Mark Ṃ Given Dec 1926 by W.S.M. (No 64 in Nov. Exn) Loxiaz'; album I: exhibition catalogue.

104. Pot: 'Mother Earth' exh. 1926

Pale body flecked with iron, toasted orange; white (?)slip covered in a dark iron glaze with iron decoration (incised code: '1.', painted code: '(?)62').

H $8\frac{3}{8}$ in (21.2 cm); D $9\frac{3}{8}$ in (23.9 cm)

Mark: Murray's pentagon (impressed)

By 1926 Murray had assimilated all he could learn from Oriental ceramics and from then onwards his own personality began to dominate the character of his work. This pot was referred to as 'Mother Earth' by the Dean in his General Catalogue and in the Fitzwilliam Book, and this is the name by which the pot is generally known. In the indexed notebook, however, the word 'Dis' appears. The precise meaning of this word is unknown, but it could be an alternative name. The pot was oil-fired at Wickham Road.

PROV: Paterson's, 1926(35gns); lent, 1958, and received outright on Milner-White's death, 1963 (1050/8).

EXH: Paterson's, 1926 (75); Middlesbrough, 1984-5.

LIT: Wingfield Digby, 1952, p.101, pl.19; *Handlist*, 1971 (56); Haslam (*Murray*), 1984, p.29, pl.v in colour.

MW DOC: General Catalogue: '1926 ... 11 MURRAY. Pot. Green Bronze over Cream dec. underglaze, purple-red./11 "Mother Earth" (still at the Deanery)/; Fitzwilliam Book: '7 Class I No. in Catalogue 11 No. underfoot 10 Date 1926 Pot. "Mother Earth" Green-bronze glaze over cream, with underglaze decn. flushing red. A powerful pot after the Chinese manner, yet typically Murray. From now onwards Murray's potting ceases to be "Chinese" of any school or date, & becomes purely "Murray". For all its variety, his work henceforth is recognisable at a glance by any expert; there never was a more "personal" potter than Murray; but his personality was such as to introduce something wholly new in potting history. As yet, his worth is insufficiently recognised: it is best described by "the Times" critiques of his exhibitions year by year written

not appear in any of the Milner-White documentation. The bowl was oil-fired at Wickham Road.

PROV: Paterson's, 1926(10gns); presented, January 1959 (935/65).

EXH: Paterson's, 1926 (66); Dartington, 1952 (102).

LIT: Wingfield Digby, 1952, p.101, pl.17; *Handlist*, 1971 (64).

MW DOC: General Catalogue: '1926 ... 10 MURRAY Bowl, Parchment flushed sepia, dec. threefold bulb into seven-petalled flower' and '1952 The following pots were exhibited (1) Dartington Hall ... [see No.23] ... [Murray] 10 Petals'; Fitzwilliam Book: '4. Class II No. in General Catalogue 10. No. under foot 9. Date 1926. Bowl, parchment flushed sepia dec. brush-work, threefold bulb and seven-petalled flower. A typical example of an early Murray bowl & brush-work. The "Three" & the "Seven" illustrate the mystical type of his mind.'; indexed notebook: 'MURRAY 9 BOWL B Reddish gray G. Parchment flushed sepia D Brushwork in sepia Threefold bulb issuing in seven-petalled flower H $2\frac{7}{12}$" × w $6\frac{7}{12}$" Date 1926 Mark Ṃ Purchased 1926 for £10.10 Nov. Ex. no 66'; notes on back of loose catalogue: '66 £10 Mystice[crossed out] Theotes'; invoice: Wm B. Paterson, November 1926, receipted 11

December 1926, 'W. Staite Murray's Stoneware Pottery Exhibition 1926 Nov. 10 To a Bowl, Parchment flushed sepia, brush decoration in Sepia No 66 10.10'; album I: exhibition catalogue ('Five Elementals[*sic*]' written by the entry by Milner-White in error).

103. Bowl: 'Wings' 1926

White porcelain body; form warped; white slip and iron brush-decoration (incised code: 'P.').

H 3 in (7.5 cm); D $4\frac{3}{4}$ in (12 cm)

Mark: Murray's pentagon (impressed)

This bowl is an early and unusual experiment with a porcelain body. Milner-White notes that it was 'one of the two first successful pieces in this body'. Significantly he was given the pot by Murray. It was referred to as 'wings' in the Dean's General Catalogue and indexed notebook. In the latter however, the word 'Loxiaz' has also been used, which could be an alternative name; its precise significance is unknown. The bowl was oil-fired at Wickham Road.

PROV: Given by Murray to Milner-White, December 1926; presented, 1958, and received on Milner-White's death, 1963 (1049/32).

by Marriot[sic], (to be found in my book of press-cuttings & catalogues of pottery exhibitions.); indexed notebook: 'MURRAY 10 POT. B. Reddish gray G. Green-bronze glaze over cream D. Purple red brushwork under the green-bronze glaze H 8½″ × W 9¼″ Date 1926 Mark Ṃ Purchased 1926 £36-15-0 no 75 Nov. Exn. (Desired by Eumorfopoulos.) Dis'; loose catalogue: notes on back: '75 £35 [illegible word crossed out] (?)Geologus'; invoice: Wm B. Paterson, November 1926, receipted 11 December 1926, 'W. Staite Murray's Stoneware Pottery Exhibition 1926 [November] 13 ... Pot. Purple, Bronze decoration in purple [No] 75 [£]36.15.'; album I: exhibition catalogue, and review, The Times, 15 November 1926.

105. Bowl exh. 1927

Grey body toasted orange; luminous deep-red glaze with rose oil spot, several burst air bubbles and one impurity (painted code: 'SF5').

H 4⅜ in (11 cm); D 8¾ in (22.4 cm)

Mark: Murray's pentagon (impressed)

The form and glaze of this bowl are Oriental in inspiration. The shape has warped in the kiln. Persimmon red was a favourite glaze of Murray's. The exhibition in which this pot was originally shown was Murray's first at the Beaux Arts Gallery. Frederick Lessore, the proprietor, had written to him as early as 1925 trying to entice him away from Paterson's: 'In your show at Paterson's I noticed that the rich dark-tones of your pots were lost in the darkness of the room and the dark warm colour of the background.'[1] Apart from the more sympathetic surroundings at Bruton Place, a major attraction for Murray would have been exhibiting with painters, thus showing his work in its rightful context: this exhibition was shared with Ben Nicholson and Christopher Wood. Murray had met Nicholson somewhere around 1924 and the painter was to have an enormous influence on his treatment of surface decoration.

PROV: Beaux Arts Gallery, 1927(10gns); presented, January 1959 (935/44).

EXH: Beaux Arts Gallery, 1927 (Murray ?45, Murray's pots not listed in catalogue); Rotterdam, 1960 (76).

LIT: Handlist, 1971 (65).

MW DOC: General Catalogue: '1927 ... 28. MURRAY. Bowl, red and gold.'; Fitzwilliam Book: '11. Class II No. in Catalogue 28 No. underfoot

105

106

107

14 Date 1927 Bowl, Red and Gold. diameter 8⅝ in. A bowl of typical Murray form, no decoration, but the gold 'oil spot' modifying the dark crimson glaze, esp. on the exterior.'; indexed notebook: 'MURRAY. 15 BOWL B. Reddish grey. G. Red-gold. H 4″ × 8½″ Date 1927 (early) Mark Ṃ Purchased Apr. 1927 £10-10-0 Beaux Art[sic] Gallery Exhibn'; invoice: Beaux Arts Gallery, 1 July 1927, receipted 4 July 1927, 'Ap 21 W.S. Murray's Stoneware Pottery … [?] Bowls. No. 45 10.10.0'; album I: exhibition catalogue.

1. Quoted by Haslam (Murray), 1984, p.32.

106. Bowl: 'Starry Jacinth' exh. 1927

White body with tiny iron flecks, toasted orange, heat blisters; white slip covered with transparent and slightly crackled, watery-green glaze, brush-decoration in olive-green, tessha and dark-green glaze.

H 2¾ in (7 cm); D 6⅞ in (17.4 cm)

Mark: Murray's pentagon (impressed)

Murray gave names to most of his pots, or rather he waited for the names to reveal themselves as they had a mystical significance for him. He regarded his work as an inquiry into the essence of life. In each piece he was trying to understand and experience the intangible yet real relationship between man and his material, and, through that, life itself. In a written commentary on his poem 'Pot and Potter' he says of the making of a pot on the potter's wheel: 'The clay spirals upwards in the hands of the potter, this spiral formation allows the clay to expand and unfold, for a pot grows from within, much as the whorled rose unfolds her petals, and all forms of organic life unfold their spiral construction in growing. The potter's wheel establishes the fact that spinning earth is a vast potter's wheel, moulding organic forms out of earth and water.'

PROV: Paterson's, 1927 (8gns); presented, January 1959 (935/38).

EXH: Paterson's, 1927 (26, 'starry jacinth').

LIT: Wingfield Digby, 1952, pl.18; Handlist, 1971 (60).

MW DOC: General Catalogue: '1927 … 41 MURRAY. Bowl water green dec. red and black.'; Fitzwilliam Book: '16 (Class II – raise to) Class I No. in Catalogue 41 No. underfoot. 20. Date 1927 BOWL, water-green, decorated red and black, floral suggestion. Irregular crackle, back & front. A beautiful piece both of potting & decoration. Murray in his less austere and masculine mood. Diameter 6¾ in.'; indexed

notebook: MURRAY 19 BOWL (DISH) B. Reddish-grey G. Water Green D. Crackled. Brush decoration v. thick, within cup, red, black & green 2¾ × 6¾ Mark Ṃ Date 1927 (late) Purchased £8.8. Nov. '27 Paterson's Exn. 'Starry Jacinth'; copy invoice: Wm B. Paterson, 8 November 1927, receipted 22 December 1927, '[To a] water green Bowl decorated red & black 26 8.8. '; album I: exhibition catalogue.

107. Bowl exh. 1927

Pale body with tiny iron specks and heat blisters; white slip covered with parchment glaze and iron brush-decoration (incised code: ?'1.'; painted code: '42.').

H 3⅜ in (8.7 cm); D 9½ in (24.1 cm)

Mark: Murray's pentagon (impressed)

In form, this bowl was clearly inspired by the Oriental tradition, yet its vigorous and well-placed abstract iron brush-decoration has more to do with European 'Modernism' than the Orient: in 1927 Murray was elected a member of the Seven and Five Society, having been proposed by Ben Nicholson, whose artistic theories dominated the group. Milner-White wrote under the entry for this pot in his Fitzwilliam Book: 'For Murray's work, 1927 is a peak year. The potting was superb, & not so heavy or over-large as his output tended to become later. The glazing and decoration was sure, astonishingly varied, original and refined. No future year showed so rich a profusion of idea'. The cream glaze, usually described as parchment, is typical of many of Murray's pots.

PROV: Paterson's or perhaps purchased from Murray direct after the exhibition, 1927(5gns reduced from 20gns and therefore, according to Milner-White, 'Given'); presented, January 1959 (935/43).

EXH: Paterson's, 1927 (100, 20gns).

LIT: Handlist, 1971 (59).

MW DOC: General Catalogue: '1927 … 42 MURRAY Bowl, parchment, sepia brush decn.; Fitzwilliam Book: '17 Class (III or) II No. in Catalogue 42 No. underfoot 21. Date 1927. BOWL. Parchment glaze, heavy sepia brush decoration. Diameter 9½ in. (For Murray's work, 1927 is a peak year … [as above]); indexed notebook: 'MURRAY 20 BOWL (Dish) B. Brownish-grey G. Parchment D. Strong brush Decn. 3⅜ × 9½ Mark Ṃ Date 1927 (late) Given (as to £15 15) by W.S.M. (as to £5.5 bought), Patersons[sic] Exhibn. Dec. '27'; loose catalogue (indicipherable word by catalogue entry); album I: exhibition catalogue.

108

108. Pot exh. 1927

Pale white-grey body with tiny iron specks; tenmoku glaze, incised diagonal lines through to the body, with iron brush-decoration (incised code: illegible).

H 7½ in (18.9 cm); D 6⅞ in (17.4 cm)

Mark: Murray's pentagon nearly obliterated by glaze (impressed)

It is recorded that Hamada sent Murray a recipe for a tenmoku glaze in or by 1923.[1] The tenmoku glaze used on this pot may well have been made from this recipe. Milner-White writes of No.108 in the Fitzwilliam Book: 'This pot marks Murray's nearest approach to the Japanese; & forms the link between his work and that of Hamada, for whose potting he has great respect'.

PROV: Paterson's, 1927(10gns); presented, January 1959 (935/50).

EXH: Paterson's, 1927 (144); Stockholm, 1939.

LIT: Handlist, 1971 (68).

MW DOC: General Catalogue: '1927 … 38 MURRAY Pot, blue black with yellow vertical lines and bronze markings' and '1939. Collection Lent to Stockholm at the request of the Government. [MURRAY] ''Blue Black with yellow vertical lines & bronze markings'' [Insured for £]20'; Fitzwilliam Book: '14 Class III No. in Catalogue 38 No. underfoot. 18. Date. 1927. POT, blue-black with yellow vertical lines and red-bronze lip and markings. (This pot marks Murray's nearest approach … [as above])'; indexed notebook: 'MURRAY. 24 POT. B. Brownish grey G.

109

Blue-black, red lip. D. Incised yellow vertical lines; bronze brush markings. $7\frac{3}{8} \times 6\frac{1}{2}$ Mark. Imperfect? M̦ Date 1927 (late) Purchased Nov. 27 £10-10-0 Paterson's Exhibn. "Murray's nearest approach to Hamada"; notes on back of loose catalogue: '144 Iron slip underneath (black) incised thro' [the] slip, biscuited (=fired). decorated with brush marks, & fired 3rd time'; copy invoice: Wm B. Paterson, 8 November 1927, receipted 22 December 1927, '[To a] blue black pot with yellow vertical lines & bronze markings 144 10.10. '; album I: exhibition catalogue.

1. Haslam (Murray), 1984, p.17.

109. Bowl: 'Cloud Petals' exh. 1927

Pale grey body with tiny iron specks, toasted orange and blistered; parchment glaze streaked creamy-white with brown and blue brush-decoration (painted code: '45.').

H 3 in (7.8 cm); D $4\frac{5}{8}$ in (11.7 cm)

Mark: Murray's pentagon (impressed)

As with so many of Murray's pots, the name of this bowl well suits its form and decoration. Milner-White wrote of it in the Fitzwilliam book: 'A small and inconspicuous piece which was a first favourite of Murray himself.' Like No.107, this bowl is covered with one of Murray's cream glazes generally described as parchment.

PROV: Paterson's, 1927 (10gns); presented, January 1959 (935/56).

EXH: Paterson's, 1927 (1); Dartington, 1952 (100).

LIT: Handlist, 1971 (79).

MW DOC: General Catalogue: '1927 ... 36 MURRAY Bowl, parchment dec. brown & blue.' and '1952 The following pots were exhibited (1) Dartington Hall ... [see No.23] ... [Murray] 36 Cloud Petals'; Fitzwilliam Book: '13 Class II No. in Catalogue 36. No. underfoot. 17 Date 1927 BOWL, parchment glaze, dec. brush-work brown and blue. A small ... [as above].'; indexed notebook: MURRAY 17 BOWL. B. Reddish Grey G Parchment D Brush decoration brown and blue H $3'' \times 4\frac{1}{2}''$ Mark M̦ Date 1927 (late) Purchased £10.10. Paterson's Exhibn Nov. 1927 (a great exhibition, from which I bought Eight pieces & was given one); copy invoice: Wm B. Paterson, 8 November 1927, receipted 22 December 1927, 'To a parchment glazed Bowl decoration brown & blue No 1 10.10. '; album I: exhibition catalogue.

110. Vase: 'Cadence' exh. 1927 (colour XVII)

Pale body, similar to that on No.125 but not so coarse, with iron specks; white (?)slip, ivory glaze breaking to warm white with brush-decoration in sepia and blue glazes.

H $13\frac{3}{4}$ in (34.9 cm); D $6\frac{7}{8}$ in (17.5 cm)

Mark: Murray's pentagon (impressed)

Murray asked 100 guineas for Cadence, nearly twice the price of the next most expensive pot in the 1927 Paterson exhibition.[1] Indeed the majority of the other 300 pots were priced at under 15 guineas. The sum of 100 guineas was a huge amount of money to ask for a pot in the 1920s, especially in view of the depressed economic climate. However, Murray considered Cadence to be his masterpiece at that time and Milner-White supported him by paying the price. In common with his other pots to date, it was Oriental in inspiration. Murray greatly admired the Chinese potters' facility with brush-decoration. Hamada had taught him how to wield a brush in the Oriental way and in Cadence was the evidence that the lesson had been absorbed. Decoratively, this pot owes much to Hamada but the pot is not derivative: although the inspiration is clearly Oriental, it has been incorporated into Murray's unique vision. Eschewing bright colours in favour of a restrained colour-scheme, he believed that 'mood' or abstract emotion was an important quality in a pot. Cadence typifies this aspect of his philosophy: as the name indicates, Murray was seeking to suggest in tones and colour something akin to the falling-away character of a phrase of music.

PROV: Paterson's, 1927 (100gns); presented, January 1959 (935/64).

EXH: Paterson's, 1927 (141, 'cadence'); Middlesbrough, 1984-5.

LIT: (?Charles Marriott), 'Art Exhibitions', The Times, 11 November 1927; P.G.K(onody), 'Poetry in Pottery', Daily Mail, 14 November 1927; anon., 1927, ill. p.284; Marriott, 1943, p.36; Wingfield Digby, 1952, p.101, pl.17; anon., obituary, The Times, 21 February 1962; Handlist, 1971 (69); Webber, 1975, ill. p.32; Bennett, 1980, p.98; Haslam (Murray), 1984, p.30, pl.x in colour.

MW DOC: General Catalogue: '1927 ... 34 MURRAY. Pot, "Cadence" ivory, brush decn. sepia & blue'; Fitzwilliam Book: '12. Class I. No. in Catalogue 34 No. underfoot. 15. Date 1927 POT. "Cadence". Ivory glaze, brush decoration sepia & blue. Illustrated in Apollo. Dec. 1927 Illustration prepared for Encyclopedia Brittanica[sic] 1929, but finally omitted. Murray considered this his masterpiece to-date, and put a price of £105 on it. "... Cadence – the falling-away character, as of a musical phrase, of the form being continued by the brush-decoration in two tones of colour." The Times Nov. 11. 1927.'; indexed notebook: MURRAY 21 POT. B Brownish grey. G. Parchment D. Brush, sepia and blue grey $13\frac{1}{2} \times 7$ Mark M̦ Date 1927 (late) Purchased, Nov. '27, 100 guineas Paterson Exhn. Illustrated in "Apollo". Dec. 27 "Cadence" '; copy invoice: Wm B. Paterson, 8 November 1927, 'To a parchment glaze Pot, brush decoration in Sepia & blue grey (Cadence) 141 £105. . '; album I: exhibition catalogue, review, The Times, 11 November 1927, and letter, from the Encyclopaedia Britannica, 15 May 1928, requesting permission to reproduce 'Five Elementals'[sic],[2] Cadence and 'The Bird Cage' [No.111] in a new edition; Murray's album: review, Daily Mail, 14 November 1927.

1. Fawn cost 55 guineas.
2. Five Elements is missing from the Collection, presumed stolen: see Appendix B4 (935/33).

111. Jar: 'Birdcage' late 1927

Creamy-grey body, speckled cinnamon; incised decoration of five birds in a cage, inlaid with rust and white slip, the whole covered in a cream-grey glaze, with iron glaze around the lip.

H $9\frac{7}{8}$ in (25.2 cm); D $10\frac{3}{8}$ in (26.4 cm)

Mark: Murray's pentagon (painted)

Birdcage is a sister pot to The Roundabout (No.101), and to the Crinolines bowl.[1] Inlaid decoration, a feature of all three, does not appear on its own in Murray's decoration after this date. A very heavy pot, it was oil-fired at Wickham Road.

PROV: Paterson's 1927 (37gns); presented, January 1959 (935/66).

EXH: Paterson's, 1927 (150); Manchester, 1988 (49).

111

112

LIT: (?)*Encyclopaedia Britannica*, Encyclopaedia Britannica Co. Ltd, 1929, ill.; anon., 1952, ill.; Wingfield Digby, 1952, p.72; Ingamells (*Preview*), 1959 p.439, ill. p.440; Ingamells (*Museums Journal*), 1959, p.125, fig.32; *Handlist*, 1971 (61); Webber, 1975, ill. p.30; Bennett, 1980, pp.98-9; Haslam (*Murray*), 1984, pl.13.

MW DOC: General Catalogue: '1927 35 MURRAY. Pot. "Birdcage" inlaid decn. red & white'; Fitzwilliam Book: '10 Class 1 No. in Catalogue 35 No. underfoot 16 Date 1927. POT. "Bird-cage" Cold gray, inlaid decoration brown & white of birds in cages. "Two strongly contrasted pieces – except in colour – 'The Bird Cage' and 'The Sea' ... illustrate very well the way an abstract art can be given naturalistic 'point' by suggested movement, the one pot being made static by lines at right-angles, the other waving throughout in contours and decoration." The Times Nov. 11. 1927 (Eumorfopoulos bought "The Sea") (I had the chance of buying it in the sale after his wife's death in April 1944, but it was distinctly inferior to my two pieces)'; indexed notebook: 'MURRAY. 23. POT. B. Brownish grey G. Stonegrey (goldish) D. Inlaid red-brown and white, design of birds in cage; red-brown lip. 9¾ × 10 Mark M̦ Date 1927 (late) Purchased, Nov. 27 £38-17-0 Paterson Exhibn. The Bird-cage.'; notes on back of loose catalogue: '150 Celadon type of glaze. two different clays inlaid in the body one a clay without iron the other a slip clay with a percentage of iron in it'; copy invoice: Wm B. Paterson, 8 November 1927, receipted 22 December 1927, '[To a] grey pot inlay decoration dark red & white (The Bird Cage) 150 [£]38.17[s].'; album I: exhibition catalogue, review, *The Times*, 11 November 1927, and letter from the *Encyclopaedia Britannica*, 15 May 1928, asking permission to reproduce 'Five Elementals'[sic],[2] *Cadence* [No.110] and 'The Bird Cage' in a new edition; album II: review, *Yorkshire Gazette*, 22 February 1952.

1. Private collection, ill. Haslam (*Murray*), 1984, pl.12.
2. See No.110, n.2.

112. Tea-Bowl 1928

Pale body with iron specks, toasted orange; parchment glaze with flushed sepia brush-decoration, touches of blue and (probably wax-resist) dedication around the rim: 'Father Eric his Tea Bowl. King'[s] College Cambridge – 1928.'

H 3⅛ in (8 cm); D 3¾ in (9.6 cm)

Mark: Murray's pentagon (impressed)

This tea-bowl is a touching expression of the friendship between Murray and Milner-White, for whom it was specially made. The Dean was Murray's major patron, acquiring

113

114

113. Bowl exh. 1928

Pale body with iron flecks, toasted orange; form warped; silver-blue glaze with iron decoration on the exterior (more toasted on one side than the other) and a flushed purple mark on the interior; (incised code: 'GT'; painted code: '1D').

H 3 in (7.5 cm); D 4½ in (11.3 cm)

Mark: Murray's pentagon (impressed)

This bowl clearly demonstrates the great trouble Murray had in controlling his materials. The critic writing in *Apollo*, November 1927, wondered why several of Murray's pots were warped when others were of an exceptionally high technical standard.[1] Murray's art, sparked by a desire to recreate ancient Chinese glazes, had to be based upon experimentation. As he himself put it, 'Surrounded by influences, both Eastern and Western, of extraordinary beauty and technical perfection, with qualities that have taken generations to evolve, their beauty of form, depth of quality and richness of colour are obvious, but the technical reason is not readily revealed.'[2] Much trial and error was involved in arriving at the desired result and many technically bad pots were made alongside the successful ones.

PROV: Paterson's, 1928 (4gns); presented, May 1959 (935/95).

EXH: Paterson's, 1928 (261).

LIT: *Handlist*, 1971 (66); Webber, 1975, ill. p.27 in colour.

MW DOC: General Catalogue: '1928 ... 61 MURRAY, Bowl, Grey d. in lustrous bronze, inside flushed purple red.'; Fitzwilliam Book: '20 Class III No. in Catalogue 61 No. underfoot 27 Date 1928. Small Bowl, blue-grey; exterior, brush-decn in lustrous bronze; interior, copper-flush, purple-red. (Murray rarely uses a copper glaze) (Another small piece which grows in attraction on acquaintance); invoice: Wm B. Paterson, 1 November 1928, receipted 2 April 1929, 'W. Staite Murray. Pottery Exhibition 1928 'No 261. [To a] bowl Grey glaze, decorated in lustrous bronze, inside flushed purple red[£]4.4.; album I: exhibition catalogue.

1. Anon., 'Art News and Notes', *Apollo*, vi, no.35, November 1927, p.232.
2. W. Staite Murray, 'Pottery from the Artist's Point of View', *Artwork*, i, no.4, May-August 1925, p.201.

114. Beaker: 'Dark Lagoon' c.1928

Pale body with tiny flecks of iron, toasted orange; ferruginous brown over thick parchment glaze, red-rust brush-decoration of four tulips (painted code: '4/6.').

H 4⅜ in (11.1 cm); D 3¾ in (9.7 cm)

Mark: Murray's pentagon (impressed)

This beaker is an unusual form for Murray. The decoration recalls his training as a bulb and seed merchant in the Netherlands.

PROV: Unknown, but probably Paterson's, 1928; presented, 1958 and received on Milner-White's death, 1963 (1049/38).

EXH: (?)Paterson's, 1928 (not in catalogue).

LIT: Wingfield Digby, 1952, p.101, pl.18.

MW DOC: General Catalogue: Probably '1928 ... 49 MURRAY. Cup, parchment flushed sepia, brush decn./(49 Still at the Deanery)'; Fitzwilliam Book: '18 Class II No. in Catalogue 49 No. underfoot. 23 Date 1928. Cup. "Dark Lagoon" Parchment glaze, flushed sepia, with brush decn. (A very simple & straightforward piece, with a subtle power of attraction. In form unlike anything else Murray has done.)'; album I: exhibition catalogue and review, *The Times*, 3 November 1928.

115. Bowl: 'Blossom' exh. 1929

Pale body flecked with iron; ochre ground with floral brush-decoration of blossoms in concentric circles of seven and six with one in the centre (painted code: '?5.').

H 3½ in (8.7 cm); D 8 in (20.3 cm)

Mark: Murray's pentagon (impressed)

Blossom was one of the first pots made at Bray. In 1929 the Murrays moved from Wickham Road to Court Cottage, Bray. Here Murray built a two-chambered oil-fired kiln, like the one at Wickham Road, only larger. His workshop was in a greenhouse, where he was to make all his pots for the remainder of his career.

Although Murray exhibited 123 pots, including *Blossom*, at Paterson's Gallery in 1929 he was not entirely happy about doing so, as a letter to Milner-White dated 19 December 1928 makes clear: 'they [the pots] always are so much better away from the gallery they seem caged and unhappy for want of light and air. It depresses me, and yet I have booked the Gallery for November next, & that after considering other Galleries, for an annual show is necessary if one is to continue working'. In fact

a total of fifty-seven pots, thirty-three of them by 1928, the year this tea-bowl was given to him.[1] Murray thus had good reason to be grateful to Milner-White, writing to him on 19 December 1928: 'I am no less grateful to you for buying my work than you are to me in "giving you pleasure by the beauty I create" for without buyers my work as a Potter would cease.'

PROV: Given by Murray to Milner-White, presumably 1928; presented, 1958, and received on Milner-White's death, 1963 (1049/33).

LIT: *Handlist*, 1971 (58).

1. Numbers based on information in MS General Catalogue only.

Murray's one-man show of 1929 was the last to be held at Paterson's and it was considerably smaller than those preceding it (300 pieces in 1927 and 264 in 1928). The reduction in quantity, as Haslam has pointed out, was probably due to the disruption caused by the move from Wickham Road and to the mechanical trouble which Murray was experiencing with his new kiln at Bray; a letter from Combustions Ltd, dated 16 January 1930, refers to 'uneven heating that you have experienced'.[1]

PROV: Paterson's, 1929(15gns); presented, January 1959 (935/53).

EXH: Paterson's, 1929 (71); Stockholm, 1939.

LIT: Wingfield Digby, 1952, pp.72, 101, pl.18; *Handlist*, 1971 (74).

MW DOC: General Catalogue: '1929 ... 92 MURRAY Bowl "Blossom" 15[gns]' and '1939. Collection Lent to Stockholm at the request of the Government. [MURRAY] "Blossom" [Insured for £]20'; Fitzwilliam Book: '23 Class (III or) II No. in Catalogue 92 No. underfoot Date 1929 Bowl. Blossom. Diameter 7¾ in. Brown and red floral decn on grey glaze, flowers in concentric circles, seven, five, one.'; invoice: Wm B. Paterson, 12 December 1929, 'Nov.20 To Pottery by W. Staite Murray. [no.] 71 [Bowl,] Blossom 15.15'; album I: exhibition catalogue.

1. Haslam (*Murray*), 1984, p.32.

116. Bowl: 'Vortex' exh. 1929 (*colour XVI*)

Pale body with tiny iron specks; parchment glaze with sepia brush-decoration.

H 3¼ in (8.3 cm); D 7½ in (19 cm)

Mark: Murray's pentagon (impressed)

Vortex is generally regarded as one of Murray's greatest works. The Oriental form is finely thrown with complete control. The footring is one of the nicest to be found on a Murray bowl. Everything has come together in this pot. The brushed iron decoration, in a Western idiom and at the same time both delicate and vigorous, places this bowl firmly in the forefront of early twentieth-century avant-garde art. It is a triumphant exemplar of Murray's artistic philosophy.

When asked by Muriel Rose in a questionnaire for her book, *Artist-Potters in England*, why he had taken up pottery making, Murray replied: 'Experiments of that time in abstract painting and abstract sculpture interested me, and it was I think an insight into pottery as a fundamental abstract art

115

that led me to take up pottery making.'[1] This was at a time when Sung-dynasty pottery was being acclaimed in London for its purely abstract values of form and colour, while there was a general demand that painting and sculpture be liberated from the tyranny of representation in response to progressive Continental art. Murray was closely allied to the artistic avant-garde, in particular to the Vorticists through his association with C.F.Hamilton at the Yeoman pottery. The Vorticists were developing the grammar and vocabulary of art as visual music and the vortex was their central theme of power and energy.

PROV: Paterson's, 1929(15gns); presented, January 1959 (935/59).

EXH: Paterson's, 1929 (60); Middlesbrough, 1984-5.

LIT: E.A.Lane, *Style in Pottery*, Oxford University Press, Oxford 1948, pl.35; Wingfield Digby, 1952, pp.72, 101, pl.19; *Handlist*, 1971 (72); Webber, 1975, ill. p.27 in colour; Bennett, 1980, p.99; Haslam (*Antique Dealer*), 1984, p.65; Haslam (*Murray*), 1984, p.38, pl.19.

MW DOC: General Catalogue: '1929 ... 91 MURRAY. Bowl. "Vortex" 15[gns]'; Fitzwilliam Book: '22 Class I. No. in Catalogue 91 No. underfoot. 29. Date 1929. BOWL. "Vortex" Line and zigzag brushwork, sepia on cold grey-white; sepia lip. (A perfect example of true pottery decn.) (and finely potted)'; receipt: Wm B. Paterson, 12 December 1929, 'Nov. 20 To Pottery by W. Staite Murray. [No.] 60 Bowl, Vortex. 15.15'; album I: exhibition catalogue.

1. Quoted by Haslam (*Antique Dealer*), 1964, p.65.

117. Jar: 'Mist early Morning' exh. 1929 (*colour XVIII*)

Pale body with tiny flecks of iron; one side more toasted than the other; grey streaked pearly-white glaze with iron brush-decoration of two ducks, reeds and rings.

H 17⅜ in (44.2 cm); D 13½ in (34.3 cm)

Mark: Murray's pentagon (impressed)

Mist early Morning is one of Murray's finest pots. The form is strong and original and the decoration extraordinarily subtle. Oriental-inspired brushwork loaded with iron is applied in a vigorous and powerful manner and the decoration (whose subject matter is not Oriental) is particularly well placed for the shape of the pot. The name alludes to the intangible qualities which Murray sought to convey. Ian Bennett included this pot among 'Murray's greatest pieces' which he considered to 'represent a major contribution to ceramic art' (the others being *Vortex* and *Cow*).

The duck on one side of the pot is dark and hot, whilst that on the other is paler and cooler in colour: the dark side must have been more greatly exposed to heat in the kiln than the cooler side. This is a clear indication of the uneven heating Murray was experiencing with his new kiln at Bray. Nevertheless *Mist early Morning* remains one of Murray's most successful pots.

PROV: Paterson's, 1929(£105); presented, January 1959 (935/84)

EXH: Paterson's, 1929 (29); Dartington, 1952 (106); Rotterdam, 1960 (72); Middlesbrough, 1984-5.

LIT: Anon., 'Christmas Art Pottery', *Daily Mail*, 29 November 1929; Marsh, 1944, ill. p.107; Wingfield Digby, 1952, p.102, pl.21; *Handlist*, 1971 (75); Webber, 1975, ill. p.27 in colour; Bennett, 1980, p.99; Haslam (*Murray*), 1984, p.72, pl.20.

MW DOC: General Catalogue: '1929 ... 90 MURRAY. Pot. "Mist, Early Morning" 100[gns]' and '1952 The following pots were exhibited (1) Dartington Hall ... [see No.23] ... [Murray] 90 Mist, Early Morning'; Fitzwilliam Book: '21 Class I No. in Catalogue 91 [actually 90] No. underfoot 28. Date 1929 Large POT "Mist, Early Morning." A powerful pot with broad brushwork design of wild duck swimming and taking flight on ivory glaze ground'; receipt: Wm B. Paterson, 12 December 1929, 'Nov. 20 To Pottery by W. Staite Murray. No. 29 Pot, Mist, early morning [£]105 - -'; album I: exhibition catalogue and photograph; Murray's album: review, *Daily Mail*, 29 November 1929.

118.   Tall Jar: 'The Bather' 1930
(*colour XXII*)

Cream glaze streaked pearly white with decoration of iron-rust red bands approximately 1 in (2.5 cm) wide, and thin, cobalt lines approximately $\frac{1}{8}$ in (0.3 cm) above and below each band, 'birth mark' spot in iron 4 in (10 cm) from bottom.

H $27\frac{7}{8}$ in (70.8 cm); D $5\frac{3}{4}$ in (14.7 cm)

Mark: Murray's pentagon (impressed)

The late 1920s saw the culmination of Murray's development as a potter of brilliant inventiveness and originality. *The Bather*, exhibited in 1930, is generally regarded as one of Murray's great pots. Made in the new kiln at Bray, its size possibly reflects the extra space available in this kiln. Its shape is evidence of Murray's interest in the intrinsic qualities of form coupled with the belief that a pot could possess an inner life, and is faintly anthropomorphic. Robins Millar wrote of this and another pot of the same shape and height (illustrated together), at the time of the 1930 Lefevre exhibition, that they 'indicate how the potter has thought of the form of a woman as he shaped the clay on his wheel. He conceives a vase that subtly moulds itself into curves which seem to contain the feminine figure without evolving into actual realism of limbs and head.' Ronald G. Cooper in 1947 captioned the same two pots as 'Two Women'. In contrast to earlier elongated forms, this pot has been given a firm and substantial base. Milner-White writes that the pot was 'Unique as an instance of a throw in one piece' and that

117

'Murray accomplished it at the 69th attempt!' The origin of this new form (which was to be recurrent in his work) is not clear. It could have developed from Murray's growing acquaintance with the sculptor Henry Moore, whose work was displaying similar metamorphoses of the human figure. Moore had been an instructor in sculpture at the Royal College of Art since 1924, and Murray probably met him, although it is not clear when. At the same time, a black and white striped tall pot of the Sung dynasty is at the Fitzwilliam Museum, Cambridge, and Murray might well have known this piece through Milner-White, who was Dean of King's College from 1918 until 1941. Murray's decoration of bands of iron-rust red over cream features his two most favourite colours. This striped decoration reminiscent of a long striped bathing costume coupled with the tall slim form provide a rare example of humour in Murray's art. The foot of *The Bather* was damaged in 1988; it was restored in 1989 by Judith Larney of London.

A similar pot, *Laughing Water*, is in Paisley Museum and Art Gallery (201-1960).

PROV: Lefevre, 1930(50gns); presented, January 1959 (935/83).

EXH: Lefevre, 1930 (12); Hayward Gallery, 1979 (2.80); Middlesbrough, 1984-5; Manchester, 1988 (164).

LIT: Robins Millar, 'Potter and Poet: An ancient Craft with a modern Message', (Glasgow) *Evening News*, 16 December 1930, ill.; Forsyth, 1936, ill. p.64; Cooper, 1947, p.IV, pl.37; Ingamells (*Museums Journal*), 1959, fig.33 (in group shot); *Handlist*, 1971 (62); Webber, 1975, ill. p.30; Bennett, 1980, pp.13, 98-9; Haslam (Murray), 1984, p.32, pl.XII in colour; Hyne, 1985, ill. p.10 in colour; Haslam, 1986, ill. p.1605 in colour.

MW DOC: General Catalogue: '1930 ... 97 MURRAY. Pot. The Bather. 50[gns]/97 Unique as an instance of a throw in one piece – Murray accomplished it at the 69th attempt'; Fitzwilliam Book: '25 Class II No. in Catalogue 97 No. underfoot Date 1930 POT. "The Bather" Height 2ft 4.in. A tall slender pot – itself a miracle of throwing – with ivory glaze and broad regular bands of red-brown decn. Illustrated in many papers; and in Gordon Forsyth's "XXth Century Ceramics" (1936) Murray made no fewer than sixty attempts before succeeding in throwing this pot.'; invoice: Alex. Reid & Lefevre Ltd, December 1930, receipted for part payment 13 January 1931, '1930 Nov. 6 To pottery by W Staite Murray. 1 Pot. Bather. 52.10'; album I: exhibition catalogue and photograph; Murray's album: review, (Glasgow) *Evening News*, 16 December 1930.

119. Tall Jar: 'Water Birds' exh. 1930

Pale body flecked with iron; toasted orange, heat blisters; streaked creamy-white glaze over fine parchment-coloured ground, brush-decoration of three cranes and wavy bands in iron with touches of cobalt.

H $21\frac{3}{8}$ in (54.4 cm); D $10\frac{3}{8}$ in (26.3 cm)

Mark: Murray's pentagon (impressed)

Water Birds is one of Murray's great pots made in 1930. Large, stable and elegant in form, it makes use of Murray's favourite iron glaze applied with bold, vigorous brush-strokes in a decidedly painterly manner. The decoration of three cranes beautifully reinforces the shape of the pot. Murray explained his approach to decoration in an article in *Artwork*, 1925: 'The treatment is largely determined by the pot, which presents a wide but limited scope demanding high skill in the decorating for there is no question of erasion, and in brush work, direct and vigorous handling is required, emphasising the vitality of the pot.'[1] It seems likely that Murray's more figurative painterly approach evolved at least partly through his association with con-

temporary avant-garde painters such as Ben Nicholson and Cedric Morris, with whom he exhibited. It is known that around 1928 Cedric Morris made some designs for application to Murray's pots: *Wading Birds* of 1930, now in Buckinghamshire County Museum (449.1984), was among the resulting pieces.

PROV: Lefevre, 1930(80gns); presented, January 1959 (935/87).

LIT: Wingfield Digby, 1952, p.102, pl.26 and dust jacket; Ingamells (*Museums Journal*), 1959, p.125, fig.34 (in group shot); *Handlist*, 1971 (67); Webber, 1975, ill. p.27 in colour.

EXH: Lefevre, 1930 (49); Stockholm, 1939; Wakefield, 1987.

MW DOC: General Catalogue: '1930 ... 102 MURRAY Pot Water Birds 80[gns]' and '1939. Collection Lent to Stockholm at the request of the Government. [MURRAY] "Water Birds" [Insured for £]84'; Fitzwilliam Book: '24 Class I No. in Catalogue. 102 No.underfoot 36 Date 1930 Large POT "Water Birds." Brown-ivory glaze, design in brushwork of three cranes, red-sepia; red-sepia lip and broad wavy bands about neck.'; invoice: Alex. Reid & Lefevre Ltd, December 1930, receipted for part payment 13 January 1931, '1930 Nov: 6 To Pottery by W Staite Murray ... 1 [Pot] "Water Birds" [£]84 ..'; album I: exhibition catalogue.

1. W Staite Murray, 'Pottery from the Artist's Point of View', *Artwork*, i, no.4, May-August 1925, p.201.

120. Tea-Bowl c.1930

Coarse pale body flecked with iron; heat blister; grey glaze speckled with iron and cobalt brush-decoration, pale blue flush to the interior.

H $2\frac{3}{4}$ in (7 cm); D $3\frac{1}{2}$ in (8.8 cm)

Mark: Murray's pentagon (impressed)

The clay body in this tea-bowl is iron rich, the speckled effect being caused by the iron in the clay reacting under intense heat to reveal itself. The form is rather awkward, an example of Murray's constant experimentation. This tea-bowl was purchased as one of a set of nine; No.121 in this catalogue and three Murray bowls lent to Milner-White's executors in 1963 (see Appendix B3) are likely to be part of the same set.

PROV: Presumably Lefevre, 1930, as one of a set of nine (10gns the set); presented, May 1959 (935/96).

EXH: Lefevre, 1930 (134, the set of nine).

LIT: *Handlist*, 1971 (77).

MW DOC: General Catalogue: (presumably) '1930 ... 100 MURRAY Set of nine tea-cups 2 given away 10[gns]/100 At the Deanery, v. pleasant but hardly museum pieces'; invoice: Alex. Reid & Lefevre Ltd, December 1930, receipted for part payment 13 January 1931, 'Nov. 6 To Pottery by W Staite Murray ... 1 Set of Nine Tea Bowls 10.10.; album I: exhibition catalogue.

121. Tea-Bowl c.1930

Coarse pale body heavily speckled with iron; two heat blisters; parchment glaze speckled with iron from the clay body with iron brush-decoration of three flower pots.

H 3 in (7.8 cm); D $3\frac{5}{8}$ in (9.2 cm)

Mark: Murray's pentagon (impressed)

See No.120. A similar tea-bowl is in the Crafts Study Centre, Bath (P.74.190).

PROV: Presumably Lefevre, 1930, as one of a set of nine (10gns the set); presented, May 1959 (935/97).

EXH: Lefevre, 1930 (134, the set of nine).

LIT: *Handlist*, 1971 (73).

MW DOC: See No.120.

122. Tall Jar: 'Mare' exh. 1931

Grey body flecked with iron; heat blisters, one side more toasted than the other; incised decoration with iron splashes over a whitish glaze.

H $16\frac{1}{2}$ in (41.8 cm); D $10\frac{1}{2}$ in (26.7 cm)

Mark: Murray's pentagon (impressed)

Mare and *Persian Garden* (No.123) are formed and decorated in the same manner. Milner-White wrote that they were 'the only two pots in this "manner" that Murray has done' but he was not entirely correct: *Persian Bird*, for example, also has incised and splashed iron decoration.[1] This type of decoration is, however, rare in Murray's œuvre. Although it has been generally admired, the critic for the *Morning Post*, writing at the time of the 1931 exhibition, did not share this view: 'Mr. Murray as a potter excels himself, but, alas, he has added to his sins as a decorator. Some of his finest works are so covered with incised or painted designs that the shape and surface quality of vase or pot are almost hidden. It is like spoiling the beauty of a young woman's face by tattooing her cheeks.' On the other hand, the form of *Mare* was praised by the same critic: 'Note particularly the superbly

120

121

formed "Mare," ... '.[2] This was echoed by Milner-White: 'The form of this pot is of remarkable strength, squareness rather than rotundity receiving emphasis from its high shoulders.' Mare means sea in Latin and Italian, although the pot was captioned as 'Swimming Fish' by Ernest Marsh in his article on Murray in *Apollo*, 1944. A pot decorated in a similar style is to be found in the Crafts Study Centre, Bath (P.74.42).

PROV: Lefevre, 1931 (80gns); presented, January 1959 (935/42).

EXH: Lefevre, 1931 (36); Stockholm, 1939; Rotterdam, 1960 (75).

LIT: Anon., 'Pottery and Paintings', *Morning Post*, 7 November 1931; Marsh, 1944, ill. p.108 (as 'Swimming Fish'); Wingfield Digby, 1952, p.102, pl.25; *Handlist*, 1971 (52); Bennett, 1980, pp.13, 99.

MW DOC: General Catalogue: '1931 ... 114 MURRAY "Mare" (Sea) ... 80[gns]' and '1939. Collection Lent to Stockholm at the request of the Government. [MURRAY.] "Mare" [Insured for

122

123. Jar: 'Persian Garden' 1931
(colour XIX)

Pale grey body with orange iron flecks, heat blisters; incised decoration of three cranes with leaf-petals and grasses brushed in iron over a whitish glaze, iron glaze also around the lip.

H 22¼ in (56.5 cm); D 12 in (30.5 cm)

Mark: Murray's pentagon (impressed)

Persian Garden is one of Murray's most famous pots. It was made in 1931 at a period when his inventiveness and originality were at a peak. One of this largest pots, it was also one of his most expensive, being priced at 120 guineas. In the Milner-White collection only *Kwan Yin* (No.127) was more expensive, costing 150 guineas in 1958.

Persian Garden was formed and decorated in the same manner as *Mare* (No.122). The incised and splashed iron decoration is strong and vigorous. The *Morning Post*, at the time of the 1931 exhibition, criticized Murray for spoiling the shape and surface quality of his work by an indulgence in decoration, but specifically excepted *Persian Garden* as being 'less objectional in this respect'. Technically, however, the pot is flawed. Too much clay has been used for the size, the form has warped and there are two heat blisters caused by subjection of the clay to too high a temperature. Additionally, the pot has not been fired evenly: one side is a beautifully milky white and the other a hot grey-brown. According to Leach, Murray claimed to fire at 1600°c in the early 1920s. Hamada's knowledge of Chinese glazes fired at 1300-1350°c would have helped him, but this pot demonstrates that even in the early 1930s he was still having trouble controlling his material.

Despite these deficiencies, *Persian Garden* is generally regarded as one of Murray's greatest pots. Milner-White wrote of it as 'Probably Murray's masterpiece – he so considers it,' while the anonymous critic of the *Yorkshire Gazette*, writing in 1952, deemed it to be one of 'the two rivals for the title of the finest of all modern pots' (amongst those then exhibited at York, the other being an unspecified piece by Hamada, probably No.26). 'Inspiration transcends craftsmanship,' wrote Ingamells in 1959.[1] Though technically imperfect, *Persian Garden* remains a powerful and dynamic creation.

According to Bennett, *Persian Bird* (with similar incised decoration)[2] was intended as a companion piece to *Persian Garden* and the

£]84'; Fitzwilliam Book: '29 Class I No. in Catalogue 114 No. underfoot. 37 Date 1931 Large POT. "Mare" A sister-pot to "Persian Garden" ... the only two pots in this "manner" that Murray has done White glaze, shading into cream-grey: incised decoration and brush-work fishes and waves in warm brown: brown lip. The form of this pot is of remarkable strength, squareness rather than rotundity receiving emphasis from its high shoulders. As in the case of "Roundabout" & "Bird Cage", there is

nothing remotely resembling these two pots in ceramic history'; invoice: Alex. Reid & Lefevre, December 1931, ' 1931. Novr. 5 Stoneware Pots, by Staite Murray ... "Mare" [£]200 [with Persian Garden]; album I: exhibition catalogue; Murray's album: review, *Morning Post*, 7 November 1931.

1. Exh. Christopher Wood Gallery, 1980 (42, ill. p.68).
2. Anon., 'Pottery and Painting', *Morning Post*, 7 November 1931.

two were shown side by side at the Lefevre exhibition of 1931. However, the title *Persian Bird* does not appear in the catalogue of the exhibition.

PROV: Lefevre, 1931 (120gns); presented, January 1959 (935/85).

EXH: Lefevre, 1931 (9); Dartington, 1952 (107); Rotterdam, 1960 (74); Hayward Gallery, 1979 (2.79); Crafts Council, 1982 (MC34, ill. p.79); Middlesbrough, 1984-5; Manchester, 1989.

LIT: Anon., 'Artists who favour Symbolism', *Birmingham Daily Post*, 4 November 1931; anon., 'Pottery and Paintings', *Morning Post*, 7 November 1931; anon., 'Master-Potters', *Observer*, 22 November 1931; Rowan Williams, 'La vie artistique à Londres', *Bulletin du Palais des Beaux-Arts de Bruxelles*, no.228, 15 January 1937, ill.; anon., 1952, ill.; Wingfield Digby, 1952, p.102, pl.22; Ingamells (*Preview*), 1959, p.439, ill. p.442; Ingamells (*Museums Journal*), 1959, p.125, fig.34 (in group shot); *Handlist*, 1971 (53); Webber, 1975, ill. p.29; Bennett, 1980, pp.13, 38, 99; Hyne, 1985, ill. p.10 in colour; Richard Green, 'Eric Milner-White (1884-1963) and York City Art Gallery', *Clay*, no.15, 1981, p.19, ill. back cover.

MW DOC: General Catalogue: '1931 ... 113 MURRAY "Persian Garden" 120[gns]' and '1952 The following lots were exhibited (1) Dartington Hall ... [see No.23] ... Murray 113 Persian Garden'; Fitzwilliam Book: '28 Class 1 No. in Catalogue 113 No underfoot 39 Date. 1931. Large POT. "Persian Garden" Thrown in one piece. Probably Murray's masterpiece – he so considers it. White glaze, shading into cream-grey. Incised decoration of cranes & brushwork decn in warm brown of leaf-petals. Lip also warm-brown.'; invoice: Alex. Reid & Lefevre, December 1931, '1931 Novr. 5 Stoneware Pots, by Staite Murray. "Persian Garden" [£]200 . . [with Mare]'; album I: exhibition catalogue; album II: reviews, *Bulletin du Palais des Beaux-Arts de Bruxelles*, no. 228, 15 January 1937, and *Yorkshire Gazette*, 22 February 1952; Murray's album: reviews, *Morning Post*, 7 November 1931, *Birmingham Daily Post*, 14 November 1931, and *Observer*, 22 November 1931.

1. Ingamells (*Preview*), 1959, p.439.
2. Last exhibited Christopher Wood Gallery, 1980 (42, ill. p.68).

124. Bowl: 'Peach Flush' 1935

Coarse orange body; transmutation glaze (incised code: 's.K.s.', painted code: 'FRICH').

H 4⅞ in (12.4 cm); D 6⅝ in (16.9 cm)

Mark: Murray's pentagon (impressed)

124

The form of *Peach Flush* is characteristic of a type of bowl produced by Murray in the mid-1930s – strong in shape, tending towards the clumsy with a very heavy, even obtrusive, foot. Another example is illustrated in the catalogue of the 1958 Leicester Galleries exhibition of Murray's work as *Winter* (no.42). The glaze effect on this pot is probably that characterized by Ernest Marsh as 'rich jewel-like colourings radiating from a centre pool of colour in the inside of the bowls'.[1] Murray was reputedly very proud of the glaze effect on this pot: Milner-White refers to it as a 'supreme piece of glazing, which Murray thinks he has never excelled.' He goes on to state that the pot was broken to pieces by a fall and repaired skilfully by Murray himself. The only visual evidence of damage is a small repair to the inside of the top lip. Another pot in the 1935 Lefevre exhibition was also called *Peach Flush* (no.79).

PROV: Lefevre, 1935 (25gns); presented, January 1959 (935/52).

EXH: Lefevre, 1935 (65).

MW DOC: General Catalogue: '1935 ... 174 MURRAY Bowl "Peach Flush" 25[gns]'; Fitzwilliam Book: '34 Class III ?II No. in

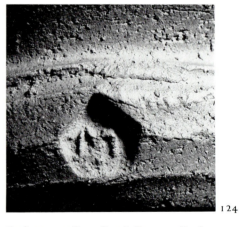

124

Catalogue 174. No on Foot 65 Date 1935 Bowl "Peach Flush" A supreme piece of glazing, which Murray thinks he has never excelled. The shape is possibly a little clumsy with a heavy foot. It was broken to pieces by a fall, & repaired with unusual skill by Murray himself.'; invoice: Alex Reid & Lefevre Ltd, May 1936, receipted, 26 May 1936, '1935 Novr. 12 Pottery by W. Staite Murray ... "Peach Flush" [£]26.5.'; album II: exhibition catalogue.

1. Marsh, 1944, p.107.

125. Pot: 'Grecian Mode' 1935

Pale coarse body flecked with iron; red-brown glaze over cream slip (incised codes: 'K1' and 'AG').

H 13¼ in (33.7 cm); D 10⅜ in (26.4 cm)

Mark: Murray's pentagon (impressed)

By 1932 the economic depression was beginning to bite and it was becoming difficult for Murray to find buyers for his highly-priced pots. In 1933 he did not have an exhibition. By 1934 he was decorating fewer and fewer of his pots with figurative designs. Abstraction was more apparent, probably reflecting the fact that the Seven and Five Group, of which he was still a member, had in that year become the '7 & 5 Abstract Group' with a rule that exhibitions consist of non-representational art only. It is possible that Murray began to lose his way artistically at this time. At any event the mid-1930s were a time of stylistic experimentation for him. The influence of ancient Greek and English medieval ceramics was apparent in many pieces. That of the former is clearly evident in the present pot and also in *Aulos*, now at Southampton Art Gallery. Another pot entitled *Grecian Mode* was in the 1958 Leicester Galleries exhibition of Murray's work (no.145).

PROV: Lefevre, 1935(40gns); presented, 1958, and received on Milner-White's death, 1963 (1049/27).

EXH: Lefevre, 1935 (35); Stockholm, 1939; Manchester, 1989.

LIT: Wingfield Digby, 1952, p.73; *Handlist*, 1971 (57); Bennett, 1980, p.99.

MW DOC: General Catalogue: '1935 ... 173 MURRAY Pot. "Grecian Mode" 40[gns]'/173 Still at Deanery. Quiet but good' and '1939. Collection Lent to Stockhom at the request of the Government. MURRAY. "Grecian Mode" Insured for [£]42'; Fitzwilliam Book: '33 Class [III crossed out] II No. in Catalogue 173 Date 1935. Pot. "Grecian Mode" A pot of good & unusual form, with a remarkable biscuit-brown glaze'; invoice; Alex Reid & Lefevre Ltd, May 1936, receipted, 26 May 1936, '1935 Novr. 12 Pottery by W. Staite Murray ... "Grecian Mode" [£]42 ..'; album II: exhibition catalogue.

126. Jar: 'Motet for Strings' 1937-9
(colour XX)

Iron glaze, incised and brushed decoration of three stringed instruments in blue, brown and white (incised code: '[?]MP.1 10.', painted code: '[?]SMG').

125

H 20¼ in (50.3 cm); D 11 in (28.2 cm)

Mark: Murray's pentagon (impressed)

Motet for Strings is one of the great Murray pots which together constitute a unique and original contribution to British art of the 1930s. Of all his pots, this and *Vortex* (No.116) are the ones most in tune with the artistic avant-garde of the time. From 1934, in accordance with the rule of the newly named '7 & 5 Abstract Group', Murray was decorating fewer and fewer pots with figurative designs. He was developing an abstract style of brushed and incised decora-

tion, which was becoming looser and more fluid. This pot, which indicates a clear reference to Ben Nicholson's paintings, not least in the use of the stringed instruments, displays a near-abstract and powerfully vigorous brush-decoration. It also demonstrates a mastery of the use of iron glaze. Milner-White links *Sonata*, *Wheel of Life*, *Flame*, *Motet for Strings*, and *Alpha* as 'a "family" of great beauty of colour, iron-red & black, with over-glazes in cream & white'.

PROV: Leicester Galleries, 1958(£126); lent from 1958, presented on Milner-White's death, 1963 (1050/9).

EXH: Leicester Galleries, 1958 (82);
Middlesbrough, 1984-5; Wakefield, 1987;
Manchester, 1988 (55).

LIT: Ingamells (*Museums Journal*), 1959, p.125,
fig.34 (in group shot); *Handlist*, 1971 (54);
Haslam (*Murray*), 1984, p.74, pl.xx in colour.

MW DOC: General Catalogue: '1958 ... STAITE
MURRAY'S FINAL SHOW at the Leicester Galleries
Nov. 1958 257. MOTET FOR STRINGS Catalogue No
82 £126/257 At the Art Gallery'; loose
catalogue: (following introduction) '7. 18. 86.
82. 103 [*Sonata, Wheel of Life, Flame, Motet for Strings,
Alpha*] are a "family" of great beauty of colour
iron-red & black, with over-glazes in cream &
white In daylight I prefer 7 to 103 – both
medium small pots of [illegible word] shape &
decoration.' and (by catalogue entry) 'bought E
M-W. £120.'; invoice: Leicester Galleries, 19
December 1958, receipted 24 December 1958,
'82 "Motet for Strings" by W. Staite Murray
[£]126 - -'; album II: exhibition catalogue and
private view card.

127. Very tall Pot: 'Kwan Yin' 1937-9
(colour XXIII)

Coarse pale body; thrown in three sections
and jointed; white slip with burst air bubbles (incised code: 'K14 G8A').

H 40 in (101.8 cm); D 9¼ in (23.5 cm)

Mark: Murray's pentagon (impressed)

Kwan Yin is perhaps the most idiosyncratic
Murray pot in the collection. Together with
Ra it is among the largest pieces he made.
Even though it has been thrown in three
sections, jointed and fired as one, it is technically impressive, the end result combining
elegance, strength and power. All of Murray's tallest anthropomorphic pots have
names associated with Buddhism. *Kwan Yin* is
no exception, taking its name from a Buddhist goddess. It is difficult to be precise
about the dating of this pot. Although
clearly a work of the mid- to late-1930s, it
is virtually certain that it was not in Murray's 1936 exhibition (his penultimate),
since its name does not appear in the catalogue and, had it been, it is likely that

Milner-White would have bought it there
and then (and not in 1958). On this evidence it would seem probable that the pot
was made some time between 1937 and
1939 when Murray resigned his post at the
Royal College of Art and left for Rhodesia.
This trip was ostensibly for three months
but circumstances overtook him and he was
only to return briefly to England in 1957 to
organize the sale of those pieces left behind
and stored in his studio at Bray. Murray died
of cancer in 1962, having made no pots for
the last twenty-three years of his life.
Maurice Collis, in his introduction to the
catalogue of the 1958 Leicester Galleries
exhibition, wrote of the pots shown:
'Among them are some of the best he ever
made, particularly noticeable being the
great pot *Ra* and the tall slender white pots,
vessels which are both delicate and strong,
quite unique, for no other potter of today,
to my knowledge, has attempted such a difficult task.' Another of these tall slender
pots, *Standing Buddha* (no.94 in the exhibition), was illustrated as the frontispiece to
the catalogue; the present whereabouts of
this and *Ra* are unknown.

PROV: Leicester Galleries, 1958 (150gns);
presented, January 1959 (935/86).

EXH: Leicester, 1958 (96); Middlesbrough,
1984-5.

LIT: *Pottery Quarterly*, v, no.20, winter 1958, pl.2b;
Heber Mathews, 'W. Staite Murray, Leicester
Galleries, November', *Pottery Quarterly*, vi, no.21,
spring 1959, pp.29-30; *Handlist*, 1971 (100);
Bennett, 1980, p.99; Haslam (*Murray*), 1984,
pl.30.

MW DOC: General Catalogue: '1958 ... STAITE
MURRAY'S FINAL SHOW at the Leicester Galleries
Nov. 1958 258 KWAN-YIN C.No. 96 £157-10';
invoice: Ernest Brown & Phillips, Leicester
Galleries, 19 December 1958, receipted 24
December 1958, '96 "Kwai-Yin" [by W. Staite
Murray] 157.10 -'; loose catalogue ('150 bt.
EMW 150' written beside entry by Milner-
White); album II: exhibition catalogue.

Johannes Knud Ove Nielsen
Danish 1885-1961

A painter, sculptor and ceramicist, Jais Nielsen (as he was known, Jais being a shortened form of Johannes) was born in Copenhagen and trained there first as a painter's apprentice and subsequently, from 1906 to 1909, at the Kristian Zahrtmann and Johan Rohde art schools. He then spent three years in Paris, where he was able to study museum collections of Chinese, Egyptian and Persian ceramics. Around 1915 he began making ceramics, initially having his work fired at Eifrig's pottery works at Valby, a suburb of Copenhagen. From 1921 he was employed at the Royal Copenhagen Porcelain Manufactory and started to make stoneware. His works formed part of the Royal Copenhagen display at the International Exhibition in Paris of 1925, where they were awarded the *Grand Prix*. Nielsen was strongly influenced by archaic Greek and Byzantine art as well as by 'Modernism'. He combined these influences to develop an intensely personal style characterized by strong simple line and massive, sometimes monumental, form. His dishes and pots are often painted, usually with a blue colour on grey glaze or with an iron colour directly on a rough chamotte body. His output consisted of dishes, vases and bowls on the one hand and sculptural or relief modelling on the other. The former category was often decorated with scenes from the Bible, which also frequently provided inspiration for the latter. Neilsen was a prolific pioneer of Danish stoneware.

128

128. Squared Bowl 1928

Dark blue glaze with a head motif painted within, and chevron decoration incised without.

H 3½ in (8.8 cm); D 5¾ in (14.6 cm)

Marks: 'PROVE', unidentified mark associated with Nielsen, 'JAIS 1 - 3 - 28' and Royal Copenhagen mark (all painted)

This was made at Royal Copenhagen on 1 March 1928.

PROV: Probably Royal Copenhagen Porcelain Manufactory, 1936; presented, 1958, and received on Milner-White's death, 1963 (1049/53).

MW DOC: General Catalogue: '1936 ... DANISH. Jais Nielsen Four Sided bowl. 4[?gns]'.

128

128

Edith Helen Pincombe
British   born 1908

Although modest about her achievement, Helen Pincombe, predominantly a teacher, has been one of the leading twentieth-century promoters of hand-built pots.

Born in Darjeeling, India, and educated in Australia, Helen Pincombe came to Great Britain in 1925. She trained as an art teacher and discovered pottery through sculpture. She was then to study at the Central School of Art and the Royal College of Art. At the latter she just overlapped with Staite Murray. When he left for Rhodesia and the College moved to Ambleside for the duration of the war, Pincombe was asked to teach. The major benefit of this move was that it put her in stimulating contact with the pottery at Burton-in-Lonsdale, which continued the country slipware tradition stretching back to the eighteenth century.

After the Second World War Pincombe set up a pottery at Oxshott in Surrey close to Denise Wren. By 1955 she had given up teaching and was trying to find a focus for her work. She made slipware and tin glaze as her staple lines, but also stoneware which she preferred. Although most of her work is thrown, she took a great interest in hand-building.

At the Central School Pincombe had spent a great deal of time making pots this way. The only study she could find on the subject was one devoted to the pot makers of the Pueblo Indians – and she based her method on that. Her major contribution was to introduce professional coiling techniques to British pottery. With Ruth Duckworth she helped to alter the prevailing attitudes to the validity and worth of hand-building.

As far as can be ascertained Pincombe exhibited in only three exhibitions. The first was the Brygos Gallery exhibition *Under £10 English Pottery* of 1936, where she showed six pieces; the second was an exhibition of thrown and coiled stoneware shared with Katharine Pleydell-Bouverie at the Primavera gallery in November 1958; the third was the travelling exhibition of the Craftsmen Potters Association held in the summer of 1958. Her work was mostly sold through the Craftsmen Potters Association, Primavera and the Crafts Centre. By 1972 she had given up potting. Her major interest now is gardening.

129. Squared Bowl exh. 1958

Thrown with flattened sides; *sgraffito* decoration of lines surrounding an Oriental-style character through red-brown iron glaze to reveal cream slip.

H $3\frac{7}{8}$ in (9.8 cm); D 5 in (12.5 cm)

Mark: HP monogram (impressed)

This bowl was made for the Primavera exhibition of 1958. The decoration may derive from that of Mexican Indian pots which seems to have been a major influence on Pincombe's work. The character on the pot has no meaning to the potter. It was fired in an updraught gas kiln at Oxshott designed by Mr Skinner of the South Metropolitan Gas Company.[1]

PROV: Primavera, 1958(3gns); presented, 1958, and received on Milner-White's death, 1963 (1049/39).

EXH: Primavera, 1958 (95).

LIT: Handlist, 1971 (2).

MW DOC: General Catalogue: '1958. Pleydell Bouverie and [...] at Primavera Gallery, Sloane Sq. November 4-17 ... HELEN PINCOMBE 256 Small bowl, incised pattern red-brown iron glaze £3-3-0/256 Pleasant but hardly museum rank'; album II: private view card.

1. Verbal communication, 1988.

129

129

Katharine Pleydell-Bouverie was born on 7 June 1895 in Highworth, Wiltshire, and brought up in Coleshill House, Berkshire, the beautiful home of her well-to-do and well-connected family. She started to pot at the Central School of Art. Then in 1924 she went to St Ives to join the Leach Pottery for a year. There she laid the foundations of her craft, finding the technical lectures delivered by the Japanese potter Tsuneyoshi Matsubayashi (Matsu) of particular help. She very soon decided to concentrate on using glazes for their own sake, taking little interest in, for example, brush-decoration. In 1925 she set up a wood-fired kiln on the estate at Coleshill and here for fifteen years, first with Ada Mason (Peter) and from 1923 with Norah Braden, she experimented extensively with wood- and vegetable-ash glazes made from trees and plants on the estate. In 1946 Coleshill was sold and 'Beano' (as she was known) moved to Kilmington Manor, Wiltshire, where she was to live and work for the rest of her life, initially using an oil-fired kiln but afterwards turning to electricity. She died there at the age of eighty-nine.

Pleydell-Bouverie's output consisted principally of vases, bottles and bowls, and she was particularly fond of making pots for flowers. Her pioneering work on ash glazes and the meticulous records of her experiments, which she kept in a special notebook, have together made a tremendous contribution to the range of ash glazes available today. Her MS Glaze Recipe Notebook together with the largest single collection of her pots may be found at the Crafts Study Centre, Holburne of Menstrie Museum, University of Bath, which she helped to establish.

130

130. Bottle c.1925-8

Floral cut decoration through iron slip, covered with clear glaze.

H 5½ in (14 cm); D 4 in (10.2 cm)

Marks: 'COLE' and 'KPB' (impressed)

This pot was made early in Pleydell-Bouverie's career at Coleshill. Though not typical of her work, the cut decoration exhibited here is not uninteresting. The original inspiration for this pot, particularly its decoration, was cut T'zŭ Chou-type ware, made in north China during the Sung dynasty. Whereas in Leach's work (see No.56) such borrowing is clear, in the case of Pleydell-Bouverie's bottle the influence has been fully integrated with her own vision to make something original. Two other bottles with cut-away decoration are in the Crafts Study Centre, Bath, both dating from 1926 (P.74.169 and P.74.170).

PROV: (?)Colnaghi; purchased, 1928 (£1 15s.); presented, January 1959 (935/18).

EXH: (?)Colnaghi, 1928 (not identifiable in catalogue); Bath, 1980-1 (159).

LIT: Handlist, 1971 (10, incorrectly as Norah Braden).

MW DOC: General Catalogue: '1928 ... 47 PLEYDELL BOUVERIE. Bottle, red-black, floral decn. cut to slip. £1.15 Given to Veronica Carpenter [crossed out] (Given away)'.

131. Small Bowl (?)exh. 1931

Hawthorn-ash glaze grey-brown, matt (incised body code: '74'; brushed glaze code: 'XLIV').

H 3⅛ in (7.8 cm); D 4⅜ in (11.1 cm)

Mark: KPB monogram in octagon (impressed)

Pleydell-Bouverie was a meticulous experimenter and usually incised the body code and brushed the glaze code on to her pots.

130

PROV: (?)National Society: Painters, Sculptors, Engravers, Potters, June 1931 (2gns); presented, 1958, received on Milner-White's death (1049/2).

EXH: (?)Royal Institute Galleries, 1931 (bowl 13, case D); Bath, 1980-1 (76).

MW DOC: (?)Receipt: National Society: Painters, Sculptors, Engravers, Potters, 16 June 1931, Bowl No. 13 Case D by Miss Pleydell Bouverie £2:2:0'; album I: reviews, *The Times*, 9 June 1931, and *Morning Post*, undated.

1. In Pleydell Bouverie's MS Glaze Recipe Notebook, under stoneware glazes for wood-fired kiln at Coleshill 1928-46, 'XLIV**' (Norah Braden's glaze) = 'Hawthorn Ash 10. Limestone 6. Potash felspar 16. Quartz 4. China clay slip 8. Ball clay slip 8. Manganese oxide 1½. Chamber 1 cream to buff, matt, takes pigment 12, 19 and 21 very well. About 1250°-60°c. Chamber 2 matt cream and takes pigment 12 well, rather short period of correct fire round 1250°c.'

132. Vase exh. 1958

Squat form: deeply carved vertical lines, matt pale-blue glaze with opaque whitish spots (incised body code: ?'276', '226' or '2215'; brushed glaze code: 'ICX').[1]

H 4 in (10.1 cm); D 4⅞ in (12.3 cm)

Mark: KPB monogram in circle (impressed)

Pleydell-Bouverie's pots of this shape were often decorated with carved or incised lines; though not in this case, these lines often curve around the body. It should be noted that the glaze code on this pot relates to earthenware glazes in the Glaze Recipe Notebook, whereas the body of this pot is stoneware. It would therefore seem that a glaze developed for earthenware has been applied to a stoneware body. Leach throws light on the opaque white spots in the glaze in *A Potter's Book*: '*Acid fumes* (such as sulphuric) may be liberated which under oxidizing conditions combine with any lime present in the clay and cause spots or scum ... If the temperature is not high the *sulphates* may remain suspended in the glaze as opaque whitish spots.'[2] This vase was made at Kilmington.

PROV: Primavera, 1958 (2½gns); presented, January 1959 (935/11).

131

132

EXH: Primavera, 1958; Bath, 1980-81 (89).

MW DOC: General Catalogue: '1958. Pleydell-Bouverie and […] at Primavera Gallery, Sloane Sq. Numbered 4-17 … 254 Small celadon-coloured pot lobed sides £2-12-6'; album II: private view card.

1. In Pleydell-Bouverie's MS Glaze Recipe Notebook, under earthenware glazes for oil kiln at Kilmington onwards from 1952, 'I.CX' = 'Petalite 60. Quartz 30. Whiting 60. Soda felspar 90. China clay 30. Frit 321 30. 712 frit 11½, red iron oxide 1. Black copper oxide ¼. Good. Same quality and texture at 4A as XXXVI and a pleasant light blue'.
2. Leach, 1940, p.164.

133. Pot exh. 1958 (*colour XXIV*)

Narrow aperture and everted lip with cut lobed panels; matt grey-white glaze (incised body code: '235'; brushed glaze code: IXXXVI').[1]

H 10⅝ in (26.9 cm); D 7 in (17.8 cm)

Mark: Obliterated by glaze (impressed)

Other examples of similar cut decoration are at the Craft Study Centre, Bath.[2] Like No.132, this stoneware pot appears to be covered with a glaze developed for earthenware bodies. It was made at Kilmington.

PROV: Primavera, 1958(6gns); presented, January 1959 (935/74.)

EXH: Primavera, 1958.

LIT: *Handlist*, 1971 (89).

MW DOC: General Catalogue: '1958. Pleydell-Bouverie and […] at Primavera Gallery, Sloane Sq. Numbered 4-17 … 253 Greenish-grey Pot, lobed sides £6-6'; album II: private view card.

1. In Pleydell-Bouverie's MS Glaze Recipe Notebook, under earthenware glazes for oil kiln at Kilmington from 1952, 'I.XXXVI*' = 'Petalite 2, quartz 1, whiting 2, sodar felspar 3, china clay 1, frit 321.1. Fired around 1150°C. A good matt grey white in reduction. <u>Later</u> in the electric kiln it is a very good matt white at Cone 4A'.
2. Several are illustrated in Crafts Council, *Katharine Pleydell-Bouverie: A Potter's Life 1895-1985*, Crafts Council, 1986, e.g. pp.35 & 48, in colour.

134. Vase exh. 1958

Crackled cream-white glaze (incised body code: '233.').

H 9 in (22.8 cm); D 9 in (22.9 cm)

Mark: KPB monogram in circle (impressed)

Although this pot has no painted code, the glaze is perhaps that described by Leach in

134

A *Potter's Book* as being made from the ashes of grass, reeds, nettles and lavender, which is 'White or very pale grey, rather sugary in texture and heavily crackled if used thick,'[1] as seen here. The section on wood-ash glazes in this book was based on advice given by Pleydell-Bouverie. This vase was made at Kilmington.

PROV: Primavera, 1958(7gns); lent, 1958, and presented on Milner-White's death, 1963 (1050/1).

EXH: Primavera, 1958; Bath, 1980-1 (99).

LIT: *Handlist*, 1971 (14).

MW DOC: General Catalogue: '1958. Pleydell-Bouverie and […] at Primavera Gallery, Sloane Sq. Numbered 4-17 252 PLEYDELL-BOUVERIE Cream-white Pot, crackled Still at Deanery £7-7'; album II: private view card.

1. Leach, 1940, p.163.

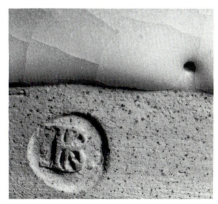

134

Margaret Enid Rey
British   born 1911

Margaret Rey was born on 10 August 1911 in Dinas Powis, near Cardiff, and brought up in Bognor Regis in Sussex. She trained at the Royal College of Art under William Staite Murray from 1932 to 1935. In common with that of many of his pupils, Rey's work is heavily influenced by Murray's and can sometimes be mistaken for it. Like Murray's, some of her pots were given names and were conceived as independent works of art. Her philosophy was, however, less rigid than Murray's in this respect and, for example, she did not object to her vases being used for flowers, while a proportion of her output had a more direct functional use. From 1934 to 1939 she had a studio in Raynes Park, Wimbledon, which Sam Haile (q.v.) a fellow student at the Royal College shared for a while. She exhibited with the Englishwoman Exhibition in 1934 and 1936, at the Wertheim Gallery in 1935 and the Brygos Gallery in 1937. In 1938 she had her first one-woman show at the Brygos Gallery. In the same year, her work was also included in the exhibition of English potters' work at the Galerie Rouard in Paris, in exchange for an exhibition of the work of French potters at the Brygos Gallery in London. Additionally she exhibited in Canada.

She worked in both earthenware and stoneware, making a wide variety of items including bowls, coffee-beakers, and beer-mugs but specializing mainly in large pots. Her work received critical acclaim before the Second World War and examples were purchased by the Contemporary Art Society. After the war, however, she made very few pots and worked mainly as a designer and sculptress from her home in Forest Green, Surrey.

A large vase by Rey was purchased for the collection (as a Staite Murray) in 1966 (1126); its painted mark, and not that of No.135 (which is unclear), is the one illustrated here.

135. Lidded Tobacco-Jar 1938 or earlier

Squared sides: predominantly dark-brown glaze with sand and cast grey interior.

H 4⅜ in (11.2 cm); D 5¼ in (13.5 cm)

Mark: MR monogram (impressed)

This tobacco-jar was presumably made specially for Rey's one-woman exhibition at the Brygos Gallery in 1938, which marked the apex of her potting career.

PROV: Brygos Gallery, 1938 (15s. 6d.); presented, 1958, and received on Milner-White's death, 1963 (1049/42).

EXH: Brygos Gallery, *Stoneware by Margaret Rey*, 17 March - 7 April 1938 (64).

MW DOC: General Catalogue: '1938. 195 REY (Miss Margaret) Tobacco Jar (Pleasant) Still at Deanery 15[s.]-6[d.].'; album II: exhibition catalogue.

135

Frances Emma Richards
British c.1869-1931

Frances E. Richards, along with W. B. Dalton and Reginald Wells, was one of the earliest pioneers of the studio pottery movement. She worked in stoneware and earthenware using a kiln in her garden at various addresses in Highgate, London. Between 1898 and 1900 she was at 39 Claremont Road; from 1901 she lived at 33 Archway Road and in 1912 at 3 Prestwood Mansions, Archway Road, whilst by 1915 she was exhibiting from 178 Archway Road. She produced both thrown and hand-built pots, simple in form and decorated with experimental glazes. She exhibited regularly with the Arts and Crafts Exhibition Society from 1916 and with the Englishwoman Exhibition. She also showed her work in 1922 at the *Exhibition of Pottery produced in London between the Years 1872-1922* at the South London Art Gallery and Museum, and in 1928 had a one-woman show at the Three Shields Gallery. Her work was purchased by the Contemporary Art Society and is represented at the Victoria and Albert Museum and Southampton, although the largest collection of her pots is at the University College of Wales, Aberystwyth.

Very little is known about this potter. She seems to have lived in poverty and worked on her own, producing remarkable pots given her isolation and lack of technical knowledge. She died at the Royal Northern Hospital, London, on 30 August 1931, at the age of sixty-two.

Milner-White and Richards

Milner-White probably first came across Frances E. Richards's work in 1926, when he saw examples in the Arts and Crafts Exhibition Society's show at the Royal Academy: although he wrote 'Goodish – but vulgar after L & M [presumably Leach and Murray]' against the catalogue entry for one of her pots,[1] he also wrote 'Keep eyes upon Dalton, Richards, Fox-Stra[ngeways]' at the top of the same page. In fact his interest in these potters was not sustained. Only two works by Dalton and three by Richards, and none at all by Fox-Strangeways are listed in the Dean's General Catalogue. There are two letters in the Gallery file from Richards to Milner-White. The first, dated 27 July 1927, in reply to a letter from the Dean, promises she will notify him when she has produced something 'of my best'; the second, dated only 22 November but presumably of 1927 or later, mentions two exhibitions in which she is showing and encloses invitation cards for them.

1. No. 134 (w) on p.48 of the Arts and Craft Exhibition Society's catalogue for 1926.

136. Vase 1927

Pale body; deep-brown mottled glaze.

H 7⅛ in (18 cm); D 4¾ in (12.1 cm)

Mark: Richards's monogram with date 1927 (incised)

This vase was made for Richards's only one-woman exhibition. In common with much pioneer pottery it is heavier than it need be.

PROV: Three Shields Gallery, 1928 (£1½gns); presented, 1958, and received on Milner-White's death, 1963 (1049/41).

EXH: Three Shields Gallery, *Pottery made by Frances E. Richards*, 22 May - 12 June 1928 (54).

MW DOC: General Catalogue: '1928 ... 46 RICHARDS. Pot, deep brown./At Deanery, used for flowers'; invoice: Three Shields, 26 May 1928, receipted, 16 June 1928, 'Brown Pot. [No] 54. £1.11.6'; album I: exhibition catalogue.

137. Dish 1928

Pale body ; incised spiral decoration within, radiating petal-like incised lines without, the whole covered with green-yellow glaze and brown stippled splashes.

H 2½ in (6.5 cm) ; D 10 in (25.5 cm)

Mark : Richards's monogram with date 1928 (incised)

This dish was made for Richards's only one-woman exhibition. Particularly noteworthy is the individual manner in which the brown splashes of glaze have been applied. In common with much pioneer work, this pot is heavier than it need be.

PROV : Three Shields Gallery, 1928 (2gns) ; presented, 1958, and received on Milner-White's death, 1963 (1049/40).

EXH : Three Shields Gallery, *Pottery made by Frances E. Richards*, 22 May - 12 June 1928 (4).

MW DOC : General Catalogue : '1928. 45. RICHARDS. Dish, brown, incised dec.' ; invoice : Three Shields, 26 May 1928, receipted, 16 June 1928, 'Brown Dish No 4 £2.2.0' ; album I : exhibition catalogue.

137

136

Axel Salto

Danish 1889-1961

Axel Salto was a prolific and versatile artist who worked as a painter, lithographer and ceramicist. Born in Copenhagen, he trained there as a painter at the Royal Academy of Fine Arts. In 1913 he set up his own studio, where he practised painting and book design, at the same time as working for Bing and Grøndahl in porcelain. In 1929 he started to work in stoneware, a body which suited him better. His first works were fired at Carl Halier's factory. Later he worked with Natalie Krebs (q.v.) and Bode Willumsen (q.v.). From the early 1930s until his death in 1961 he was attached to the Royal Copenhagen Porcelain Manufactory, for whom he produced a long series of outstanding pots.

A highly original artist, Salto had no intention of making purely functional pots, although functional shapes provided a starting point. His innovation was in ornamentation, using a variety of colour and glaze effects. Initially he exploited the way in which a glaze ran through cut or scratched lines in the body : the glaze collected thickly in the hollows and thinly on the raised parts, thereby bringing the surface alive. Later on colour variations were achieved over modelled bodies : in characteristic work from this period he was inspired by the shapes of fruit and other plant-forms such as sweetcorn, pineapples and pine cones. He sought to draw inspiration from nature rather than imitate it directly. He divided his work into the fluted, the budding and the sprouting styles. Salto's control over the way glaze runs was exceptional and ensured him a place as one of the greatest decorative ceramicists of his time.

138. Bowl c.1946 (*colour XXVIII*)

Grey 'hare's fur' glaze within, incised foliage ribs covered with a golden glaze without.

H 3 in (7.5 cm) ; D 7 in (18 cm)

Marks : 'SALTO' (carved), Royal Copenhagen symbol (painted) and an unidentified mark (painted)

This bowl was made at the Royal Copenhagen Porcelain Manufactory from Salto's design. It can be grouped with his first style of work in stoneware. A similar pot is illustrated in *Dansk Kunsthåndvaerker Leksikon*, Rhodos, Copenhagen 1979, p.518, where it is dated 1946.

PROV : Possibly Copenhagen Porcelain Manufacturing Depot; purchased 1946(12gns) ; presented, 1958, and received on Milner-White's death, 1963 (1049/51).

MW DOC : General Catalogue : '1946 ... DANISH 224 SALTO. (Copenhagen) Bowl, Grey Hare's Fur & iron-red pool within incised foliage-rib in gold on chestnut red 12.12'.

138

Séraphin Soudbinine
Russian   1870-1944

Séraphin Soudbinine was arguably the greatest potter working in France in the twentieth century. Born at Nijni-
Novgorod in Russia, where he first worked as an actor and
learnt to sculpt, Soudbinine came to live in Paris at the turn
of the century. There he became an assistant to Auguste
Rodin and spent some thirty years as a sculptor. In the early
1930s he visited New York and was much impressed by the
Chinese and Japanese ceramics at the Metropolitan Museum.
On his return to Paris he started to make ceramics. His working methods often tended towards the sculptural: for
instance many pots are carved from a block of clay rather
than thrown on the wheel. He was also an avid experimenter
in glazes. The synthesis of Russian and Oriental influences in
Soudbinine's work resulted in a wonderfully original art of
great beauty. However, his costs were not covered by sales.
At the beginning of the Second World War his studio was
destroyed and he died of starvation. Although collected in
England during the 1930s, his work is not known to be
represented in any other British public collection. The largest
collection in public hands is in the Musée National de
Céramique at Sèvres in France.

Milner-White and Soudbinine
Soudbinine had just one exhibition in England, a one-man
show at the Brygos Gallery in 1937, from which Milner-
White bought three pieces. Two are now in the collection
at York City Art Gallery but the whereabouts of the third pot,
which did not come to the Gallery, are unknown. No.60 in
the exhibition, priced at 35 guineas and paid for on 5
October 1937, it was recorded by the Dean in his MS catalogue as '189A ... Stoneware Tortoise Carved Bowl'.

139

140

140

139. Dish 1937 or earlier (*colour XXVII*)

Pale body ; vortex decoration and five large fish in iron and pale green glazes on a dark green glaze.

H 3⅜ in (8.5 cm) ; D 15¼ in (38.8 cm)

Mark : 'SERA PHIN' design and 'Soudbinine' (incised)

This dish was the most expensive of the three pieces of Soudbinine's work purchased by Milner-White from the Brygos Gallery exhibition of 1937 and in fact one of the most expensive pieces in the whole exhibition. It is thrown, although many of Soudbinine's pots are carved. The body is very close to porcelain. A strikingly original and powerfully decorated dish, it clearly reveals the influences of Soudbinine's Russian background in the handling of the darkly vibrant and relentless vortex. The dish has an almost icon-like quality.

PROV : Brygos Gallery, 1937(40gns) ; presented, January 1959 (935/31).

EXH : Brygos Gallery, *Soudbinine : An Exhibition of Pottery*, 19 May - 8 June 1937 (4, 'Loaned – Not for sale', according to receipt, but more probably 31).

MW DOC : General Catalogue : '1937 ... 189B SOUDBININE Dish with fish design 40.[gns]' ; invoice : Brygos Gallery, 29 June 1937, receipted 29 July 1937, '[SOUDBININE] No.4, Plate, [£]42.0.0' ; album II : exhibition catalogue (31 underlined and 'Dish with Fish Design' written alongside by Milner-White).

140. Bowl 1937 or earlier

White porcelain body ; dull green glaze over (?)iron-based glaze without, fish frieze towards top.

H 5 in (12.6 cm) ; D 8⅝ in (21.9 cm)

Mark : 'Soudbinine' (incised)

Soudbinine usually employed either a dark-brown stoneware body or a porcelain body. The body here is porcelain, and is finely controlled except that the bottom has become too thin and has had to be plugged. Although his pots are frequently carved from a block of clay, this one is thrown. The decoration is a subtle synthesis of Oriental and Russian influences.

PROV : Brygos Gallery, 1938(15gns) ; presented, January 1959 (935/39).

EXH : Brygos Gallery, *Soudbinine : An Exhibition of Pottery*, 19 May - 8 June 1937 (19).

LIT : *Handlist*, 1971 (97).

MW DOC : General Catalogue : '1938 ... 195D RUSSIAN SOUDBININE Bowl, fish decoration 15.15.0/Continental Pieces Date uncertain but at least a year before my purchase' ; receipted invoice : Brygos Gallery, undated, '1 piece (bowl) by S. Soudbinine £15.15.0' ; album II : exhibition catalogue (19 underlined and 'Bowl, Fish Decoration' written alongside by Milner-White).

Charles Vyse and Nell Vyse

British 1882-1971
British 1892-1967

Charles Vyse came from a Staffordshire pottery background. He trained as a designer and modeller, starting his career as a sculptor. When he and Nell married they set up together in Chelsea making original figurines based on London types. They produced two or three new designs a year which became very popular. By 1928 they were also making bowls and vases derived from Chinese ceramics of the Sung dynasty. This was in line with the current enthusiasm for Oriental ceramics brought about by the influx of such wares into the country in the early years of the century. Nell was an experienced chemist and together the Vyses experimented tirelessly in order to reproduce the glazes on these early pots. Their most noted discovery was that a blue used by the Chinese was not in fact derived from copper, as had been believed, but from iron. From around 1935 original designs started to appear, their form often based on traditional prototypes (such as beer-mugs) and their decoration usually inspired by the traditions of the circus and the fairground. From 1928

until 1938 the Vyses had an annual exhibition at Walker's Galleries, 48 New Bond Street. Their work was bought by the Contemporary Art Society and important collectors like George Eumorfopoulos and Eric Milner-White. After the war the Vyses parted. Charles continued to work and exhibit but did not attract the same attention. He taught for a while at Farnham, and then retired to Deal in Kent.

Milner–White and the Vyses

After Hamada, Leach, and Murray, Milner-White purchased more pots by the Vyses than by any other potters (between thirty-seven and thirty-nine, his last in 1938). He also gave away more pots by the Vyses than by any of the others.

Three of the pots in the collection are signed 'C V'. All works, however, are catalogued as by both Charles and Nell Vyse, as it is believed that Nell was mostly responsible for mixing and applying the glazes.

---

141. Plate 1929 or earlier

Black glaze, with blue and yellow flecked glaze and star motifs (probably wax-resist) within.

H $1\frac{5}{8}$ in (4.2 cm); D 7 in (17.8 cm)

Mark: Any mark obliterated by glaze

This is an early experiment in the Oriental style.

PROV: Walker's Galleries, 1930 (4gns); presented, 1958, and received on Milner-White's death, 1963 (1049/50).

EXH: Walker's Galleries, *Pottery, Stoneware and Hard Porcelain by Mr. and Mrs. Charles Vyse* (their second annual exhibition), 20 November - 18 December 1929 (46).

MW DOC: General Catalogue: '1929 ... 84 VYSE Plate, Temmoku, green, star decorn.'; invoice: Walker's Galleries, 25 February 1930, receipted 3 March 1930, '[No.] 46. Plate. Temmoku type, 4.4.0'; album I: exhibition catalogue.

142. Bowl 1930

Light golden-brown background with dark green radiating brush marks.

H $2\frac{1}{8}$ in (5.5 cm); D 7 in (17.6 cm)

Mark: 'C V 1930' (incised)

This bowl was inspired by early Oriental pottery, the glazes of which it imitates. According to a note in Milner-White's MS catalogue it was broken in 1938. It was presumably mended soon after.

141

PROV: Walker's Galleries, 1930 (4gns); presented, 1958, and received on Milner-White's death, 1963 (1049/45).

EXH: Walker's Galleries, *Pottery, Stoneware and Hard Porcelain by Mr. and Mrs. Charles Vyse* (their third annual exhibition), 26 November - 17 December 1930 (53).

MW DOC: General Catalogue: '1930 ... 103 VYSE Dish, red, gold & green Broken 1938 Mended? 4[gns]'; album I: exhibition catalogue (53 underlined and '(Broken)' written beside entry by Milner-White).

143. Bowl 1933

Mirror black glaze made from mineral lime with iron-red splashes.

H $3\frac{7}{8}$ in (9.8 cm); D 7 in (17.7 cm)

Mark: 'C V/1933' (incised)

This bowl was inspired by early Oriental pottery, the glazes of which it imitates. Pots in this style are characterized by *The Times* critic's review of the Vyses' 1932 exhibition at Walker's Galleries: 'The forms they produce are well enough, not very imaginative but generally well proportioned, but the special character of their work is in the quality of the glazes. One would say that a pot exists for them chiefly as a support for

142

144

143

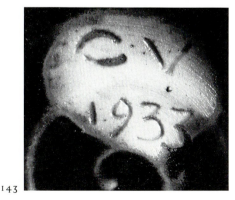

143

MW DOC: General Catalogue: '1933 ... 160 VYSE
Bowl, mirror black, red splashes 8[gns]/160
used as a lamp. Glaze remarkable, but form poor.
In use at Deanery'; invoice: Walker's Galleries,
29 December 1933, '[No.] 90. Bowl. Mirror
black, red splashes, 8.8.0'; undated note from
Walker's Galleries on glazes: '90. Mineral
lime'; album II: exhibition catalogue; letter from Arden
Constant, 20 December 1933.

1. (?)Charles Marriott, 'New Pottery Glazes' *The
Times*, date unknown but probably November or
December 1932 (cutting in Milner-White's
album II).

144. Minute Pot 1933

Brown brush-decoration of fishes on grey
glaze speckled with iron from the clay body
(incised code: '18').

H $1\frac{7}{8}$ in (4.7 cm); D $2\frac{1}{8}$ in (5.5 cm)

Mark: 'C V 1933' (incised)

This was a trial piece.

PROV: Walker's Galleries, 1933($\frac{1}{2}$gn); presented,
1958, and received on Milner-White's death,
1963 (1049/62).

EXH: Walker's Galleries, *Stoneware Pottery, Hard
Porcelains and Figures by Mr. and Mrs. Charles Vyse* (their
sixth annual exhibition), 29 November-19
December 1933 'A collection of trial pieces: ...
c.–Half-a-guinea each.')

MW DOC: General Catalogue: '1933 ... 163 VYSE
Minute pot, grey with brown decoration $\frac{1}{2}$[gn.] /
163 Still at Deanery'; invoice: Walker's Galleries,
29 December 1933, 'c ... 10[s.].6[d.]'; album II:
exhibition catalogue (c underlined and 'Minute
Pot' written beside entry by Milner-White).

surface treatment.'[1] Arden Constant wrote
to Milner-White on 20 December 1933:
'I feel that No 90 is the best piece in the
exhibition and apparently you think so too!
What a glaze; what richness and quality.!'

PROV: Walker's Galleries, 1933(8gns); presented,
1958, and received on Milner-White's death,
1963 (1049/43).

EXH: Walker's Galleries, *Stoneware Pottery, Hard
Porcelains and Figures by Mr. and Mrs. Charles Vyse* (their
sixth annual exhibition), 29 November-19
December, 1933 (90).

LIT: *Handlist*, 1971 (94).

145

145. Vase: 'Olympia' 1935 (colour IX)

Iron brush-decoration on grey glaze depicting a circus man and woman standing on the backs of horses with title 'OLYMPIA'.

H 16⅜ in (41.5 cm); D 10¼ in (25.9 cm)

Mark: 'VYSE/1935' (incised)

This vase is a fine example of the Vyses' work influenced by English traditions and the fairground. Despite its appearance, which suggest the use of a stencil, the decoration was applied free-hand. *The Times* review of the Vyses' 1935 exhibition at Walker's Galleries noted: 'In this exhibition there are some interesting attempts to get away from the Chinese model – which is playing for safety – in some pots, jugs and mugs of English character, with Olympia Circus and Barnet Fair decorations in rust on grey.' Another pot decorated with circus horses is in the City Museum and Art Gallery, Stoke-on-Trent (499P1942); this vase is also dated 1935.

PROV: Walker's Galleries, 1936(30gns); presented, January 1959 (935/54).

EXH: Walker's Galleries, *Stoneware Pottery and Figures by Mr. and Mrs. Charles Vyse* (their eighth annual exhibition), 2-21 December 1935 (1, 'Olympia').

LIT: (?)Charles Marriott, 'Decorative Pottery: Artistic Sensibility', *The Times*, 19 December 1935; *Handlist*, 1971 (90).

MW DOC: General Catalogue: '1935 ... 175 VYSE. Pot "Olympia" 30[gns]'; invoice: Walker's Galleries, 15 January 1936, 'No. 1. "Olympia". Pot, 31.10.0'; album II: exhibition catalogue, review, *The Times*, 19 December 1935, photograph of the Vyses working with *Olympia* on their work table, and reproduction of a photograph showing *Olympia* and three other Vyse pots.

146

146. Beer-Mug 1935

Brush-decoration with text: 'WHAT YOU FANCY DOES YOU GOOD.'

H 5¼ in (13.3 cm); D 4½ in (11 cm); maximum width including handle 6¼ in (15.9 cm)

Marks: 'VYSE' and '1935' (incised)

This was one of the Vyses' earliest designs based on English tradition, rather than the Chinese, and is typical of the many beer-mugs made by them. Milner-White bought another Vyse beer-mug from their 1937 exhibition at Walker's Galleries (127), which was also given to York Art Gallery. It had a combed decoration and, according to an MS note by Milner-White in the catalogue, was glazed with 'Rose Ash from Bencant Wood'; it has been stolen from the collection.[1]

PROV: Walker's Galleries, 1936(2gns); presented, January 1959 (935/55).

EXH: Walker's Galleries, *Stoneware Pottery and Figures by Mr. and Mrs. Charles Vyse* (their eighth annual exhibition), 2-21 December 1935 (67).

LIT: *Handlist*, 1971 (92).

MW DOC: General Catalogue: '1935 ... 177 VYSE Mug. "What you fancy does you good". 2 [gns]'; invoice: Walker's Galleries, 15 January 1936, '[No.] 67. Mug, 2.2.0'; album II: exhibition catalogue and review, *The Times*, 19 December 1935.

1. See Appendix B4 (935/58).

147. Vase 1935

In the form of a figure based on a Cretan kore; painted decoration.

H 15⅛ in (38.5 cm); D 6 in (15.2 cm)

Mark: 'VYSE 1935' (incised)

This vase is a humorous piece based on English fairground traditions. From the photograph of Nell Vyse in Milner-White's album II, the head of this figure would seem to have been modelled upon her.

PROV: National Society, 1935(10?gns); presumably given by Milner-White to Mrs V.J.Long, York, by whom presented, October 1963 (1058/63).

148

147

EXH: Royal Institute Galleries, sixth annual exhibition of the National Society: Painters, Sculptors, Engravers, Potters, 11 February - 4 March 1935 (in group, 240: Table c).

LIT: *Handlist*, 1971 (99).

MW DOC: General Catalogue: '1935 ... 168 VYSE Pot, woman's figure 10[?gns]/168 In use as a light-standard at the Deanery in Guest Bedroom. Is it good – or worthless??'; receipt: National Society, 4 March 1935, '240 c/5, C Vyse 240 c/ 10 [C Vyse] £14.14.0'; album II: exhibition catalogue, reproduction of a photograph of the Vyses at work with No.147 on the work table; letter from Charles Vyse, 6 March 1935: 'I have brought the two pots [No.147 probably being one of them] to the studio, & I hope to pack them off to you either today or to-morrow. Our purveyor of "Wood-wool" packing has been burnt out, & hence the slight delay!'

148. Bowl 1938

Faceted octagonal cut body on four feet; butterfly motif on tenmoku and elm-ash glaze.

H 3 in (7.7 cm); D $4\frac{3}{4}$ in (12.1 cm)

Mark: 'VYSE/1938' (incised)

This bowl is made in the Oriental manner, showing complicated glaze effects. The Vyses experimented widely to improve their understanding and control of glazes to great effect. Much of their work, like this example, employed wood-ash glazes.[1]

PROV: Walker's Galleries, 1938 (3gns); presented, January 1959 (935/49).

EXH: Walker's Galleries, *Stoneware Pottery and Figures by Mr. and Mrs. Charles Vyse* (their eleventh and last annual exhibition), 30 November - 20 December 1938 (22).

MW DOC: General Catalogue: Probably '1938 …
198 VYSE. Temmoku Facetted [sic] Bowl, Elm Ash
3.3.0'; invoice: Walker's Gallery, 20 December
1938, receipted 31 January 1939, 'Exhibition of
Pottery by Mr. & Mrs. Charles Vyse No. 22
Facetted [sic] Temmoku 3.3.-'; album II:
exhibition catalogue.

1. See review by (?)Charles Marriott of Walker's
Galleries' *Vyse* exhibition of 1932, *The Times*,
November or December 1932, in Milner-White's
album II.

149. Octagonal Bowl probably 1938

Red and blue poplar-ash glaze.

H $2\frac{5}{8}$ in (6.6 cm); D $6\frac{7}{8}$ in (17.4 cm)

Mark: 'VYSE 1938' (incised)

This bowl is made in the Oriental manner.

PROV: Walker's Galleries, 1938($1\frac{1}{2}$gns);
presented, 1958, and received on Milner-White's
death, 1963 (1049/48).

EXH: Walker's Galleries, *Stoneware Pottery and Figures
by Mr. and Mrs. Charles Vyse* (their eleventh and last
annual exhibition), 30 November-20 December
1938 (24).

MW DOC: General Catalogue: Probably '1938 …
199 VYSE Octagonal Red Bowl (Poplar Glaze)
1.10.6'; invoice: Walker's Galleries, 30
December 1938, receipted 31 January 1939,
'Exhibition of Pottery by Mr. & Mrs. Charles Vyse,
[No.] 24 Octagonal red bowl 1.11.6'; album II:
exhibition catalogue.

149

Philip Smeale Wadsworth
British born 1910

Philip Wadsworth was born on 8 July 1910 in Draycott-le-Moors, Stoke-on-Trent. He was educated at Malvern College and then at Chelsea School of Art from 1929 until 1931. From 1931 he studied at the Royal College of Art, where he was a pupil of William Staite Murray during the period 1932 to 1936. He was greatly impressed by his teacher and, like him, did not think of his pots as functional. Working in stoneware, he was particularly fond of celadon glazes. He exhibited pots in the *Stoneware and Earthenware* show at the Brygos Gallery in 1937 which was to be his sole exhibition. He taught at a succession of colleges before and after the war including Poole School of Art and the Southern College of Art, where he was Head and Head of the Pottery Faculty respectively. His work is represented in the Victoria and Albert Museum, the City Museum and Art Gallery, Stoke-on-Trent, and other museums both in Great Britain and abroad. He made very few pots after the war, and retired from teaching in 1966. By 1967 he was living in France. There he helped to set up a small experimental pottery studio at Can Damm, Coustouges (Pyrénées Orientales). In 1970 he returned to Malvern and since then has divided his time between this country and France.

150. Lidded Tea Canister 1937 or earlier

Press-handled lid; olive-green glaze breaking to iron-red.

H 5¾ in (14.6 cm); D 4½ in (11.5 cm)

Mark: 'PSW' (incised)

This jar was made for the Brygos exhibition of 1937 just after Wadsworth had left the Royal College.

PROV: Brygos Gallery, 1937 (4gns); presented, January 1959 (935/17).

EXH: Brygos Gallery, *Stoneware and Earthenware*, 10 February - 1 March 1937 (152).

MW DOC: General Catalogue: '1937. 189 WADSWORTH. Brown & black pot with cover, tea canister. 4[gns]'; invoice: Brygos Gallery, 5 March 1937, receipted 4 March 1937, '1 Pot (Wadsworth) ... £4.4.-'; album II: exhibition catalogue.

150

150

Reginald Fairfax Wells
British 1877-1951

Reginald Wells was one of the earliest pioneers of studio pottery in the twentieth century. He trained as a sculptor at Camberwell and at the Royal College of Art in the late 1890s, and set up his first pottery in the spirit of the Arts and Crafts Movement at Coldrum near Wrotham in Kent. Coldrum was the birthplace of Kentish seventeenth-century slipware which Wells took as his inspiration, making traditional slip-decorated brown and white earthenware. His earliest known dated piece was produced in 1909, which means that Wells was the first artist-potter to turn to English traditions for his inspiration. By 1910 he had moved to College Street in Chelsea and was producing Coldrum ware, which demonstrated a more original use of glazes and forms. His work was interrupted by the First World War (during which he became involved in aircraft manufacture), but afterwards, in 1918, he took up new premises in the King's Road and embarked upon his most exciting creative period. Stimulated no doubt by the flurry of interest in Chinese stoneware from the Sung dynasty he began experimenting. Paying great attention to the body of his pots he tried new mixtures of clays; he strove to control the glazes to reveal and give emphasis to the clay body. He also experimented widely with glaze effects to achieve subtle gradations in tone, colour and surface texture, often by firing and re-firing at different temperatures. He called these productions Soon ware. The precise connection between 'Soon' and 'Sung' is not clear. In addition to pots, which vary in size from huge sculptured vases to tiny vessels, Wells made tiles and rugged ceramic sculptures, including farm animals, of great charm. In 1925 he moved to Storrington in Sussex where he continued to work until his death in 1951.

Most of Wells's output is very experimental in character. It clearly exemplifies the struggle of the pioneers in controlling their medium. Large collections of Wells's pots are in the Victoria and Albert Museum and the National Museums and Galleries on Merseyside.

Milner-White and Wells

The jar No.151, acquired in 1925, was the very first pot (by anyone) that Milner-White purchased. He later recalled: 'The people interested in the work of Wells, Murray, Leach, during the '20s could be counted on the finger[s] of one hand – Eumorphopoulos[sic], Marriott the A[rt] – C[ritic] of the Times, Bernard Rackham, head of the department of Ceramics at the V&A. & that young & poor & unknown clergyman which was myself!'[1] He also bought a 'Horse' and a 'Ram' by Wells from the Eumorfopoulos sale in 1944 but, sadly, these rare pieces have been stolen from the collection[2] and No.151 is now the only representation of Wells at York.

1. MS notes.
2. See Appendix B4 (935/1 and 935/3).

151

151. Two-handled Jar exh. 1925
(colour II)

Mottled salmon-rose glaze over a low-toned underglaze.

H 8⅞ in (22.4 cm); D 6 in (15.1 cm)

Mark: 'SOON' (incised)

This jar was made in Wells's King's Road studio, Chelsea, during his most exciting period: stimulated by early Chinese ceramics, he was experimenting extensively with clay bodies and glazes in pursuit of subtle effects. Work from this period is incised 'SOON'. It was the very first pot that Milner-White bought.

PROV: Fine Art Society, 1925 (20gns); presented, January 1959 (935/26).

EXH: Fine Art Society, 1925.

LIT: Handlist, 1971 (88).

MW DOC: General Catalogue: '1925. 1. WELLS. Two-handled Jar, salmon-rose. "SOON" underneath. [20 gns]'; invoice: Fine Art Society, 15 December 1925, receipted, 17 December 1925,' "Soon" Pottery. Brown pot. L74 £21-.-.'; note: 'It was by pure chance c.1925. I walked into a Bond St. Gallery & saw a show of Stoneware pots by Reg. Wells. Transfixed. Sat there 2 hours – forgot lunch! – At the end, I bought (£20) ...'.

Bode Bertel Willum Willumsen
Danish   born 1895

Bode Willumsen is a Danish sculptor and ceramicist. Born in Copenhagen, he was trained by his father, J. F. Willumsen (a sculptor and painter), and worked for the Royal Copenhagen Porcelain Manufactory from 1925 to 1930 and then from 1940 to 1948. There he designed a number of vases, bowls and sculptures in stoneware. He also worked for the Bing and Grøndahl Porcelain Manufactory as a designer of technical porcelain, and had his own workshop from 1934 to 1940. He made large heavy vases, often decorated with figures or rich ornament. Willumsen's work is illustrated in the *Studio*, xciii, no.407, 15 February 1927, and 'The Studio' Year Books, *Decorative Art 1928* and *Decorative Art 1930*.

152

Milner–White and Willumsen

There are receipted invoices (or similar documents) for six Willumsen pots in the Milner-White papers. None appears in the Dean's MS catalogue, however, and only one was given to the Gallery (No.152). The whereabouts of the others are unknown.

152. Jug 1927 (*colour XXXII*)

Handle in the form of a female mountain lion.

H 9¼ in (23.5 cm) ; D 7⅛ in (18.2 cm)

Mark : BW monogram (incised), Royal Copenhagen symbol, date '29-9 1927' and an unidentified symbol (painted)

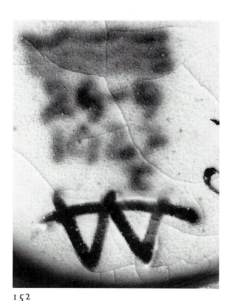

152

This jug was made during Willumsen's first period of work for the Royal Copenhagen Manufactory. The making of stoneware there was regarded as an artistic endeavour and not as the mass-production of objects for everyday use. A similar jug is illustrated in a Royal Copenhagen Porcelain Manufactory catalogue, *Stoneware*, undated but c.1930, where with other examples it is offered as a typical specimen of the fine stoneware manufactured by the firm since the beginning of the century.

PROV : Royal Copenhagen Porcelain Manufactory (London), 1928 (£7 10s.) ; presented, 1958, and received on Milner-White's death, 1963 (1049/55).

MW DOC : Invoice : Royal Copenhagen Porcelain Manufactory, 21 May 1928, receipted 8 June 1928, 'B.W. 29.9.27 1 Jar £7.10.-'.

Appendix A: Numerical concordance

Accession Number	Potter	Catalogue Number	Accession Number	Potter	Catalogue Number	Accession Number	Potter	Catalogue Number
592a	Leach	75	935/47	Murray	101	952/1	Cardew	5
592b	Leach	76	935/48	Vyse	Appendix B4	952/2	Cardew	7
935/1	Wells	Appendix B4	935/49	Vyse	148	953/3	Leach	78
935/2	Martin Brothers	92	935/50	Murray	108	1049/1	Dalton	14
			935/51	Murray	98	1049/2	Pleydell-Bouverie	131
935/3	Wells	Appendix B4	935/52	Murray	124			
935/4	Leach	69	935/53	Murray	115	1049/3	Cardew	11
935/5	Leach	70	935/54	Vyse	145	1049/4	Cardew	8
935/6	Leach	60	935/55	Vyse	146	1049/5	Cardew	6
935/7	Leach	65	935/56	Murray	109	1049/6	Cardew	9
935/8	Leach	81	935/57	Hamada	33	1049/7	Cardew	10
935/9	Leach	62	935/58	Vyse	Appendix B4	1049/8	Cardew	12
935/10	Martin Brothers	94	935/59	Murray	116	1049/9	Cardew	13
			935/62	Murray	97	1049/10	Decœur	18
935/11	Pleydell-Bouverie	132	935/63	Hamada	38	1049/11a	Hamada	29
			935/64	Murray	110	1049/11b	Hamada	30
935/12	Martin Brothers	91	935/65	Murray	102	1049/11c	Hamada	31
			935/66	Murray	111	1049/12a-f	Hamada	41
935/13	Martin Brothers	95	935/67	Hamada	34	1049/13a-f	Hamada	40
			935/68	Leach	73	1049/14	Hamada	40
935/14	Leach	Appendix B4	935/69	Leach	82	1049/15	Hamada	40
935/15	Leach	55	935/70	Leach	72	1049/16	Hamada	40
935/16	Leach	Appendix B4	935/71	Leach	66	1049/17	Hamada	44
935/17	Wadsworth	150	935/72	Martin Brothers	96	1049/18	Audu	1
935/18	Pleydell-Bouverie	130				1049/19	Audu	2
			935/73	Pleydell-Bouverie	133	1049/20	Hjorth	45
935/19	Braden	3				1049/21	Ladi Kwali	54
935/20	Martin Brothers	88	935/75	Leach	74			
			935/76	Leach	79	1049/22	Kåge	47
935/21	Leach	58	935/77	Haile	20	1049/23	Leach	84
935/22	Leach	67	935/78	Braden	4	1049/24	Leach	61
935/23	Hamada	32	935/79	Leach	68	1049/25	Leach	77
935/24	Leach	56	935/80	Hamada	35	1049/26	D. Leach	86
935/25	Hamada	21	935/81	Hamada	36	1049/27	Murray	125
935/26	Wells	151	935/82	Krebs	51	1049/28	Martin Brothers	93
935/27	Kawai	49	935/83	Murray	118			
935/28	Hamada	23	935/84	Murray	117	1049/29	Martin Brothers	90
935/29	Dring	Appendix B4	935/85	Murray	123			
935/30	Kawai	50	935/86	Murray	127	1049/30	Murray	100
935/31	Soudbinine	139	935/87	Murray	119	1049/31	Murray	99
935/32	Hamada	24	935/88a-b, d-f	Hamada	37	1049/32	Murray	103
935/33	Murray	Appendix B4				1049/33	Murray	112
935/34	Decœur	16	935/88c	Hamada	Appendix B4	1049/34	Murray	Appendix B3
935/35	Decœur	17	935/89	Hamada	25	1049/35	Murray	Appendix B3
935/36	Hamada	28	935/90a-f	Hamada	39	1049/36	Murray	Appendix B3
935/37	Kawai	48	935/91	Leach	63	1049/37	Martin Brothers	89
935/38	Murray	106	935/92	Leach	64			
935/39	Soudbinine	140	935/93	Leach	80	1049/38	Murray	114
935/40	Hamada	43	935/94	Leach	57	1049/39	Pincombe	129
935/41	Murray	Appendix B4	935/95	Murray	113	1049/40	Richards	137
935/42	Murray	122	935/96	Murray	120	1049/41	Richards	136
935/43	Murray	107	935/97	Murray	121	1049/42	Rey	135
935/44	Murray	105	935/98	Ladi Kwali	53	1049/43	Vyse	143
935/45	Hamada	22				1049/44	Vyse	Appendix B3
935/46	Hamada	27				1049/45	Vyse	142

Accession Number	Potter	Catalogue Number
1049/46	Vyse	Appendix B3
1049/47	Vyse	Appendix B3
1049/48	Vyse	149
1049/49	Vyse	Appendix B3
1049/50	Vyse	141
1049/51	Salto	138
1049/52	Krebs	52
1049/53	Nielson	128
1049/54	Lenoble	87
1049/55	Willumsen	152
1049/56	Unknown	Appendix B3
1049/57	Decœur	19
1049/58	Hoy	46
1049/59a-e	Leach	Appendix B3
1049/60	Leach	Appendix B3
1049/61	Leach	59
1049/62	Vyse	144
1049/63	Vyse	Appendix B4
1050/1	Pleydell-Bouverie	134
1050/2	Pleydell-Bouverie	Appendix B4
1050/3	Davis	15
1050/4	Hamada	26
1050/5	Hamada	42
1050/6	Leach	71
1050/7	Leach	85
1050/8	Murray	104
1050/9	Murray	126
1058/63	Vyse	147

1. Fitzwilliam Museum, Cambridge[1]
(presented 1940)

Murray

Vase: 'Cow', 1928
Grey-green and dark brown speckled glaze, brown brush-decoration of cattle
H 18½ in (47.5 cm); D 11 in (28.4 cm)
(C19-1947)

Bowl: 'Trellis', 1930
Brown and grey glaze, chestnut brush-decoration of flowers and diagonal lines within, abstract brush-decoration without
H 4½ in (11.5 cm); D 8¾ in (22.5 cm)
(C20-1947)

2. Southampton Art Gallery[2]
(presented 1939, in memory of his father)

Dring[3]

Tile: 'Parrotcage', 1937
Underglaze decoration in oxides
5⅞ in square

Haile

Bowl: 'Shepherds' Dance', 1937
Decorated in iron-oxide
D 12½ in

Pot: 'Triumphant Procession', 1937
Decorated with underglaze brush-decoration in iron, copper, cobalt- and manganese-oxides, reduction fired

Hamada

Celadon Dish, 1922
Crackled glaze engraved with a comb
D 7⅞ in

Globular Pot, 1923
Beaten sides, with kaki glaze
H 5⅞ in

Pot, before 1925
Flattened sides with incised design
H 5⅞ in

Large Pot, 1927
Tenmoku glaze with brush-decoration in iron pigment
H 10¼ in

Two small Plates, 1928
Slip-trailed decoration
H 6¼ in

Plate
Decorated with spots and bands of dark iron pigment
D 10¼ in

Jug, 1928
Iron glaze trickled round the rim
H 6¾ in

Kawai

Bowl, 1928
'Yo-Hen' tenmoku glaze, wax-resist decoration
D 8¼ in

Dish, 1931-2
Decorated with clay and wax-resist
D 7¾ in

Leach

Bottle, 1923-5
'Lavender and Rust', an iron-rich glaze with incised willow-tree
H 6½ in

Plate, 1928
Underglaze brush-decoration in blue of bracken frond
D 9½ in

Cup, 1928
Blue-grey brush-decoration of a willow-tree
H 4⅞ in

Tea-Pot, 1929
Pattern in cobalt- and iron-oxides

Tile, 1929
Underglaze brush-decoration of a bell flower in cobalt- and iron-oxides

Small Vase, 1931
Dark olive celadon glaze incised with a spiral on each of the three flattened sides
H 4¾ in

Ovoid Bottle, 1931
Bracken-ash glaze with wavy bands of dark iron pigment
H 9⅜ in

Tile: 'Leaping Antelope', 1933
Iron brush-decoration
5⅞ in square

Tile: 'Tree', 1933
Iron brush-decoration
4⅛ in square

Bottle, 1933
Long necked; indented sides, inlaid pattern and semi-matt celadon glaze
H 9½ in

Murray

Tea-Bowl: 'Clouds', 1926
Ivory-white glaze over blue-grey brush-decoration of clouds
H $3\frac{1}{4}$ in; D $5\frac{1}{4}$ in

Bowl, 1926
Delicate shallow form with a small neat foot; incised decoration
D $7\frac{3}{4}$ in

Tea-Bowl, 1926
Deep red kaki glaze
H $5\frac{1}{4}$ in

Bowl, 1927
Bright iron-red glaze over wax-resist decoration
D $7\frac{1}{4}$ in

Tall Jar: 'Sentinel', 1928
Cylindrical neck tapering to a very small foot; iron-red glaze breaking into coloured textures

Small Bowl: 'Snowdrop', 1929
Iron-oxide brush-decoration of snowdrops
H $3\frac{7}{8}$ in

Bowl: 'Lotus', 1930
Deep conical shape with heavy foot; iron brush-decoration
D $8\frac{1}{2}$ in

Bowl: 'Crater', 1932
Heavily ribbed foot; dark-grey speckled glaze
D $8\frac{7}{8}$ in

Pot: 'Aulos', 1932
Two-handled; underglaze decoration in coloured slips
H $12\frac{3}{4}$ in

Large Jar: 'Serenity', 1935
Pronounced throwing rings; semi-matt ash glaze
H $15\frac{1}{2}$ in

Large Pot: 'Alchemist', 1936
Brown glaze, double-poured in places
H $16\frac{1}{4}$ in

Tall Pot: 'Scarab', 1936
Pronounced throwing rings and heavy foot; light-grey glaze breaking to red-brown

Pleydell-Bouverie

Small Bowl, 1934
Boxwood-ash glaze with red-iron flash
D $4\frac{3}{4}$ in

Bowl, 1935
Rose-ash glaze

Small Bottle, 1935
Scotch-pine-ash glaze with iron flash
H $3\frac{1}{4}$ in

Richards

Plate, 1926
Cream flecked glaze
D $10\frac{1}{2}$ in

The Vyses

Pot, 1927
Tenmoku glaze, brushwork-decoration of foliage
H $7\frac{3}{4}$ in

Shallow Bowl, 1929
Deep green glaze, 'aventume' decoration
D $6\frac{7}{8}$ in

Shallow Bowl, 1932
Leaf decoration
D $5\frac{3}{4}$ in

Bowl, 1933
Brush-decoration in iron pigment
D $5\frac{3}{4}$ in

Bowl, 1933
Indian-style design in red iron
D $5\frac{3}{4}$ in

Large Pot: 'Coconut Shies', 1935
Cobalt- and iron-oxide underglaze brush-decoration
H $12\frac{7}{8}$ in

Dish, 1936
Design in feathered slip
D $7\frac{1}{8}$ in

Shallow Bowl, 1938
Red iron glaze, leaf decoration
D $6\frac{1}{2}$ in

3. Pottery lent from the Milner-White collection at York City Art Gallery

(received on Milner-White's death, June 1963, but placed on 'permanent loan' to his executors, July 1963)[4]

Leach

Five Cups and Saucers, c. 1927
Speckled cream and brown glazes, double 'S' and dot motifs around rims
Cup H $2\frac{1}{8}$ in; D $3\frac{3}{4}$ in
Saucer D $5\frac{1}{2}$ in
(1049/59 a-e)

Milk Jug, c. 1927
Speckled cream and brown glazes, double 'S' and dot motifs around rims
H $3\frac{1}{4}$ in
(1049/60)

Murray

Tea-Bowl, exh. 1930
Parchment and grey glazes, iron brush-decoration of foliage and flowers without
H 3 in; D $3\frac{1}{2}$ in
(1049/34)

Tea-Bowl, exh. 1930
Parchment, grey and brown glazes, brush-decoration in cream, brown and black without
H $2\frac{1}{2}$ in; D $3\frac{1}{2}$ in
(1049/35)

Tea-Bowl, exh. 1930
Parchment, grey and brown glazes, brush-decoration in brown without
H $2\frac{3}{4}$ in; D $3\frac{1}{2}$ in
(1049/36)

The Vyses

Bowl, 1931
Bird in flight decoration in gold, blue and black glazes within, black and gold glazes without
H $1\frac{1}{2}$ in; D 6 in
(1049/49)

Small Bowl, 1933
Red, sea-weed decoration
H $2\frac{1}{2}$ in; D $5\frac{1}{2}$ in
(1049/44)

Bowl, exh. 1933
Bronze and cream wax-resist decoration in a sinuous radial pattern within, purple and black without
H $2\frac{1}{2}$ in; D $6\frac{1}{2}$ in
(1049/46)

Flower Pot, exh. 1933
Octagonal on four legs: tenmoku and elm-
ash leaf decoration
H 4¼ in
(1049/47)

Unknown

Jug
Crackled cream glaze with underglaze-blue
brush-decoration including a bird
H 5¾ in
(1049/56)

4. Pottery missing from the Milner–White Collection at York City Art Gallery[5]

Dring[3]

Buckle, 1937
Two square pieces of enamelled stoneware
1½ in square (each piece)
(935/29)

Hamada

Plate (from set of six: see No.37), c.1929
Tenmoku glaze over cream slip, wax-resist
decoration of six-petalled flower motif in
centre of plate and wavy line around rim
H 1½ in; D 9½ in
(935/88c)

Leach

Bowl, 1926
Grey with brush-decoration in cobalt, iron
and reduced copper
H 2 in; D 3¾ in
(935/14)

Bowl, 1956
Red and black without, cream glaze within
and brush-decoration of an owl
H 2 in; D 4¾ in
(935/16)

Murray

Bowl: 'Five Elements', 1926
Parchment glaze, with sepia brush-
decoration without
H 2¾ in; D 6 in
(935/33)

Jar, 1924
Narrow neck, red-brown glaze
H 5½ in; D 3⅜ in
(935/41)

Pleydell–Bouverie

Bowl, exh. 1958
Cream glaze
H 2½ in; D 5½ in
(1050/2)

The Vyses

Bowl, 1928
Tenmoku glaze with green, gold and black
star decoration
H 1¾ in; D 7⅛ in
(935/48)

Beer-Mug, 1937
Grey with red decoration, using a rose ash
from Bencourt Wood
H 5¾ in; D 4½ in
(935/58)

Minute Pot, exh. 1936
Speckled grey with brown and blue
decoration
H 1½ in
(1049/63)

Wells

Horse, 1925
Blue, green and brown mottled glazes
H 5¾ in; D 5¾ in
(935/1)

Ram, 1925
White grey mottled glaze
H 4¾ in; D 5¾ in
(935/3)

1. Details supplied by the Museum.
2. Details taken mostly from Ruth J. Bulford, *The Milner-White Collection of Stoneware at Southampton*, unpublished illustrated essay, Southampton College of Art, 1976; full technical details not available; dates to be treated with caution.
3. Charles James Dring, British 1905-1985, not represented in the main body of this Catalogue.
4. Details from Gallery records.
5. Ditto.

Appendix C: Dealers patronized by Milner-White[1]

Appendix D:

The Artificers' Guild (*F.L. Eley*)
7 (& 8) King's Parade, Cambridge:
1927 (Leach), 1929 (Hamada), 1933
(Cardew, Harding,[2] Leach)

Beaux Arts Gallery (*Frederick Lessore*)
1 Bruton Place, New Bond Street, London
W1:
1927 (Murray), 1928 (Leach), 1929
(Kawai), 1931 (Leach), 1933 (Leach),
1952 (Hamada, Leach)

Berkeley Galleries 20 Davies Street,
London W1:
1946 (Leach), 1959 (Cardew, Kwali), 1962
(Audu, Cardew, Kwali)

Brygos Gallery (*Ulick Browne*)
73 New Bond Street, London W1:
1936 (Haile), 1937 (Dring,[3] Haile, Soudbinine, Wadsworth), 1938 (Decœur,
Lenoble, Rey, Soudbinine)

P. & D. Colnaghi & Co. (*O.C.H. Gutekunst,
G. Mayer*)
144-6 New Bond Street, London W1:
1927 (Hamada, Leach), 1928 (Dalton,
Pleydell-Bouverie), 1929 (Leach)

**The Royal Copenhagen Porcelain
Manufactory, Depot for British Empire**
2 Old Bond Street, London W1:
1927 (Willumsen), 1928 (Willumsen),
1929 (Willumsen)

The Fine Art Society Ltd
148 New Bond Street, London W1:
1925 (Wells), 1927 (Hopkins[4])

**Alex Reid & Lefevre Ltd (The Lefevre
Galleries)** (*Ernest A. Lefevre, A.J. McNeill Reid,
D.M. Macdonald; by 1931, A.J. McNeill Reid,
D.M. Macdonald; by 1933 A.J. McNeill Reid,
D.M. Macdonald, T.J. Honeyman*)
1a King Street, St James's, London SW1:
1928 (Murray), 1930 (Murray), 1931
(Murray), 1932 (Murray), 1935 (Murray),
1936 (Murray)

The Leicester Galleries (*Wilfrid L. Phillips,
Cecil L. Phillips, Oliver F. Brown; by 1929 Cecil
L. Phillips, Oliver F. Brown; by 1958, Oliver
F. Brown, Patrick L. Phillips, Nicholas E. Brown,
E.C. Phillips*)
Leicester Square, London WC2:
1926 (Murray), 1929 (Pleydell-Bouverie),
1936 (Beek[5]), 1958 (Murray)

Liberty
Regent Street, London W1:
1956 (Leach)

The Little Gallery (*Muriel Rose, M.K. Turnbull*)
3 Ellis Street, Sloane Street, London SW1:
1929 (Pleydell-Bouverie), 1931 (Leach),
1935 (Braden), 1936 (Leach), 1937
(Hamada)

William Paterson's Gallery (*William
B. Paterson; by 1929, William B Paterson, Max
Morris*)
5 Old Bond Street, London W1:
1926 (Hamada, Leach, Murray), 1927
(Leach, Murray), 1928 (Murray), 1929
(Hamada, Murray), 1931 (Hamada)

Primavera
149 Sloane Street, London SW1:
1958 (Pincombe, Pleydell-Bouverie)

Rembrandt Gallery (*P. Dunthorne, C.E. Peers,
A. Yockney*)
5 Vigo Street, London W1:
1936 (Pleydell-Bouverie)

The Three Shields Gallery (*D. Hutton*)
8 Holland Street, Church Street, Kensington,
London W8:
1927 (Leach), 1928 (Richards)

Walker's Galleries (*A.J. Walker,
W.H. Walker, R. Whitehead, J.H. Downey*)
118 New Bond Street, London W1:
1929 (Vyses), 1930 (Vyses), 1933 (Vyses),
1935 (Vyses), 1936 (Vyses), 1937 (Vyses),
1938 (Vyses), 1942 (Martinware)

Yamanaka & Co. Ltd
127 New Bond Street, London W1:
1932 (Kawai)

Zwemmer Gallery (*A. Zwemmer*)
26 Litchfield Street, London WC2:
1936 (Halpern[6])

Chart

plotting Milner-White's pots by maker against year of acquisition

(based on information in
his MS General Catalogue only)

Potters not appearing in the main body of the
Catalogue

1. Frank Barber, British c.1912-1933
2. Jan Bontjes von Beek, German
3. (?) Vanessa Bell (née Stephen), British
   1879-1961
4. Charles James Dring, British 1905-1985
5. Lea H. Halpern, Dutch
6. Alfred G. Hopkins, British
7. Reginald H. Marlow, British
8. (?) Cathinka Olsen, Danish
9. Constance E. Dunn (née Wade), British

1. Information taken in the main from receipts.
2. Deborah N. Harding, British.
3. Charles James Dring, British 1905-1985.
4. Alfred G. Hopkins, British.
5. Jan Bontjes von Beek, German.
6. Lea H. Halpern, Dutch.

1930

PHOTOGRAPH: Murray's *The Bather* with another tall Murray pot and a small Murray bowl.

EXHIBITION CATALOGUE: Alex. Reid & Lefevre, Ltd, *Pottery, Paintings and Furniture by Staite Murray* (with a foreword 'The Appreciation of Pottery' by 'X.X.'), November 1930.

REVIEW: (?Charles Marriott), 'Mr. Staite Murray', *The Times*, 7 November 1930.

ARTICLE: E.M. [?Ernest Marsh], 'Catalogue of Pottery Figure Subjects by Mr. and Mrs. Charles Vyse of Chelsea', *Walker's Monthly*, December 1930.

EXHIBITION CATALOGUE: Walker's Galleries, *Pottery, Stoneware and Hard Porcelain by Mr. and Mrs. Charles Vyse*, 26 November-17 December 1930.

EXHIBITION CATALOGUE: Beaux Arts Gallery, *Stoneware Pottery and Porcelain by Kenkichi Tomimoto (of Tokyo) and Bernard Leach* (with a foreword by Bernard Leach), 5-22 May 1930.

REVIEW: Anon., 'An ancient Craft with a modern Message.', *Evening News: Glasgow*, 16 December 1930.

1931

REVIEW: (?Charles Marriott), 'The National Society', *The Times*, 9 June 1931.

REVIEW: Anon., 'Excellent second Exhibition', (?)*Morning Post*, n.d., 1931.

REVIEW: Unidentified newspaper review, 'Winchcombe Pottery'.

REVIEW: (?Charles Marriott), 'Stoneware Pottery', *The Times*, 29 October 1931.

REVIEW: Anon., 'A Master Potter: Splendid Examples by a Japanese Craftsman: Traditions based on beauty', *Morning Post*, 2 November 1931.

EXHIBITION CATALOGUE: Paterson's Gallery, *Pottery by Shoji Hamada* (with a foreword by M. Yanagi), 31 October-28 November 1931.

REVIEW: (?Charles Marriott), 'The R.B.A.', *The Times*, 10 November 1931.

REVIEW: R. M., '"Clay that Sings": Staite Murray's Pottery', *Evening News: Glasgow*, 8 December 1931.

EXHIBITION CATALOGUE: Alex. Reid & Lefevre, Ltd, *New Pottery and Paintings by Staite Murray*, November 1931.

REVIEW: (?Charles Marriott), 'Mr. and Mrs. Vyse', *The Times*, 2 December 1931.

PERIODICAL: *Walker's Monthly*, no.48, December 1931 (including: Ernest Marsh, 'The fourth Exhibition of Stoneware Pottery, Hard Porcelains and Figures by Mr. and Mrs. Charles Vyse of Chelsea 30th November to 19th December, 1931').

Album II

1932

ARTICLE: Philip James, 'Modern Fireplace Tiles', *Country Life*, 13 February 1932, p.XXXVI.

REVIEW: (?Charles Marriott), 'Stoneware Pottery', *The Times*, 23 May 1932.

EXHIBITION CATALOGUE: Yamanaka & Co. Ltd, *Stoneware Pottery by Kanjiro Kawai*, October 1932.

REVIEW: (?Charles Marriott), 'Lefevre Galleries', *The Times*, 7 November 1932.

EXHIBITION CATALOGUE: Alex. Reid & Lefevre, Ltd, *New Pottery, Paintings & Sculpture by Staite Murray* (with a foreword 'Clay that Sings' by Robins Millar), November 1932.

REVIEW: (?Charles Marriott), 'New Pottery Glazes', (?)*The Times*, n.d.

EXHIBITION CATALOGUE: Walker's Galleries, *Stoneware Pottery Hard Porcelains and Figures by Mr. and Mrs. Charles Vyse* (with a foreword by Wallace B. Nichols), 28 November-17 December 1932.

1933

REVIEW: (?Charles Marriott), 'Mr. Bernard Leach', *The Times*, 5 December 1933.

PRIVATE VIEW INVITATION AND EXHIBITION CATALOGUE COMBINED: Beaux Arts Gallery, *Stoneware Pottery by Bernard Leach*, 15 November-2 December (?)1933.

REPRODUCTION OF PHOTOGRAPH: Four Vyse pots.

EXHIBITION CATALOGUE: Walker's Galleries, *Stoneware Pottery, Hard Porcelains and Figures by Mr. and Mrs. Charles Vyse*, 29 November-19 December 1933.

1934

EXHIBITION CATALOGUE: Alex. Reid & Lefevre, Ltd, *Pottery and Paintings by Staite Murray*, April-May 1934.

REPRODUCTION OF PHOTOGRAPH: The Vyses at work.

1935

EXHIBITION CATALOGUE (incomplete): Royal Institute Galleries, *National Society: Painters, Sculptors, Engravers, Potters: Sixth annual Exhibition*, 11 February-4 March 1935.

EXHIBITION ANNOUNCEMENT CARD: Little Gallery, *K. Pleydell-Bouverie and D. K. N. Braden: Stoneware*, 28 October-9 November (?)1935.

REVIEW: (?Charles Marriott), 'Representative Shows', *The Times*, 15 November 1935.

EXHIBITION CATALOGUE: Alex. Reid & Lefevre, Ltd, *Pots, Paintings and Drawings by Staite Murray*, November 1935.

REPRODUCTION OF PHOTOGRAPH: Four Vyse pots, including *Olympia*.

REVIEW: (?Charles Marriott), 'Decorative Pottery: Artistic Sensibility', *The Times*, 19 December 1935.

PHOTOGRAPH: The Vyses at work.

EXHIBITION CATALOGUE: Walker's Galleries, *Stoneware Pottery and Figures by Mr. and Mrs. Charles Vyse*, 2-21 December 1935.

1936

EXHIBITION ANNOUNCEMENT CARD: Little Gallery, *Stoneware & Slipware by Bernard Leach*, 20 April-3 May 1936.

REVIEW: (?Charles Marriott), 'Mr. Bernard Leach', *The Times*, n.d.

REVIEW: (?Charles Marriott), 'New Dutch Pottery: Departure from standard Forms', *The Times*, 1 July 1936.

EXHIBITION CATALOGUE: Zwemmer Gallery, *Lea H. Halpern*, 26 June-25 July 1936.

1937

ARTICLE: Rowan Williams, 'La vie artistique à Londres', *Bulletin du Palais des Beaux-Arts de Bruxelles*, no.228, 15 January 1937.

1936

EXHIBITION CATALOGUE: Alex. Reid & Lefevre, Ltd, *Pottery and Paintings by Staite Murray* (with a foreword by Maurice Collis), November 1936.

REPRODUCTION OF PHOTOGRAPH: 'Group of decorated Pots and Bowls in Rose, Evergreen and Scotch Fir Glazes' by the Vyses.

REPRODUCTION OF PHOTOGRAPH: 'Group of Beer Jugs and Mugs in a Variety of Shapes and Colourings' by the Vyses.

REVIEW: Anon., 'The Vyses', *Observer*, 13 December 1936.

REPRODUCTION OF PHOTOGRAPH: 'Group of modelled Shapes in golden Elm, Apple and Ivy Glazes' by the Vyses.

EXHIBITION CATALOGUE: Walker's Galleries, *Stoneware Pottery and Figures by Mr. and Mrs. Charles Vyse*, 25 November - 19 December 1936.

REVIEW: (?Charles Marriott), 'Terra-Cottas and Pottery', *The Times*, 5 December 1936.

REVIEW: Anon., 'The Brygos Gallery', *Observer*, 13 December 1936.

EXHIBITION CATALOGUE: Brygos Gallery, *Under £10 English Pottery*, 26 November - 19 December 1936.

NEWSPAPER OR MAGAZINE CUTTING: Cartoon with caption, 'Well, which is it, Sam — a lovely old vase or a hideous modern one?'

PRIVATE VIEW CARD: Rembrandt Gallery, *Stoneware by K. Pleydell-Bouverie*, 10 December 1936.

REVIEW: (?Charles Marriott), untitled, *The Times*, 16 December 1936.

1937

EXHIBITION CATALOGUE: Brygos Gallery, *Stoneware and Earthenware*, 10 February - 1 March 1937.

EXHIBITION CATALOGUE: Wertheim Gallery, *Contemporary Georgian Exhibition*, May 1937.

EXHIBITION ANNOUNCEMENT CARD: Little Gallery, *Recent Work by Five Japanese Craftsmen*, 1 - 19 June (?)1937.

EXHIBITION CATALOGUE: Brygos Gallery, *Soudbinine: An Exhibition of Pottery*, 19 May - 8 June 1937.

ARTICLE: Anon., 'The Tenth Exhibition of Stoneware Pottery and Figures by the Vyses of Chelsea — November 24th to December 18th, 1937', *Walker's Monthly*, no.120, December 1937.

EXHIBITION CATALOGUE: Walker's Galleries, *Stoneware Pottery and Figures by Mr. and Mrs. Charles Vyse*, 24 November - 18 December 1937.

EXHIBITION CATALOGUE: Brygos Gallery, *Stoneware Pottery by T.S. Haile and decorated Plates and Tiles by C.J. Dring*, 10 December - 1 January 1937.

1938

EXHIBITION CATALOGUE: Brygos Gallery, *Stoneware Birds and Figures by Tyra Lundgren and Works in Enamel and enamelled Jewellery by Stefa Rawitz* (with forewords by Louis Vauxcelles and Nikolaus Pevsner), 1 - 22 February 1938.

EXHIBITION CATALOGUE: Brygos Gallery, *Stoneware by Margaret Rey*, 17 March - 7 April 1938.

EXHIBITION CATALOGUE: Brygos Gallery, *Contemporary French Pottery by Members of the Group of 'Artisans Francais Contemporains'* (with a preface by Ernest Marsh), 20 April - 20 May 1938.

EXHIBITION CATALOGUE: Walker's Galleries, *Stoneware Pottery and Figures by Mr. and Mrs. Charles Vyse*, 30 November - 20 December 1938.

1939

REVIEW: (?Charles Marriott), 'A Civic Art Centre: Southampton's New Gallery', *The Times*, 27 April 1939.

1942

EXHIBITION CATALOGUE: Walker's Galleries, *Martin Ware from the Collection of the late Frank Knight* (with a prefatory note 'The salt-glazed Stoneware of the Martin Brothers' by 'G.K.S.'), 30 November - 19 December 1942.

1958

ARTICLE: Anon., 'Exquisite Martinware Pottery', *The Times*, 19 April 1958.

1946

OUTSIDE PAGES OF PUBLICITY BROCHURE: Berkley[sic] Galleries, *Leach Pottery*, June 1946.

1952

POSTER: City of York Art Gallery, *The Dean's Taste: An Exhibition of Stoneware Pottery and modern Paintings from the Collection of the Very Rev. E. Milner-White, D.S.O.*, February 1952.

REVIEW: Anon., 'The Dean's Taste: A York Exhibition', *Yorkshire Gazette*, 22 February 1952.

EXHIBITION LEAFLET: E. Milner-White, *Stoneware: An Explanation of the Exhibits*, City of York Art Gallery, York, February 1952.

1951

LETTER: Muriel Rose, British Council, to Milner-White, 6 February 1951.

FLYER: Bernard Leach, *A Potter's Portfolio*, Lund Humphries, 1951.

1952

EXHIBITION CATALOGUE: Dartington Hall in collaboration with, the Arts Council of Great Britain, *Pottery and Textiles 1920-1952* (with a foreword by Peter Cox), June - November 1952.

PRIVATE VIEW LEAFLET: Edinburgh College of Art, *Pottery and Textiles 1920-1952*, 15 August 1952.

PRIVATE VIEW CARD: New Burlington Galleries, *Modern British Pottery and Textiles made by Artist Craftsmen 1920-1952*, 10 September 1952.

PUBLICITY BROCHURE: Leach Pottery, *The Leach Pottery 1920-1952*, August 1952.

PRIVATE VIEW CARD: Beaux Arts Gallery, *Bernard Leach and Shoji Hamada*, 16 September (?)1952.

1953

LETTER: William Staite Murray to Milner-White, 1 September 1953.

TYPESCRIPT BOOKLET: Six poems by Murray with a photograph of him.

1958

PRIVATE VIEW CARD: Leicester Galleries, *Staite Murray: Stoneware Pottery; Merlyn Evans: New Paintings; Vlaminck: Early Wood-cuts, Lithographs and Etchings*, 29 October 1958.

EXHIBITION CATALOGUE: Leicester Galleries, *Stoneware Pottery by William Staite Murray* (with a preface by Maurice Collis), November 1958.

PRIVATE VIEW CARD: Primavera, *Thrown and Coiled Stoneware by Katharine Pleydell-Bouverie & Helen Pincombe*, 4 November (?)1958.

Appendix F: Books and periodicals relating to ceramics formerly in Milner-White's library and now at York City Art Gallery

An asterisk indicates a book plate, MS notes or other evidence of Milner-White's ownership.

Aoyama, Jiro, *Ceramics by Shoji Hamada*, Koseikai, Tokyo 1933.

Flor, Kai, *Jais Nielsen: Keramik* (Dansk Kunst, vi), Arthur Jensens, Copenhagen 1938.*

Forsyth, Gordon, *20th Century Ceramics*, The Studio, London & New York, n.d. [1936].*

Hetherington, A.L, *The Early Ceramic Wares of China* (abridged edition of work of 1922), Ernest Benn, London 1924.*

Hetherington, A.L., *Chinese Ceramic Glazes* (reprint of first edition of 1937), Courtauld Institute of Art/Cambridge University Press, Cambridge 1937.*

Hannover, Emil, ed. Rackham, Bernard, *Pottery & Porcelain: A Handbook for Collectors*, 2 vols, Ernest Benn, London 1925.*

Holme, C. Geoffrey, & Wainwright, Shirley B. (eds), *Decorative Art 1928* ('The Studio' Year Book), The Studio, London 1928.*

Holme, C. Geoffrey, & Wainwright, S.B. (eds), *Decorative Art 1930* ('The Studio' Year Book), The Studio, London 1930.

Leach, Bernard, *A Potter's Book*, Faber and Faber, London 1940.*

Piccolpasso, Cipriano, with translation and introduction by Rackham, Bernard, and Van de Put, Albert, *The Three Books of the Potter's Art*, Victoria and Albert Museum, London 1934.*

Shikiba, Ryūzaburō, *Bernard Leach*, Kensetsu-sha, Tokyo 1934.*

Solon, M.L., *The Ancient Art Stoneware of the Low Countries and Germany*, 2 vols, privately published by the author, Stoke-on-Trent 1892.*

Apollo, i, no.5, May 1925, pp.283-290 only (including Ernest Marsh, 'R.F. Wells – Sculptor and Potter').*

Apollo, xxxvii, no.216, January 1943 (including Ernest Marsh, 'Bernard Leach, Potter', pp.14-16).*

Apollo, xxxvii, no.220, May 1943 (including Ernest Marsh, 'Michael Cardew, Potter, of Winchcombe, Gloucestershire', pp.129-131).*

Apollo, xxxviii, no.222, July 1943 (including Ernest Marsh, 'Charles and Nell Vyse, Studio Pottery of Chelsea', pp.12-14).*

Apollo, xxxvii, no.227, December 1943 (including Ernest Marsh, 'Studio Potters of Coleshill, Wilts: Miss K. Pleydell-Bouverie and Miss D. K. N. Braden').*

Apollo, xxxix, no.231, April 1944 (including Ernest Marsh, 'W. Staite Murray, Studio Potter of Bray, Berkshire', pp.107-9).*

Apollo, xl, no.237, November 1944 (including Ernest Marsh, 'The Martin Brothers, Studio Potters of London and Southall, Middlesex – Part II' together with loose pages bearing 'Part I' from Apollo, xl, no.236, October, 1944, pp.94-6).*

Arts and Crafts, iii, no.1 (new series), June 1929 (including A.E. Poulter, 'The Work of Frank Barber, pp.39-40).*

Art et Décoration, xxviii, no.266, February 1924 (including Guillaume Janneau, 'Les céramiques d'Emile Decœur', pp.37-44).*

Art et Décoration, xxviii, no.274, October 1924 (including Léon Deshairs, 'Emile Lenoble', pp.97-106).*

Artwork, no.7, summer 1926 (including W.A. Thorpe, 'Form in Pottery', pp.162-70).*

Kōgei (Crafts), no.53, May 1935 (including Bernard Leach, 'Thoughts on Japanese Crafts', 'Impressions of Japan after fourteen Years' and 'A Letter to England', pp.1-41).*

Mobilier et Décoration, vii, no.2, January 1927 (including Gabriel Henriot, 'La dixième exposition des artisans français contemporains', pp.16-32).*

Porslin (publication of the Gustavsberg factory, Stockholm), no.1-2, 1951-2.*

The Studio, xcii, no.404, 15 November 1926 (including Dora E. Hedges, 'Sophie Verryn Stuart – Artist Potter [of Amsterdam]', pp.335-6, and anon., 'London', pp.335-6, referring to and reproducing two pots by R. Marlow).*

The Studio, cxi, no.518, May 1936 (devoted to 'The Art of Denmark', including Ivan Munk Olsen, '3. Sculpture and Ceramics', pp.255-63).*

STONEWARE

AN EXPLANATION OF THE EXHIBITS

There are four distinctive provinces of the ceramic craft.

1. **Earthenware** or soft pottery: vessels of clay fired at a low temperature.

2. **Stoneware:** clay fired at a temperature above 1,200 centigrade. For reason of the risks attendant upon the greater heat, and the different and deeper colour effects obtainable from the mineral glazes, this has always been regarded as the aristocrat of ceramic wares—its highest art.

3. **Porcelain,** popularly known in England as "china," is also fired very high; it is not a pure clay substance, but moulded out of the kneaded mass of clay, kaolin and other mineral ingredients; when you hold it to the light it is to some degree transparent.

4. **Figure modelling** in any of these materials, mostly perhaps in porcelain. This is not so much pottery as sculpture, usually coloured, and of an idealistic, humorous or dainty character.

In the collection on view there is no piece which is not true STONEWARE, the ceramic responsible for the grace and beauty of the most exquisite and noble pottery ever made—during the two SUNG dynasties of China, A.D. 960–1280. All the pieces here, however, are modern; all date between the two wars. A few, for comparison, are works of the leading continental artist-potters, but most are by English artists; or by Japanese influenced directly by them.

For the remarkable truth, still not recognised by this country, even in artistic circles, is that, for the first time in history, English pottery during those twenty years led the world, not only on its technical side but also on its imaginative and creative side. And actually was able to teach the East ! The Japanese potter SHOJI HAMADA, when young, came to learn his art under BERNARD LEACH at St. Ives, Cornwall. Recognised now as the first potter of the Far East, he has introduced and naturalised those forms and decorative modes—especially that called "slip"—which he learned in England from the love which he caught from Leach of our 17th century earthenware (Toft, etc.).

That England has been able to give back to the East—after first learning from the East—has been due to two great potters, by some miracle arising (like Turner and Constable a century earlier in the sphere of painting) independently and contemporaneously, WILLIAM STAITE MURRAY and BERNARD LEACH. Their influence on East and West alike has been tremendous. With Shoji Hamada they compose a trio unsurpassed by any potters in modern centuries. All three are still living.

The best work of each is represented in this collection.

Let us add a few words on what to look for in a good pot.

A leaflet written by Milner-White to accompany an exhibition of his pots at York Art Gallery in February 1952

First and foremost, FORM. Look first at *shape*, and then see how expressive it can be—powerful, delicate, lively or what not, simply from its *form*. A fine pot is *abstract sculpture*. In these days, both painting and sculpture proper are making agonised efforts to be abstract. It is still doubtful how far they can be; but in pottery abstract form is natural, inevitable, at home.

Secondly, observe the GLAZE. As pottery can go beyond sculpture in freedom of form, so it can, far beyond, in colour. The most brilliant art of colour is stained glass—painting on light itself; the deepest and profoundest, and the most unexpected in its phases and blends, is a mineral glaze of a stoneware pot created in the burning fiery furnace.

Thirdly, there is a DECORATION, especially a brush decoration, as abstract as either the form or the colour of a pot and equally proper to it.—Not the painting of a picture on the vessel as if it were another kind of canvas, even when the designs are as lovely in themselves as on Persian software, Italian majolica or the *famille rose* of China; these are and remain a type of *pictorial* art. Potting decoration must belong to the pot itself, a brush stroke, an incised line, a device to expound and emphasise the "movement" or the meaning or the life of the formed pot. Form, Glaze, Decoration should combine into a perfect unity.

Lastly, as you go round, studying Form and Glaze and Decoration, notice one more point which no factory-made pottery or porcelain can have at all—the SURFACE, given an almost invisible enchantment by the slight irregularities made *by the potter's hands or fingers*. Not only is the pot or bowl thus given its subtle quality, but somehow, magically, the individual potter cannot fail to express his dreams of beauty, and himself, in his creation.

E. M.-W.

THE LEACH POTTERY
SAINT IVES, CORNWALL
ALL COMMUNICATIONS TO BE
ADDRESSED TO THE SECRETARY   7.7.27

Dear Mr. Milner White,

Curiously enough I got one of Hamada's rare letters this morning asking me to send, together with Murray & Mrs Mairet & Miss Barron, for an autumn exhibition in Tokio. I am replying at once & I shall tell him of your wish & that I have given you his address in order that you may make your request direct.

Shoji Hamada,   C/o H. Inagaki Esq
                74 Susaki machi
                Honjo Ku
                          Tokio

He & my other Japanese craft friends are putting their prices down & down, in a warm brotherly spirit of the general good, & consequent personal health, so £25 will go a good way.

He says :— " We have come nearer to understand what is the real craft & what is the right craftsmanship, & Yanagi (my great philosopher mystic friend) is even going to think that communion would be the best way to produce the real craft, not being done by individual artists. (Monastery of craftsmen) He is studying the mediaeval guilds & their lives with great interest.

This is a great change & means the passing of the stage of self-assertion in art.   As a whole we are not yet ready for that & as a nation I think they are still less so.

              Yours sincerely
                          Bernard Leach

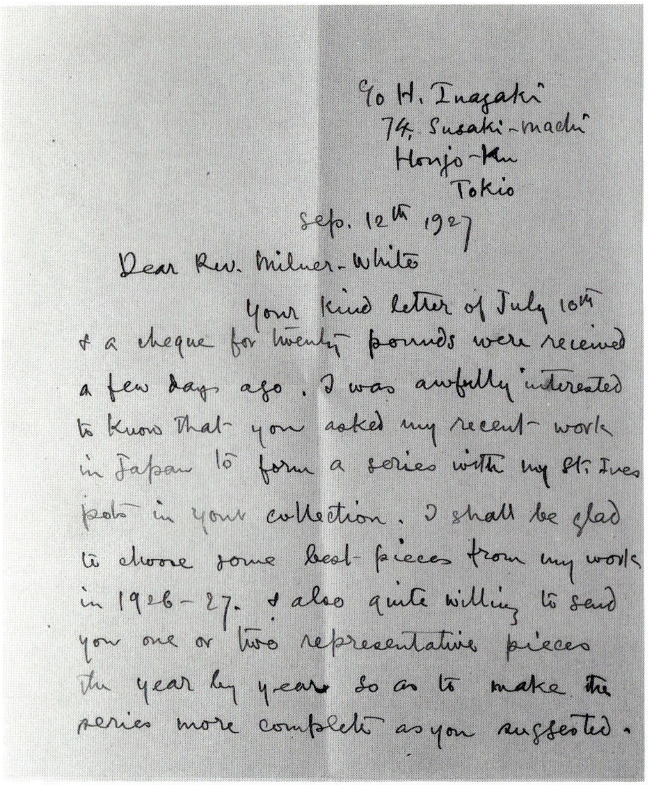

℅ H. Inagaki
74, Susaki-machi
Honjo-Ku
Tokio

Sep. 12th 1927

Dear Rev. Milner-White

Your kind letter of July 10th
& a cheque for twenty pounds were received
a few days ago. I was awfully interested
to know that you asked my recent work
in Japan to form a series with my St. Ives
pots in your collection. I shall be glad
to choose some best pieces from my works
in 1926 - 27. & also quite willing to send
you one or two representative pieces
the year by year so as to make the
series more complete as you suggested.

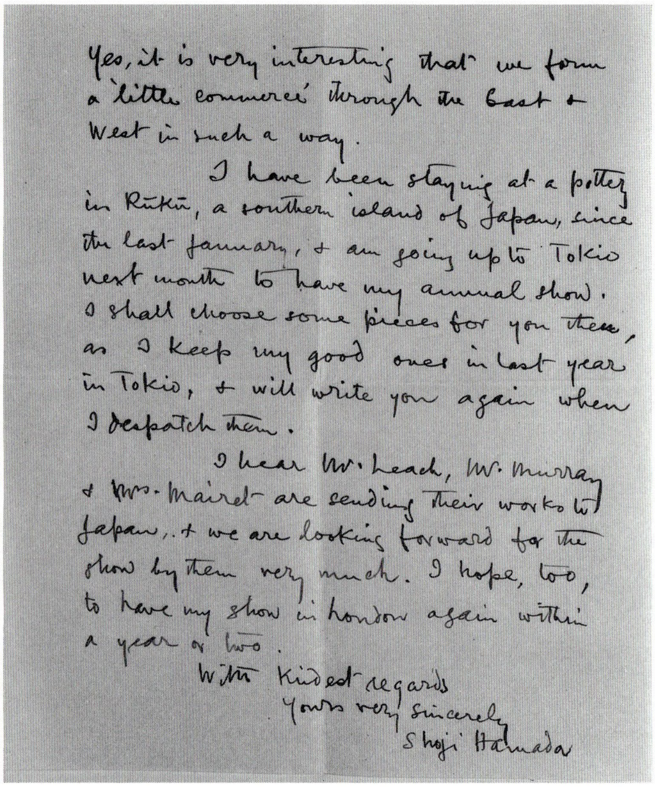

Yes, it is very interesting that we form
a 'little commerce' through the East &
West in such a way.

I have been staying at a pottery
in Rikū, a southern island of Japan, since
the last January, & am going up to Tokio
next month to have my annual show.
I shall choose some pieces for you there,
as I keep my good ones in Last year
in Tokio, & will write you again when
I despatch them.

I hear Mr. Leach, Mr. Murray
& Mrs. Mairet are sending their works to
Japan, & we are looking forward for the
show by them very much. I hope, too,
to have my show in London again within
a year or two.

With kindest regards
Yours very sincerely
Shoji Hamada

90 H. Inagaki
74, Susaki-machi
Honjo-Ku, Tokio

June 3rd 1928

Dear Rev. Milner-White

    I sent you two of my
pots about a week ago through
Messrs. Kaiten-sha & Co, as I
received the answer from Mr. Henry
Bergen in which he suggested to
have my show in London in next
spring, as Mr. Murray is going to
have his annual one through
this November at the Paterson
gallery. I am sorry I have
not been able to send them
before. One of the
pots like this was
made at Mashiko
in 1926, & the other

at Ryukyu in 1927.
They are both representative
ones at the each
Kiln. I hope they
will arrive safely.

    I have just returned
Mashiko again, & am going
to try rough porcelain as a
new line.

    With kindest regards
    Yours sincerely
    S. Hamada.

14A Cheyne Row.
Chelsea -
SW 3 -
Mch 6 1935

Dear Mr Milner-White,
          I am very grateful
to you for your letter & appreciation.
So very few have understood our
attempt to break away in a
new direction, & it is heartening
to feel that you are in sympathy
with it.
      I have brought the two pots to
the Studio, & I hope to pack them
off to you either today or to-morrow.
Our purveyor of "wood-wool"
packing has been burnt out, &

hence the slight delay!
      With kind regards,
          I am,
              Yours very sincerely,
                  Charles Vyse
                      P.P.B.

24th May 1959.

Pottery Training Centre
Abuja, via Minna
Northern Nigeria.

Dear Mr. Milner White

Thank you very much for your very kind letter of 13th May. I am sorry the invitation to the private view of my last show (Berkeley Galleries, Feb. 1958) reached you too late. It was not the fault of the Gallery — Mr. Ohly begged me to postpone the opening date because of a delay in producing the Catalogue; but I insisted on keeping to the original dates because I had to be back in West Africa by a certain date. So the invitations only reached recipients after the show had begun.

Now I am having a second exhibition at the Berkeley Galleries, 15th Sept. to 12th Oct. 1959, — I am packing the pots for it now. It should be a better exhibition than the 1958 one. I have promised the gallery to get the catalogue & invitations out in good time. What I suggest is that I mark 2 or 3 of the best pots & 1 or 2 of my pupils' best, as (provisionally) sold to you, in case you are unable to be in London for the opening day.

Of course I very much hope that you will be able to come to London for the while the exhibition is on, & you could then make

your own choice. But if that proves to be impossible I will choose what I think are the best. & also get (but not necessarily take!) good advice from friends (e.g. Wingfield Digby, Catherine Pleydell-Bouverie.)

I should very much like to see your famous collection. In the past I have been more or less non-mobile when home on leave, because I had no car; but now I have a small one, so I will try to visit York at last. Catherine Pleydell-Bouverie wrote to me several months ago telling me of her visit to you.

I do promise to let you have the best from this year's exhibition: as much for the sake of seeing Nigerian potters honoured as for myself.

Yours sincerely
Michael Cardew

6th Sept 1959. Monday.

Wenford Bridge Pottery
St Tudy, Bodmin
Cornwall.

My dear Dean Milner White

I can't think why the Berkeley Galleries have not yet sent out the invitations for the 'Abuja' pottery exhibition: it is getting late.

The opening is at 3 p.m. on Wed. 16th Sept. only just over a week from now. It will be opened by Malam Abba Habib, Minister for Trade & Industry Northern Nigeria.

I do hope you will find it possible to visit London during the exhibition — it goes on until Sat. 10th October. But in any case I will reserve 2 good pots for you; in case you are not able to come. — a good Ladi Kwali 'built' pot of Nigerian traditional design, and the best M.C. pot I can find.

Last week we unpacked a kiln here, of pots made by me in 1952 - 1955. Some of the people who have been at my Pottery Course here, (just

finished) have suggested you might like to see one or two of the best of these, so I have chosen a 'Bread Pot' and a Wine Jar, which I will take up to London with me this week. If you are not able to come to London I may be able to bring them to York for you to see before I have to return to Nigeria (i.e. before 20th October).

But I am still hoping we may be able to meet in London.

Yours sincerely
Michael Cardew

Back of an envelope from Shoji Hamada addressed to Milner-White